Anti-Machiavel: or, an examination of Machiavel's Prince. With notes historical and political. Published by Mr. de Voltaire. Translated from the French.

King of Prussia Frederick II

ECCO
PRINT EDITIONS

Eighteenth Century
Collections Online
Print Editions

Gale ECCO Print Editions

Relive history with *Eighteenth Century Collections Online*, now available in print for the independent historian and collector. This series includes the most significant English-language and foreign-language works printed in Great Britain during the eighteenth century, and is organized in seven different subject areas including literature and language; medicine, science, and technology; and religion and philosophy. The collection also includes thousands of important works from the Americas.

The eighteenth century has been called "The Age of Enlightenment." It was a period of rapid advance in print culture and publishing, in world exploration, and in the rapid growth of science and technology – all of which had a profound impact on the political and cultural landscape. At the end of the century the American Revolution, French Revolution and Industrial Revolution, perhaps three of the most significant events in modern history, set in motion developments that eventually dominated world political, economic, and social life.

In a groundbreaking effort, Gale initiated a revolution of its own: digitization of epic proportions to preserve these invaluable works in the largest online archive of its kind. Contributions from major world libraries constitute over 175,000 original printed works. Scanned images of the actual pages, rather than transcriptions, recreate the works *as they first appeared.*

Now for the first time, these high-quality digital scans of original works are available via print-on-demand, making them readily accessible to libraries, students, independent scholars, and readers of all ages.

For our initial release we have created seven robust collections to form one the world's most comprehensive catalogs of 18th century works.

Initial Gale ECCO Print Editions collections include:

History and Geography
Rich in titles on English life and social history, this collection spans the world as it was known to eighteenth-century historians and explorers. Titles include a wealth of travel accounts and diaries, histories of nations from throughout the world, and maps and charts of a world that was still being discovered. Students of the War of American Independence will find fascinating accounts from the British side of conflict.

Social Science

Delve into what it was like to live during the eighteenth century by reading the first-hand accounts of everyday people, including city dwellers and farmers, businessmen and bankers, artisans and merchants, artists and their patrons, politicians and their constituents. Original texts make the American, French, and Industrial revolutions vividly contemporary.

Medicine, Science and Technology

Medical theory and practice of the 1700s developed rapidly, as is evidenced by the extensive collection, which includes descriptions of diseases, their conditions, and treatments. Books on science and technology, agriculture, military technology, natural philosophy, even cookbooks, are all contained here.

Literature and Language

Western literary study flows out of eighteenth-century works by Alexander Pope, Daniel Defoe, Henry Fielding, Frances Burney, Denis Diderot, Johann Gottfried Herder, Johann Wolfgang von Goethe, and others. Experience the birth of the modern novel, or compare the development of language using dictionaries and grammar discourses.

Religion and Philosophy

The Age of Enlightenment profoundly enriched religious and philosophical understanding and continues to influence present-day thinking. Works collected here include masterpieces by David Hume, Immanuel Kant, and Jean-Jacques Rousseau, as well as religious sermons and moral debates on the issues of the day, such as the slave trade. The Age of Reason saw conflict between Protestantism and Catholicism transformed into one between faith and logic -- a debate that continues in the twenty-first century.

Law and Reference

This collection reveals the history of English common law and Empire law in a vastly changing world of British expansion. Dominating the legal field is the *Commentaries of the Law of England* by Sir William Blackstone, which first appeared in 1765. Reference works such as almanacs and catalogues continue to educate us by revealing the day-to-day workings of society.

Fine Arts

The eighteenth-century fascination with Greek and Roman antiquity followed the systematic excavation of the ruins at Pompeii and Herculaneum in southern Italy; and after 1750 a neoclassical style dominated all artistic fields. The titles here trace developments in mostly English-language works on painting, sculpture, architecture, music, theater, and other disciplines. Instructional works on musical instruments, catalogs of art objects, comic operas, and more are also included.

The BiblioLife Network

This project was made possible in part by the BiblioLife Network (BLN), a project aimed at addressing some of the huge challenges facing book preservationists around the world. The BLN includes libraries, library networks, archives, subject matter experts, online communities and library service providers. We believe every book ever published should be available as a high-quality print reproduction; printed on-demand anywhere in the world. This insures the ongoing accessibility of the content and helps generate sustainable revenue for the libraries and organizations that work to preserve these important materials.

The following book is in the "public domain" and represents an authentic reproduction of the text as printed by the original publisher. While we have attempted to accurately maintain the integrity of the original work, there are sometimes problems with the original work or the micro-film from which the books were digitized. This can result in minor errors in reproduction. Possible imperfections include missing and blurred pages, poor pictures, markings and other reproduction issues beyond our control. Because this work is culturally important, we have made it available as part of our commitment to protecting, preserving, and promoting the world's literature.

GUIDE TO FOLD-OUTS MAPS and OVERSIZED IMAGES

The book you are reading was digitized from microfilm captured over the past thirty to forty years. Years after the creation of the original microfilm, the book was converted to digital files and made available in an online database.

In an online database, page images do not need to conform to the size restrictions found in a printed book. When converting these images back into a printed bound book, the page sizes are standardized in ways that maintain the detail of the original. For large images, such as fold-out maps, the original page image is split into two or more pages

Guidelines used to determine how to split the page image follows:

• Some images are split vertically; large images require vertical and horizontal splits.
• For horizontal splits, the content is split left to right.
• For vertical splits, the content is split from top to bottom.
• For both vertical and horizontal splits, the image is processed from top left to bottom right.

Dowdall Pigott

Trin Coll apud Cantab
Soc et Med Templi apud Londin Armig

ANTI-MACHIAVEL:

OR, AN

EXAMINATION

OF

Machiavel's PRINCE.

WITH

NOTES *Historical* and *Political.*

PUBLISHED BY

Mr. DE *VOLTAIRE.*

TRANSLATED *from the* FRENCH.

LONDON·

Printed for T. WOODWARD, at the *Half-Moon,* between the *Two Temple Gates,* *Fleet-street.* MDCCXLI.

Advertiſement.

IT may not be improper to acquaint the Reader, that the following Tranſlation of Machiavel's PRINCE is newly made from the Original; and that the Quotations from Tacitus and other Authors are tranſlated into Engliſh, to make this Book of more general Uſe.

There are already two Engliſh Tranſlations of the PRINCE; the one by Dacres, though not unfaithful, is literal and antiquated; the other, by an unknown Hand, is more intelligible and ſpirited, but much leſs correct than the former; it has too much the Nature of a Paraphraſe, and departs from that Simplicity of Style which Machiavel keeps up through the whole Book, and which we have endeavoured to imitate. There is a Tranſlation of this Piece in French by Mr. Amelot de la Houſſaye, which has ſeveral Beauties; but they are rather his own than his Author's; and we did not think ourſelves allowed to abridge and

curtail

curtail Machiavel ſo much as that Gentleman has done.

As for the ANTI-MACHIA-VEL, the Author, who is ſaid to be a Perſon of the higheſt Rank, has but little regarded his Stile: Nevertheleſs we have followed it as much as we could; and have not preſumed to take any Freedoms but ſuch as we thought abſolutely neceſſary. It is hoped, that the Sentiments of Liberty, Humanity and Virtue, and the great Abhorrence of Tyranny, Cruelty, Craftineſs, and every Abuſe of Power, which run through the Whole of this Piece, and are ſo worthy of the Royal Author to whom the Publick aſcribes it, will not fail to make it intereſting and acceptable to all Engliſh Readers.

Nor can we forbear to take Notice of his touching ſo often upon Engliſh Affairs, and of the great Eſteem he ſhews for the Britiſh Conſtitution, which he expreſsly prefers to every other Form of Government.

INTRO-

INTRODUCTION.

MACHIAVEL's PRINCE is in point of Morality, what *Spinoza*'s Work is with regard to Faith: *Spinoza* fapped the Foundations of Faith, and aimed at nothing lefs than overturning the whole Fabrick of Religion; *Machiavel* corrupted Politicks, and undertook to deftroy the Precepts of found Morality: The Errors of the one were but Errors in Speculation; thofe of the other regarded Practice: We find, neverthelefs, that Divines have called out to Arms and founded the Charge againft *Spinoza*; that his Work has been formally refuted, and his Attacks oppofed upon Principles of Divinity; whilft *Machiavel* has only been annoyed by a few Moralifts, and has been able, in fpite of them, and of his perni-

A 3

cious

cious Doctrines, to maintain his Political System, down to our Days.

I venture to undertake the Defence of Humanity against this Monster, who would destroy it, to oppose Reason and Justice to criminal Sophistry, and publish my Remarks on *Machiavel's Prince*, Chapter by Chapter, that the Antidote may be found immediately after the Poison.

I have always looked upon that Work as one of the most dangerous that ever appeared in the World: 'Tis a Book that must naturally come into the Hands of Princes, and of those who have a Taste for Politicks: A young, ambitious Man, whose Heart and Judgment are not yet sufficiently formed to distinguish exactly between Right and Wrong, is but too liable to be corrupted by Maxims which so greatly flatter his Passions.

But if it is criminal to debauch the Sentiments of a private Person, who

has

has but a small Influence upon the Affairs of the World; it is infinitely more so to corrupt the Morals of Princes, whose Business it is to govern Nations, to administer Justice, and to set Examples of Justice to their Subjects; and who by their Magnanimity, Mercy and Goodness, ought to be the living Images of the Deity.

Inundations which ravage Countries, Thunder and Lightning that reduce Cities to Ashes, the Pestilence which lays whole Provinces waste, are less fatal to the World than the vicious Morals and unbridled Passions of Princes. The Plagues of Heaven continue but for a Time; they only ravage some Countries; and these Losses, however grievous, are nevertheless repaired; whereas the Crimes of Kings entail a lasting Misery upon whole Nations.

As Kings have the Power to do Good or Evil according to their Choice

and

and Inclination, how deplorable is the Condition of that People who have every thing to fear from the Abuse of Majesty, whose Properties are a Prey to the Avarice of their Prince, their Liberty to his Caprice, their Repose to his Ambition, their Safety to his Perfidiousness, and their Lives to his Cruelty? Such would be the tragical Situation of a Country governed by a Prince of *Machiavel*'s forming.

I must not conclude this Introduction without saying a few Words to those who believe that *Machiavel* rather describes what Princes do, than what they ought to do: A Notion which has pleased many, purely because it is satirical.

Those who pass this peremptory Judgment upon Sovereigns, are no doubt misled by the Examples of some wicked Princes, the Cotemporaries of *Machiavel* who cites them, and by the Lives of some Tyrants who have

have indeed been the Difgrace of Human Nature. I befeech thefe cenforious Perfons to confider, that, as the Temptations to which a King is liable are very powerful, it requires a more than ordinary Degree of Virtue to refift them; and therefore it is not furprifing, if, in fo great a Number of Princes, there fhould be a Mixture of bad ones among the good. In the Lift of the *Roman* Emperors, where a *Nero*, a *Caligula*, and a *Tiberius* appear, the World ftill reflects with Pleafure on the facred Names of a *Titus*, a *Trajan*, and an *Antoninus*.

It is therefore a cruel Injuftice to impute to a whole Body of Men what is only applicable to fome of them. As in Hiftory the Names of good Princes ought to be preferved, fo thofe of all others fhould be fuffered to fink in Oblivion, with their Indolence, Acts of Injuftice, and other Crimes. This indeed would leffen the Number

of

of Hiſtorical Books, but Mankind would gain by it: The Honour of living in Hiſtory, and of ſeeing one's Name tranſmitted to all future Ages, would then only be the Reward of Virtue: *Machiavel*'s Book would no longer infect the Schools of Politicks: His continual Contradictions would be treated with Contempt; and the World would be perſuaded, that the true Policy of Kings, which is ſolely grounded on Juſtice, Prudence and Goodneſs, is in all reſpects preferable to that inconſiſtent and horrible Syſtem, which *Machiavel* has been ſo bold as to offer the Publick.

PREFACE
TO
MACHIAVEL's PRINCE,
BY
Amelot de la Houssaye.

Containing some apologetical Remarks upon that Piece.

A S *Machiavel* is an Author whom few People read, and fewer underftand, it is not furprifing that the Vulgar fhould be prejudiced againft him. I fay, prejudiced; for you will find, that thofe who cenfure him, either own that they never read him; or if they pretend to have read him, never underftood his Meaning; as is evident from the literal Senfe they put upon feveral Paffages which Politicians explain in a very different manner. The Truth is, *Machiavel* is cenfured only becaufe he is ill underftood; and ill underftood by many who are capable of underftanding him better, only becaufe they read him with a fort of Prejudice; whereas, if they read him like impartial Judges, I mean, if they held the

Balance

Balance even between him and his Adversaries, they would perceive, that most of his Maxims are absolutely necessary to Princes, who, as was said by the great *Cosmo de Medicis*, cannot always govern their States with their Beads in their Hand [a]. *We must suppose*, says *Wicquefort* [*], *that he almost every-where describes what Princes do, not what they ought to do* It is therefore condemning the Conduct of Princes, to condemn what *Machiavel* says, if it be true that he describes what they do, or, to speak more properly, what they are sometimes forced to do. For *the Man*, says he, Chap XV of his Prince, *that makes a Conscience of being strictly honest on all Occasions, must needs be undone among the many who act upon different Principles. A Prince therefore must learn, for his own Security, to be virtuous or vicious according*

to

---

[a] *Che gli stati non si tengono con pater-nostri* Machiavel, Book 7 of his History Francis, who was afterwards Great-Duke of *Tuscany*, being at the Court of *Spain*, and a Gentleman blaming some Command of his as unjust, answered in the following Words of *Ezekiel*, Is not my way equal, and are not your ways unequal? (Ezek Chap xviii) giving him to understand, that there are things which seem unjust to private Persons, because they do not know the Reasons which oblige a Prince to order them

[*] Book I. of his Embassador, Section 7.

to the Exigence of his Affairs [b]. And in his
18th Chapter, after having said that a Prince
ought not to fulfil his Engagements, when
they are contrary to his Interest, he fairly
owns, that *if Men were all good, this
Maxim would be false; but that as they
are bad, and would not observe their Promises to us, we ought as little to think ourselves bound by our Engagements to them* *:
For otherwise the Prince would lose his
Power, and consequently his Reputation;
it being impossible, that a Prince who
has lost the one, should preserve the other.
Since I have happened to touch upon his
18th Chapter, which is undoubtedly the
most exceptious as well as the most dangerous
of all his Writings, I think it not unnecessary to point out here, by-the-bye, in what
Sense we ought to understand the Instruction
which he there gives to his Prince. *It is
not necessary*, says he, *that a Prince should
have all the above-mentioned Qualities;
but it is extremely requisite that he should appear to have them. Let him seem, and let*

him

---

[b] *Plutarch* says, that if all the Duties of Morality must needs be discharged, and all the Rules of Justice observed, in order to reign well, *Jupiter* himself would not be equal to the Task

See the Notes upon the 15th and 18th Chapters of his *Prince*

him actually be merciful, true to his Word,
humane, religious and sincere.---To judge of
him by his Looks and Discourse, he should
seem to be all Goodness, Sincerity, Huma-
nity, and Religion. There is nothing of
which it is more necessary to have the Ap-
pearance than of this last Quality. Upon
this Passage is grounded the prevailing Notion among the Vulgar, that *Machiavel* was
an Infidel, and even an Atheist: And indeed,
his Words might deceive weak Minds. But if
we examine the Meaning of them, we shall
find that he no-where asserts what is laid to
his Charge, *viz.* That a Prince should have
no Religion. He only says, that if he has
none, as may sometimes happen, he should
beware of shewing it, Religion being the
strongest Bond between him and his Subjects;
and the want of Religion, the most just Motive, or at least the most specious Pretence,
they can have for withdrawing their Allegiance [c]. It is infinitely better for a Prince
to be an Hypocrite than a declared Infidel;

an

---

[c] *Nec toleratitos profani*
Principis imperium, says *Ta-*
citus, Ann. 14. " People
" would never bear the
" Government of an irre-
" ligious Prince." The
Chancellor *de l Hopital* said,
That Religion had a greater
Influence upon the Minds
of Men, than all their Passions, and that the Knot with
which it tied them together,
was infinitely stronger than
all the other Bonds of civil
Society

an Evil that is concealed, being much less than one that is universally known. All the World perceive the Infidel, but few discern the Hypocrite. I take this to be *Machiavel's* Meaning, when he adds, that *all Men have the Faculty of seeing, few that of Perception; and that every one sees what you appear to be, few know what you really are.* " We see very " clearly what is before our Eyes, *said a* " Roman *Knight to* Tiberius; but it would " be in vain for us to pry into what lies con- " cealed in a Prince's Heart *d*." Besides, we ought to consider that *Machiavel* reasons every-where like a Politician, that is, according to the Interest of State, which has as absolute Power over Princes, as Princes have over their Subjects *e*. This is so true, that Princes, as an able Minister of the present Age expressed it *, chuse rather to hurt their Conscience than their Kingdom. And this is all that could be objected against *Machiavel's* Doctrines by *Justus Lipsius*, a Man

as

---

d Spectamus, quæ coram habentur, abditos Principis sensus exquirere illicitum, anceps, nec ideò adsequare Tacit Ann 6

e We are subject to the Prince, says *Cicero*, and the Prince to the Times *Nos Principi servimus, ipse temporibus* Ep Lib. 9

* Mr *de Villeroi*, Secretary of State to *Henry* IV

as eminent for his Piety and Religion; as for his Learning and Politicks. *Lipsius* frankly owns, that he values *Machiavel* more than all the other modern Politicians ƒ; which he would never have said, had he suspected *Machiavel*, in the least, either of Infidelity or Atheism. To this we may add, that *Machiavel*, who needed the Protection of the Family of *Medicis*, would never have presumed to dedicate his *Prince* to *Laurence of Medicis* in the Life-time of his Uncle Pope *Leo* X if it had been an impious Book: Neither would he have presumed, some Years after, to inscribe his History of *Florence* to Pope *Clement* VII. with an Epistle, wherein he says, that *he hopes his Holiness will cover him with the Buckler of his Ponti-*
ficcl

ƒ *Qui nuper aut heri id tentarunt non me tenent aut terrent, in quos, si verè loquendum est, Cleobuli illud conveniat Inscitia in plerisque, & sermonum multitudo. Nisi quòd imus tamen Machiavelli ingenium non contemno, acre, subtile, igneum Sed nimis sæpe deflexit, & dum commodas illas semitas intentè sequitur, aberravit à regiâ viâ* Preface to his *Doctrina Civilis* "Those who very lately "have made any Attempts "this way, neither raise my "Attention nor my Fear "To them we may truly "apply that Saying of *Cle-* "*obulus* Most of them are "grossly ignorant, and yet "abound in a Multitude of "*Words* *Machiavel* is the "only political Writer "whom I esteem, for the "Sharpness, Subtlety, and "Fire of his Genius But "while he closely follows "the Paths of Interest, he "too often deviates from the "great Highway of Truth "

ſiaſtical Approbations, had he paſſed for a Man
of no Religion. Let me obſerve, by-the-
bye, that thoſe who will take the Trouble to
read the 12th Chapter of the firſt Book of his
Diſcourſes, where he ſhews how highly neceſſary it is to keep up Divine Worſhip; and
the firſt Chapter of the third Book, where
he commends the *Franciſcans* and *Domi-
nicans*, as the Reſtorers of *Chriſtianity*,
which the bad Lives of the Prelates had intirely disfigured; will find, that however much
he deſerved the Name of a worldly wiſe Man,
he had very good Sentiments in point of Religion, and that conſequently we ought to
put a more favourable Conſtruction, than is
uſually done, upon certain State-Maxims, the
Practice of which is become in a Manner
abſolutely neceſſary, on account of the Wick-
edneſs and Perfidy of Mankind. Princes, beſides, are now grown ſo refined and ſubtle, that
it is impoſſible to deal with them in a plain
and open Manner, without being their Dupe.

I could ſay a great deal more in favour of
Machiavel; but as I am writing a Preface, not
an Apology, I leave him to be defended by thoſe
who are more intereſted in Politicks than I, or
who are better able to defend him. I ſhall only

a

add

ſ *Speraſi do che ſarà dall'e*   *tiſſimo giudicio arrivate & di-*
ermate legioni del ſuo ſan-   *feſo*

add what it is fit the Reader should know with regard to this Translation of his Prince †.

Besides several Notes, taken from the other Works of *Machiavel*, and from the Histories of *Nardi* and *Guicciardin*, I have placed under the Text several Quotations from *Tacitus*, which serve to prove, confirm, or exemplify what *Machiavel* says. This makes a sort of Concordance between the Politicks of these two Authors; from which it will appear, that it is impossible to approve or condemn the one without the other: So that if *Tacitus* is proper to be read by those who ought to learn the Art of Government, *Machiavel* is not less so; the former shewing how the *Roman* Emperors governed of old, and the latter how Princes ought to govern in our Times.

Some perhaps will ask, Whether I think that *Cæsar Borgia*, whom *Machiavel* proposes for the Imitation of Princes, is a good Model? I answer, that he is an excellent Model for new Princes, that is, for private Men who usurp a Principality, but a very bad one for Princes by Inheritance. It plainly appears from two Passages in the 7th Chapter of this Book, that *Machiavel* only proposes

---

† As the two next Paragraphs of this Preface relate only to some Peculiarities in the *French* Translation, it has been thought proper to leave them out, as foreign to the *English* Reader.

proposes *Cæsar Borgia* as an Example for
Usurpers, who indeed cannot maintain their
Usurpation, without being cruel, at least in
the Beginning; because all those who do
not find their Account in such a Change,
are of Course their Enemies; and even those
who had the chief Hand in bringing it about,
are not long their Friends, for want of being gratified in all their Pretensions. Whereas hereditary Princes, if they govern but tolerably well, have no Occasion to support
themselves by Severity and Violence, their
Subjects having been long accustomed to the
Sovereignty of their Family. As to Duke
Valentine (*Cæsar Borgia's* Title) I confess
he was a very bad Man, and deserved a thousand Deaths[h]; but at the same time it must
be acknowledged, that he was both a great General and a great Politician, and one to whom
we may justly apply what *Paterculus* said of
Cinna; viz. that his Attempts were such as
no good Man dared to make; but that he
succeeded in several Enterprizes which none
but a Man of superior Courage would have
been able to effect[i]

I

[h] *Cæsarem Borgiam vel
mille neces meritum,* says
Onufrio Panvini in his Life
of Pope *Julius* II.
[i] *De quo verè dici potest,*

*ausum eum, quæ nemo aude-
ret bonus, perfecisse quæ à
nullo, nisi fortissimo, perfici
possent* Hist 2.

I shall conclude with observing, that *Machiavel*, who is every-where represented as an Advocate for Tyranny, detested it more than any Man of his Time. This appears from the 19th Chapter of the first Book of his Discourses, where he greatly inveighs against Tyrants. *Nardi**, his Cotemporary, says that he was one of those who made Panegyricks upon Liberty, and upon Cardinal *Julius* of *Medicis*, who after the Death of *Leo* X. feigned that he would make his Country free. *Nardi* adds that *Machiavel* was suspected to be an Accomplice in the Conspiracy of *Jacopo de Diacetto*, *Zanobi Buondelmonti*, *Luigi Alamanni*, and *Cosimo Rucellai*, against that Cardinal, on account of his intimate Connexion with them and the rest of the *Libertines*; a Name which the Partisans of the Family of *Medicis* gave to those who stood up for Liberty in *Florence*. It was probably on account of this Suspicion that he was not rewarded for his History of *Florence*, which he had compiled by Order of the said Cardinal, as he himself takes Notice in the Beginning of his Dedication. This is all I think necessary to say concerning the Person and Writings of *Machiavel*, of which I leave every Man to judge as he pleases.

* Book 7. of his History of *Florence*.

Nicholas Machiavel

To the Most Illustrious

LAURENCE de MEDICIS,

Duke of Urbin, &c. *

IT is usual with those who court the Favour of a Prince, to present him either with such Things as they value most, or with those in which they see him take a peculiar Pleasure. For this Reason, he is often presented with Horses, Arms, Gold-Stuffs, precious Stones, and the like Ornaments, suitable to the Greatness of his Rank. Being therefore ambitious to appear before you with some Testimony of my humble Attachment, I could think of nothing more dear and precious to myself, than the Knowledge of the Actions of great Men, acquired by my long Experience in modern Affairs, and my continual Study of what passed in former Times. Having long and carefully examined

amined

* This Prince was Father to Catharine de Medicis, Queen of France. He died in the Year 1519.

amined this Subject, and now brought my Reflections upon it within the Compass of a small Book, I make bold to lay them at your Feet; not that I think it a Gift worthy of your Acceptance, but because from the Opinion I have of your Goodness, I flatter myself with the Hopes of your deigning to receive it especially since the richest Present I can make is, to give you an Opportunity of knowing in a very short Time what I have learned in a Course of many Years, and at the Expence of infinite Hardships and Dangers. I have not studied to recommend this Work by a Number of lofty Periods, and high-sounding Expressions, nor by any other of those outward Embellishments, and Charms with which many chuse to set off their Productions; because I had rather mine should have no Merit at all, than that this should consist in any thing but the Truth of my Reflections, and the Solidity of the Subject.

LET no Man think it Presumption, that a Person of low Rank should thus venture to prescribe Rules of Government to Princes;

for

for in the same Manner as those who draw Landskips, place themselves upon a Plain when they would observe the Nature of the Mountains, and high Grounds; but ascend to the Tops of the Mountains, in order to observe the Face of the Valleys; so, to know the Nature of the People well, it is necessary to be a Prince; and one must be a private Subject, in order to be well acquainted with the Nature of Princes.

MAY you therefore accept this small Present with the same Good will as I beg Leave to offer it! If you read and consider it carefully, you will there see how ardently I wish for your attaining to that Grandeur which Fortune and your great Qualities presage to you: And if, from that high Station in which you are placed, you should sometimes vouchsafe to look down, you will find how unjustly I stand exposed to the severe and continual Persecutions of Fortune.

CONTENTS *of the* CHAPTERS.

EXA-

EXAMINATION

OF

Machiavel's PRINCE.

CHAP. I.

The several Sorts of Principalities, and after what Manner they are acquired.

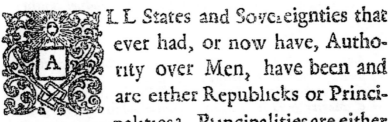

LL States and Sovereignties that ever had, or now have, Authority over Men, have been and are either Republicks or Principalities[a]. Principalities are either hereditary, where the Family of the Prince has

---

[a] This Division is founded upon the Doctrine of *Tacitus*, That a Principality and a Republick are two Opposites *Res dissociabiles, Principatum & Libertatem* In *Agricola.*

has been long in Possession b; or new. The new are either wholly so, as the Dutchy of *Milan* was to *Francis Sforza*; or they are annexed, as Members, to the hereditary States of the Prince who acquires them, as the Kingdom of *Naples* is to the King of *Spain*. Dominions thus acquired, are accustomed either to be subject to a Prince, or to be free; and are acquired either by foreign Arms, or one's own, either by Fortune or Valour.

OBSERVATIONS.

If a Man would reason well upon any Subject, he must begin with examining thoroughly the Nature of it; he must go back to the very Source and Rise of Things, in order to lay down the first Principles of them, with as much Certainty as possible; it will then be an easy matter to trace out their Progress, and all the Consequences that may follow. Instead of beginning with an Account of the different Sorts of Dominion, *Machiavel* ought, methinks,

Agricola *Romam a princi-pio Reges habuere Libertatem L Brutus instituit* Ann 1. *C Marius & L Sulla Libertatem in dominationem verterunt* Hist. 2 *Haud facile Libertas & Dominii miscentur* Hist 4. Indeed every Principality is not a Republick; but every Republick is a Principality. *Il serenissimo Principe sa saper*, says the Republick of *Venice* in its Edicts.

b 'Tis in this Sense that *Galba* said to *Piso*, *In gentibus, quæ regnantur, certa dominorum domus* Tacit Hist. 1 And *Mucianus* to *Vespasian*: *Non contra Caii aut Claudii, vel Neronis, fundatam longo imperio domum insurgimus.* Hist. 2,

methinks, to have inquired into the Rise of su-preme Power, and inlarged upon the Reasons that induced Men, who were free, to subject them-selves to a Master.

But in a Book designed to inculcate Tyranny and Crime, it would perhaps have been improper to mention what tends to destroy both : It would have ill become *Machiavel* to declare, that the People found it necessary for their own Preservation and Quiet to have Judges, who might decide their Differences; Protectors, to defend them against their Enemies, and secure them in their Possessions; and Sovereigns, to unite all their various Interests in one common Interest, and that at first they chose out of their own Number such Men to govern them as had the greatest Reputation for Wisdom, Equity, Disinterestedness, Humanity, or Valour.

A Sovereign, he should have said, was origi-nally designed for the Good of the People; this is therefore what a Prince ought to prefer to every other Consideration; and Justice alone ought to be the Guide of all his Actions. What becomes then of all those Notions of Self-Interest, Grandeur, Am-bition and Despotism; when it appears that the Sovereign, far from being the absolute Master of his People, is nothing more than their chief Ser-vant?

As I propose to refute the pernicious Principles of this Book, one by one, I shall only speak of them as the Subject of each Chapter gives Occa-sion. Here I must observe in general, from what I have said concerning the Rise of supreme Power, that an Act of Usurpation or Tyranny appears to be far more criminal than an Act of Violence; since the Prince, who sacrifices his People, and their Properties, to his Avarice and Caprice, is not only

guilty

guilty of Violence, but of a Breach of the Truſt repoſed in him : the People having veſted him with Power for no other End but that he might protect them. There are but three lawful ways of acquiring Sovereignty, either by Inheritance, or Election, or Conqueſt, as when ſome Provinces are gained from the Enemy in a War undertaken upon juſt Motives.

I would intreat thoſe for whom I deſign this Work, not to forget my Remarks upon this Chapter, ſince upon theſe all the following Remarks will depend.

CHAP. II.

Of Hereditary Principalities.

I Shall omit ſpeaking of Republicks, having diſcourſed of them elſewhere at large*: Here I ſhall only treat of Principalities, and ſhew, according to the foregoing Diviſion, how they may be governed and maintained. I ſay then, that hereditary States, and ſuch as

are

OBSERVATIONS.

Men have a ſort of ſuperſtitious Veneration for every thing that is ancient, and when the Right of Inheritance is joined with Antiquity, the Yoke it impoſes is eaſily borne, however grievous : So I would be far from denying *Machiavel* what

every

* In his Diſcourſes on Livy

are accuftomed to the Family of the Prince, are preferved with lefs Difficulty than the new[a]; becaufe it is fufficient for the Sovereign not to depart from the Order eftablifhed by his Predeceffors[b], and withal to fit himfelf to fuch Accidents as occur. So that if a Prince

every Man will grant him, that hereditary King-doms are moft eafy to govern.

I fhall only obferve, that hereditary Princes are fecured in their Poffeffions by an intimate Conne-xion which generally fubfifts between them and the principal Families in their Dominions; moft of thefe Families owing their Elevation and Eftates to the Predeceffors of the Sovereingn, and having their Fortunes fo entirely dependent upon his, that they can never forfake him, without forfaking themfelves.

In

---

a *Tacitus* obferves, that a Sovereignty got by Violence, cannot be preferved by Le-nity and Moderation *Non poffe Principatum fcele e quæ-fitum, fubita modeftia, et prifca gravitate teneri* Hift 1 Now the Rigour that is commonly neceffary for pre-ferving a State, newly con-quer'd, often caufes the Lofs of it, the Subjects growing at length impatient, and re-belling *Atque illi,* fays Ta-citus, *quamvis fervitio fueti,* patientiam abrumpunt Ann 12

b Much the fame thing was faid to *Nero,* that being no longer a Child, but of Age to govern, he needed no Mafter, nor any other In-ftruction, but the Example of his Anceftors *Finitam Neronis pueritiam, et robur juventæ adeffe, exueret ma-giftrum fatis amplis doctori-bus inftructus Majoribus fuis.* Ann 14 *Tacitus* obferves, that *Tiberius,* in the Beginning of

Prince is but tolerably induſtrious, he will always keep Poſſeſſion of his Dominions, unleſs
there be ſome extraordinary Power that deprives him of them; and even in that Caſe,
no ſooner does the leaſt Misfortune befal the
Uſurper, but the other recovers them. *Italy*
affords an Example of this, in the Duke of
Ferrara, who was able to withſtand the *Ve-*

netians,

In our Days, numerous and formidable Armies,
which Princes keep up in Times of Peace, as well as
of War, contribute likewiſe to the Security of their
States, and like naked Swords overawe their Enemies, and refrain the Ambition of neighbouring
Princes

But it is not ſufficient for a Prince to be, as *Ma-*
chiavel calls it, *di ordinaria induſtria,* tolerably induſtrious;

of his Reign, made it his
Rule to imitate the Conduct
of *Auguſtus* in every thing
Neque fas Tiberio infringere
dicta ejus Ann 1 *qui omnia*
facta, dictaque ejus, vice le-
gis obſervem Ann 1 and
that he durſt not yet treat
with Rigour, a People whom
Auguſtus had uſed with ſo
great Mildneſs *Populum per*
tot annos molliter habitum
non audebat ad duriora ver-
tere Ann 1 That *Vonones*
was deſpiſed and baniſhed by
the *Parthians,* becauſe his
Conduct had been entirely

oppoſite to that of their former Kings *Accendebat de-*
dignantes et ipſe, diverſus a
Majorum inſtitutis Ann 2.
And on the contrary, that
Italus pleaſed the *Germans*
ſo much the more, becauſe,
tho' he had been brought up
at *Rome,* yet he fell in with
them in their Debauches,
juſt as if he had always lived
with them *Lætus Germanis*
adventus, atque eo magis,
quod ſæpius violentiam ac li-
bidines, grata barbaris uſur-
paret Ann 11

netians, in the Year 1484, and Pope *Julius* II. in 1510, purely becaufe his Family had long poffeffed that Dutchy ᶜ. For
as a natural Prince has not fo much Occafion
or Neceffity to opprefs his Subjects, fo he muft
needs be more beloved by them; and unlefs
fome extraordinary Vices concur to make him
odious, his Subjects have a natural and juft
Affection

duftrious; he muft ufe all Endeavours to make
his People happy. Indeed, if they are not difcontented, they will never think of revolting; but
when a Prince makes his People happy, they will
always be more afraid of lofing him, than he
can be of lofing any Part of his Power. The
Dutch would never have revolted from *Spain*,
had not the *Spaniards* carried Oppreffion and Tyranny to fuch a Height, that the *Dutch* could not
be more miferable than they were already.

Naples, and *Sicily* too, have paffed more than
once from the *Spaniards* to the *Germans*, and from
thefe again to the *Spaniards*. Why was it always
fo eafy a matter to conquer them? The Government of both thefe Nations was equally rigorous
and oppreffive, and the People always expected a
Deliverance in a Change of Mafters.

What

ᶜ We rebel not againft the Houfe of *Auguftus*, which hath fo long poffeffed the Empire, faid *Mucianus* to *Vefpafian* (*Tacit.* Hift 2), intimating, that it was need-lefs to fear the Empire would ever return to *Vitellius*, when once he was difpoffeffed of it.

Affection for him. Besides, an old and un-
interrupted Possession of Sovereignty takes
away the Memory and Causes of Innovation;
for one Change always leaves, as in Buildings, a Toothing and Facility for establishing
another.

CHAP.

What a Difference there is between the *Neapo-
litans*, and the People of *Lorrain*! When these were
obliged to change their Sovereign, all *Lorrain* was
in Tears, and lamented the Departure of a Family, whose Predecessors had for so many Ages
possessed that flourishing Country. Some of them
had the most amiable Qualities, and were Patterns
for Kings. The Memory of Duke *Leopold* was
still so dear to the *Lorrainers*, that when his Wi-
dow was obliged to quit *Lunneville*, the whole
People fell upon their Knees before her Coach, the
Horses were often stopp'd, and nothing was heard
or seen but Cries and Tears.

For, according to *Taci-
tus*, it is always less dangerous to put up with the Prince
who is in Possession, than
look out for another *Mi-
nore: discrimine sumi princi-
pes, quam quæri* Hist 1

According to *Paterculus*,
People always improve upon
the first Examples *Non
enim ibi consistunt exempla
unde coepurunt, sed quamlibet
in tenuem recepta tramitem*

*latissime evagandi sibi viam
faciunt*, Hist 2 And that
one Change never fails to
draw on another, we have
several beautiful Instances in
*Tacitus Libertatem & Con-
sulatum L Brutus instituit.
Dictaturæ ad tempus sume-
bantur neque Decemviralis
potestas ultra biennium, neque tribunorum militum Con-
sulare jus diu valuit non
Cinnæ, non Sillæ longa dominatio*.

CHAP. III.

Of Mixt Principalities.

BUT the Difficulty lies in maintaining a Principality newly acquired. First, if it is not entirely new, but has only a new Member incorporated with it, so that

---

...natio, et Pompeii Crassique potentia cito in Cæsarem Lepidi atque Antonii arma in Augustum cessere Ann

" Lucius Brutus founded Liberty and the Consulship
" Dictators were chosen only in pressing Exigencies
" The supreme Power of the Decemvirate prevail'd little more than two Years, and the Consular Jurisdiction of the Military Tribunes not very many The Domination of Cinna was but short, that of Sylla not long The Authority of Pompey and Crassus was quickly swallow'd up in Cæsar, that of Lepidus and Antony in Augustus"
You see there a whole Series of Changes Here follows another Sulla dictator abolitis vel conversis prioribus cum plura addidisset, otium ei rei haud in longum paravit Statim turbidis Lepidi rogationibus, neque multo post

Tribunis reddita licentia quoquo vellent populum agitandi. Jamque non modo in commune, sed in singulos homines latæ quæstiones——Exin continua per viginti annos discordia, non mos, non jus Ann. 3

" Sylla the Dictator, changing or abolishing the past, added many Regulations of his own, and procured some Respite in this Matter, but not long, for presently follow'd the turbulent Suits and Proposals of Lepidus, and soon after were the Tribunes restored to their licentious Authority of throwing the People into Combustions at Pleasure And now Laws were not made for the Publick only, but for particular Men particular Laws——Henceforward for twenty Years civil Discord raged, and there was neither Law nor Settlement"

that tne whole may be called a Mixt Principality, it is expofed to Changes and Revolutions from a natural Inconveniency that arifes in all new Sovereignties; which is, that Men eafily part with their Prince, in Hopes of bettering their Condition[a]; and thefe Hopes prompt them to rebel and take Arms againft their Governor; but they are generally deceived; for they foon find by Experience, that their Condition is much worfe[b]. This again proceeds from a natural and ufual Neceffity

OBSERVATIONS.

The fifteenth Century, wherein *Machiavel* lived, was ftill rude and barbarous: the fatal Glory of making Conquefts, and of performing great Actions, that dazzle the World, and impofe a fort of Refpect, was ftill preferred to Moderation, Juftice, Clemency, and the other Virtues. In our Days

[a] *Parthos præfentibus mobiles, abfentium æquos* Ann 6 All Nations are of this Difpofition, *fervitii ingenio*, from a Capricioufnefs that accompanies Slavery, fays *Tacitus*, Ann 12

[b] Do you believe, faid a *Roman* Senator, that the Tyranny died with *Nero*? It was thought extinguifhed by the Death of *Tiberius*, and of *Caligula*, and yet we have feen a new Tyrant more cruel than thofe *An Neronem extremum dominum putatis? Idem crediderant, qui Tiberio, qui Caio, fuperftites fuerunt cum interim inteftabilior et fævior exortus eft.* Hift 4 *Claudius* therefore had Reafon to tell the *Parthian* Embaffadors, who came to ask a better King than

cessity which Princes are under to disgust their new Subjects, by oppressing them with Troops, Taxes, and a thousand other Inconveniences, which are the natural Effects of Conquest^c. Insomuch that you render all those your Enemies, whom you have wrong'd by seizing the Principality, and cannot preserve the Friendship of those who aided you, because

Days we see Humanity valued above all the Qualities of a Conqueror; the Folly of praising and encouraging those cruel Passions, that turn the World up-side down, is now at an End.

I would ask, what Reasons a Man can have for aggrandizing himself? What Right to form the Design

than the Prince who then govern'd, that frequent Changes were of no Use, and that they ought to bear with the Humours of their Kings as much as possible *Ferenda Regum ingenia, neque usui crebras mutationes* Ann. 12 All Subjects ought to adopt the Sentiments of that *Roman* Senator, who said, that he admired the Times past, without condemning the present, and that though he wished for good Princes, yet he patiently submitted to such as were bad, always remembering how necessary it is to live according to the Times.

Se meminisse temporum, quibus natus sit; ulteriora mirari, præsentia sequi, bonos Imperatores voto expetere, qualescunque tolerare Hist. 4 This is what *Machiavel* justly calls a *Golden Sentence*. *Discorsi*, lib 3 chap 6

^c *Res dura, et regni novitas me talia cogunt Moliri, et latè fines custode tueri*, says *Dido* in *Virgil* Æneid 1 *Arma*, says *Tacitus*, Ann 1 *quæ neque parari possunt, neque haberi per bonas artes* That is, It is impossible to take Arms, and at the same time to keep within the Bounds of Moderation.

becaufe you are neither able to fatisfy their Expectations, nor to treat them with Rigour, as being obliged to them: For let a Prince have ever fo powerful an Army, he muft likewife have the Favour of the Natives, if he would conquer a Province. Thus it was that *Lewis* XII. of *France* quickly fubdued *Milan*, and as quickly loft it· For the fame People that had open'd their Gates to him, finding themfelves deceived in their Hopes, and difappointed of thofe future Advantages which they expected, were not able to bear with the Haughtinefs of their new Sovereign.

It

Defign of raifing his Power upon the Ruin and Deftruction of others? Or how he can expect to make himfelf illuftrious, by rendering others miferable? The new Conquefts of a Sovereign do not enrich or improve his old Dominions; his Subjects are not the better for them; and he deceives himfelf, if he thinks they add to his Happinefs. How many Princes have, by means of their Generals, conquer'd Provinces they never faw? Thefe Conquefts are in fome refpect imaginary; imaginary

^d *Tacitus* fays, that the *Parthians* received *Tiridates* with open Arms, hoping he would ufe them better than *Artabanus* had done, and that in a little time, they hated *Tiridates* as much as they had loved him, and recalled *Artabanus* whom before they had fo much hated *Qui Artabanum ob fævitiam execrati come Tiridatis ingenium fperabant——ad Artabanum vertere, &c.* Ann 6.

It is very true, that a Country which has once rebelled, and is conquered a second time, is not so easily lost; because the Prince, after a Rebellion, is more at Liberty to secure himself, by punishing Offenders, exposeing the Suspected, and strengthening himself where he finds he is weake. So that if Duke *Lodwick** was able to recover *Milan*, the first Time, out of the Hands of the *French*, merely by making a Bustle upon its Borders; he was not able to recover it a second time,

ginary with regard to the Prince who acquires them: and yet many People must be reduced to Misery, in order to satisfy the Caprice of a single Man, who seldom deserves so much as to be known.

But suppose this Conqueror brings all the World under his Subjection; can he govern all the World, when subdued? Let him be ever so mighty a Prince, he is but a very limited Being; he can scarce remember the Names of all his Provinces, and his imaginary Grandeur will but the more expose his real Littleness.

'Tis

---

e *Tacitus* observes, that *Rhadamistus* having recover'd *Armenia*, from whence he had been expell'd by his Subjects, he treated them with excessive Rigour, looking upon them as Rebels, who only waited for a new Opportunity of revolting *Vacuam rursus Armeniam invasit, truculentior quam antea, tanquam adversus defectores, et in tempore rebellaturos.* Ann 12

* *Lodwick Sforza*, surnamed the *Moor*

time, till he had confederated all the World against them, and till their Armies were wasted, and driven out of *Italy*. And this proceeded from the Causes above-mentioned.

Nevertheless the *French* were twice dispossessed of *Milan*: The general Reasons of their losing it the first time, we have already discoursed of. It now remains, that we consider how they came to be dispossessed again, and shew what Remedies the King of *France* had, or any other Prince in his Situation may have, for securing his Conquest. I say then, that Provinces newly acquired, and join'd to the ancient Territory of the Prince who conquers them, are either of the same Country, or Language, or otherwise. In the first Case, they are easily kept, especially if the People have not been accustomed to Liberty And to secure the Possession of them, it is only necessary to extirpate the Family of the Prince who govern'd before; for if in every thing else they are allow'd to enjoy their old Customs, and provided their Manners are not intirely different from those of the other Subjects, they will acquiesce, and live quietly ; as has been seen in the Case

of

of *Burgundy*, *Bretagne*, *Gascoigne*, and *Normandy*, which have so long been subject to the Crown of *France*: For though their Language be something different, yet their Customs are alike; and therefore they are easily united into one People. Whoever therefore would preserve a Country which he has newly conquer'd, must be very careful of two things; the one, that the whole Race of the former Prince be extinguished, the other, that no new Law or Taxes be imposed: By this means it will in a very short time be incorporated with his hereditary Dominions. But here lies the great Difficulty, when a Conquest is made of a Country differing in Language, Customs and Laws; and in this Case, it can only be preserved by great Fortune, and great Industry [f]. One of the surest

'Tis not upon the Extent of a Country, that the Glory of its Sovereign depends: a few Leagues more of Land, will never make him more illustrious: for if it was otherwise, they would be the most valuable Men who had the largest Possessions.

Machiavel's Error, in this Point, may have been general in his Time; but certainly his wicked Max-

---

[f] *Ex diversitate morum crebra bella*, says *Tacitus*, Hist. 5.

fureſt and moſt effectual Expedients to keep
it, would be for the Conqueror to live there
himſelf, which would render his Poſſeſſion
more ſecure and durable; as the Great *Turk*
has done in *Greece*, who, notwithſtanding
all his Policies to preſerve that Country,
would never have ſucceeded, had he not fixed
his Reſidence there.   For when a Prince is
upon the Spot, he ſees Diſorders in their very
Riſe, and can preſently cruſh them g; whereas
if he is at ſome Diſtance, he can only be in-
form'd

Maxims were not.   Can any thing be more horrible than ſome of the Means which he propoſes
for preſerving a Conqueſt ?   And indeed, there is
not one of them, when well examined, but appears either unreaſonable or unjuſt.   *You muſt exterminate,* ſays he, *the whole Race of the Prince
who governed before.*   Is it poſſible to read ſuch
Precepts without Horror and Indignation ?   This
is trampling under Foot every thing that is ſacred
and venerable, taking off all Reſtraint upon Self-
intereſt, and paving a way for all manner of
Crimes.   If an ambitious Man has robbed a Prince
of

---

g Slight Remedies have
calmed the firſt Commo-
tions, *modicis remediis pri-
mos motus confediſſe Tacit
Ann* 14   In this Senſe it
was ſaid to *Tiberius,* that he
needed but ſhew himſelf to
the Mutinous, and they
would immediately return to
their Duty   *Ire ipſum, &
opponere majeſtatem Impera-
toriam debuiſſe, ceſſuris ubi
Principem vidiſſent Ann* 1.

form'd of them when they are got to a head, and can no longer be prevented · Besides, the Province is not liable to be pillaged by his Officers; and the Subjects having the Convenience of applying to him immediately, and without Loss of Time, rest contented, and are thus disposed to love him, if they are good; and if wicked, to fear him · If any neighbouring Power has a mind to attack his Province, it must be done with more Care and Circumspection; since a Prince can never be dispossessed of a Country where he resides, without the greatest Difficulty.

There is another Remedy, still better than the former, which is to plant Colonies in one or two Places, that may be, as it were, the Keys of such a State, either this must needs be done, or an Army of Horse and Foot be maintained in those Parts. Now Colonies are of no great Expence; the Prince sends and

of his Dominions, has he a Right to assassinate him likewise, or to poison him? But the same Conqueror, by such a Conduct, sets the World a Precedent for his own Destruction. Another more ambitious and expert than himself, will punish him by the Law of Retaliation, seize upon his Dominions, and destroy him with as much Cruelty

C

and maintains them at very little Charge; and
does Injury to none but thofe whom he is
forced to difpoffefs of their Houfes and Lands,
for the Subfiftence and Accommodation of the
new Inhabitants Befides, the Perfons injured make but a fmall Part of the State,
continue poor, and difperfed over the Province, and therefore can never hurt him;
and all the reft, who are not injured, live
peaceably and quiet, left upon any Fault they
fhould meet with the Fate of their Neighbours, who were difpoffeffed.

From whence I conclude, that thofe Colonies which are leaft chargeable, are moft
faithful and inoffenfive, and the Perfons offended, are too poor and too much difperfed,
to do any Hurt, as I faid before. Here it
muft be obferved, that Men are either to be
soothed

as he deftroyed his Predeceffor Pope *Alexander*
VI. had like to have been depofed for his Crimes;
his Baftard, *Cæfar Borgia*, was ftripp'd of all his
unjuft Poffeffions, and died in Mifery. *Galeas
Sforza* was murdered in one of the Churches of
Milan; *Ledwick Sforza*, the Ufurper, died in
France, in an iron Cage, the Princes of *York* and
Lancafter deftroyed each other by turns, as did
the Emperors of *Greece*, till at length the *Turks*
took Advantage of their Crimes, and exterminated

foothed and indulged, or utterly deftroyed [h]; becaufe flight Injuries leave them the Power of Revenge, but great ones do not: fo that an Injury ought to be fuch as removes all Fear of Revenge. But if, inftead of Colonies, an Army is kept on foot, it will be much more expenfive, and the whole Revenue of the Province will be confumed in Garifons: So that the Acquifition will become a Lofs, and rather prejudicial than ufeful, fince the whole State muft fuffer by the frequent removing of the Camp into different Parts of the Country; an Inconvenience which every Man will refent, and be ready to revenge; and of all Enemies thofe are the moft dangerous who are provoked by Infolences

nated their whole Power. If at prefent there are fewer Revolutions in *Chriftendom*, 'tis becaufe the Principles of found Morality are more univerfally known, Men are lefs favage and fierce, and their Underftanding is better cultivated, and perhaps all this is owing to Men of Learning, who have polifh'd *Europe*.

Ma-

[n] *Gli huomini grandi,* fays *Machiavel,* in the fourth Book of his Hiftory of *Florence, ò non s'hanno à toccare, ò tocchi à fpegnere*

That is, Great Men muft never be provoked, or if they are provoked, muft be killed

lences offered them in their own Houses. In all respects therefore, this sort of Guard is prejudicial, whereas that of Colonies is useful.

Besides, a Prince who gains a Province, the Language, Customs and Laws of which are different from those of his old Dominions, should make himself Head and Protector of his inferior Neighbours, use all Endeavours to weaken such as are more powerful, and take particular Care that no Stranger as powerful as himself, ever come into that Province for the Discontented will always be ready to call in some foreign Aid, either through Ambition, or Fear. Thus we see the *Romans* were brought into *Greece* by the *Etolians*, and never got footing in any Province but by means of the Natives.

What commonly happens in such Cases is this: No sooner does a foreign Potentate invade a Country, but all those who are weaker and

Machiavel's second Maxim is, That the Conqueror ought to fix his Residence in his new Dominions. There is nothing cruel in this; nay, it seems in some respects to be a wise Maxim: But it must be consider'd, that the Dominions of a great Prince are generally so situated, that he can hardly remove from the Centre, without doing a Pre-

and difcontented, join with him, out of the
Hatred they bear to thofe who are above
them: Infomuch that no Pains muft be
omitted to gain thofe inferior Lords, and
when gained, they readily and unanimoufly
fall into one Mafs with the State that is conquer'd. Only the Conqueror muft take fpe-
cial Care they grow not too ftrong, nor be
trufted with too much Authority, and then
with his own Forces, and their Affiftance,
he can eafily weaken and deprefs the others,
who are more powerful, and thus make himfelf fole Arbiter in that Province. He who
cannot put this Method in Practice, muft
quickly lofe what he has got; and, while he
holds it, will find himfelf expofed to numberlefs Difficulties and Inconveniencies. The
Romans in their new Conquefts ftrictly obferved thefe Maxims, they planted Colonies,
encouraged and protected the inferior Lords,
without

Prejudice to the Whole; for when the Sovereign,
who is the firft Principle of Activity in a State,
leaves the Centre of it, the Extremities muft needs
languifh.

The third political Maxim is, That Colonies
muft be planted in new Conquefts, for fecuring
the Fidelity of the Conquer'd.

The

without increasing their Power, depressed
and weakened the greater, and never suffered
any foreign Prince to gain Interest among
them.   I shall confine myself to the Province
of *Greece* for an Example.   They protected
the *Etolians* and *Achaians*, depressed the
Kingdom of the *Macedonians*, and expelled
Antiochus their King; and yet the Merit and
Fidelity of the *Achaians* and *Etolians* could
never procure them any Increase of Authority, nor the Solicitations of *Philip* induce
the *Romans* to be his Friends, till they had
weakened him; nor the Power of *Antiochus* prevail with them, to consent, that he
should retain any Sovereignty in *Greece*.
The *Romans* acted in this Case as all wise
Princes ought to do, who should have an Eye
to future, as well as to present Dangers and
Inconveniencies, and use all Means to prevent

The Author supports this Doctrine by the Practice of the *Romans*, but does not consider, that if
the *Romans* had not sent their Legions into those
Countries, where their Colonies were settled, they
would have quickly lost their Conquests; besides,
they had the Art of making Alliances.   The *Romans*, in the happy Times of the Commonwealth,
were the wisest Robbers that ever infested and
plunder'd the World; they preserved with Prudence,

vent them; which is eafily done, if they are
forefeen at a Diftance; whereas, if you wait
till they draw nearer, the Remedy comes too
late, and the Difeafe is incurable. The Phyficians obferve, that a Hectic Fever, in its
Beginning, is eafily cured, and hard to be
known, but when for want of being difcovered and taken in Time, it grows to a
head, it is then eafily known, but very difficult to be cured. Thus it is in Affairs of
State. Evils that are feen at a Diftance (which
can only be done by Men of Prudence and
Penetration) are quickly redreffed; but when
for want of being forefeen and prevented,
they

dence, what they had acquired with Injuftice:
But this People at length met with the Fate of all
Ufurpers, and were oppreffed in their turn.

Let us now examine whether thofe Colonies, for
the Settlement of which *Machiavel* would have his
Prince commit fo great Violence and Injuftice, are
really fo ufeful as he reprefents. The Colonies you
fend into a Country newly conquer'd, are either
powerful or weak; if powerful, you weaken yourfelf confiderably by difpeopling your old Dominions, and diflodging a great Number of your
new Subjects; if they are weak, they will not be
a fufficient Security, and, without much Advantage to yourfelf, you render all thofe miferable,
whom you have difpoffeffed.

'Tis

they come to such a Height, as to be generally known, they are past all Remedy. The
Romans therefore saw their Dangers at a
Distance, and always prevented them, they
would never put up with any Inconvenience
to avoid a War, for they knew the War was
by this means not avoided, but only deferred,
till the Enemy grew stronger. They chose
therefore to make War upon *Philip* and
Antiochus in *Greece*, that they might prevent having a War with them in *Italy* [1]:
They might, at that Time, have easily avoid
ed a War with both these Princes; but the
Romans never relished that Saying which is
every Day in the Mouths of our new Politicians, *That we ought to enjoy the Ad-*
vantages

[1] *Fuit proprium populi Ro-*
man. longe a domo bellare,
says *Cicero* " It was the
" peculiar Policy of the
" *Roman* People to make
" War at a great Distance
" from their own Country "
Tiberius always observed this
Maxim *Destinata reticere,*
consiliis & astu res externas
moliri, arma procul habere
Tacit Ann. 6 " He con-
" cealed his Designs, con-
" trived and managed fo-
" reign Affairs with Pru-
" dence and Artfulness, and
" kept War at a great Di-
" stance from home " The
Romans took this Course, in
order to preserve the Freedom and Riches of *Italy*,
for if a foreign Prince had
once got footing in it, he
might have turned the Arms
and Riches of the Country
against them, and by that
means have considerably
weakened their State And
in this Sense it was *Hannibal*
said to *Antiochus*, That the
Romans could only be conquered in *Italy*

vantages of the present Time. They trusted rather to their own Prudence and Valour than to Time, which may produce any thing, Evil as well as Good, and Good as well as Evil.

But let us return to *France,* and examine whether it has acted in this manner. I shall not speak of *Charles* VIII. but only of *Lewis* XII. as being a Prince who continued longer in Possession of *Italy,* whose Proceedings and Management are therefore more easily discerned It will appear, that he acted the very Reverse of every thing that is necessary for preserving such a Province as we now speak of *Lewis* was brought into *Italy* by the Ambition of the *Venetians,* who expected to gain half *Lombardy* by his coming. I will not blame that Expedition,

nor

'Tis therefore much better to send regular Troops into such a Country ; for if good Order and Discipline are but observed, the Soldiers will neither oppress the Natives, nor be chargeable to the Towns where they are quarter'd. But in *Machiavel*'s Time, this sort of Policy was unknown: Armies were only raised upon great Exigencies, and for the most part were nothing else but a Multitude of Vagrants and Free-booters : Standing Armies, Magazines, Caserns, and a thousand other

Re-

nor the King's Councils; for as he wanted to get footing in *Italy*, and had no Allies in that Country, as the very Gates were fhut againft him on account of the Mifmanagement of *Charles* his Predeceffor, he was obliged to take up with fuch Friends as he could get; and his Enterprize would have fucceeded, had he not committed feveral Errors. *Lewis* therefore had no fooner fubdued *Lombardy*, but he recovered all the Reputation that was loft by King *Charles*; *Genoa* fubmitted; *Florence* courted his Friendfhip; the Marquis of *Mantua*, the Duke of *Ferrara*, the *Bentivoglo's* *, the Coun-

Regulations, that fecure a State in Times of Peace, both againft its foreign and domeftic Enemies, were not yet in Ufe.

Machiavel's fourth Maxim is, That a Prince ought to make himfelf Head and Protector of the inferior Princes his Neighbours, and by fowing Diffention among them, raife or humble them, as he thinks fit. This was the Practice of *Clovis*, the firft King of *France* that embraced the Chriftian Religion: His Example has been followed by fome other Princes, not lefs cruel than himfelf. How different is this from the Conduct of a good King, who, when the neighbouring Princes are at Va-

* Lords of *Bologna*.

Countess of *Forli*, the Lords of *Faenza*, *Pesaro*, *Rimini*, *Camerini* and *Piombino*; the People of *Lucca*, *Pisa* and *Sienna*, all addressed themselves to him, for his Alliance and Friendship. Then it was the *Venetians* might have perceived their Folly; since to gain two Towns in *Lombardy*, they had made the King of *France* Master of two thirds of *Italy*. Now let any one consider with how little Difficulty the King might have kept up his Reputation in that Country, had he observed the Rules above-mentioned, and protected his Confederates, who being numerous, and yet weak, and fearing some the Pope, and some the *Venetians*, were always under a Necessity of adhering to him, and might have been the means of securing him ef-

Variance, becomes their Mediator, decides their Quarrels, and gains their Confidence by his Probity, Justice and Disinterestedness! Such a Prince is not only the Father of his People, but of his Neighbours.

Besides, it may be observed, that those Princes who raise others to a Throne by violent Means, generally undo themselves. We have two Instances of this in the present Century; one of *Charles* XII. King of *Sweden*, who raised *Stanislaus* to the Throne of *Poland*; and another, which

effectually against any Competitor whatever.
Yet no sooner had *Lewis* entered *Milan*,
but he did the very reverse, and sent Supplies
to Pope *Alexander*, to put him in Possession
of *Romagna*; not considering, that he weakened himself by disgusting his Friends, who
had thrown themselves into his Arms, and
that he aggrandized the Church, by adding to
its spiritual Authority, which was so formidable before, so great a Proportion of Temporal.   Having committed this first Error, he
was forced to go on in it; till at length, in
order to put a Stop to the Ambition of Pope
Alexander, and hinder his making himself
Master of all *Tuscany*, he was obliged to
come again into *Italy*   Nor was it enough
for him to have advanced the Interest of the
Church, and deserted his Friends; but out of
an

is still later. I conclude therefore, that true
Glory is not to be purchased by Usurpation ; that
Assassinations will always be abhorred , that a
Prince who treats his new Subjects with Injustice
and Violence, will forfeit the Esteem and Affection of all the rest , that it is impossible to justify
Crime, and that all who apologize for it, will
argue no better than *Machiavel*   To employ our
Reason against Humanity, is wounding ourselves
with a Weapon that was given us for our Defence.

an Ambition to poſſeſs himſelf of the Kingdom of *Naples*, he ſhared it with the King
of *Spain*. Thus *Lewis*, who before was
ſole Umpire of *Italy*, introduced a Partner,
to whom the Ambitious of that Province
and his own Malecontents muſt have Recourſe upon Occaſion; turned out a King of
Naples, whom he might have made a tri-
butary Prince; and put in another, powerful enough to turn out himſelf.

Certainly there is nothing more common,
or indeed more natural, than for a Prince to
deſire new Acquiſitions [k]; when he attempts
nothing but what he is able to execute he is
always applauded [l], or at leaſt not blamed:
But when his Enterprizes are too great for
his Power, and yet he purſues them, he is
then deſervedly cenſured. If the King of
France, with his own Forces alone, was able
to make himſelf Maſter of *Naples*, he ought

to

---

[k] *Vetus ac jampridem inſita mortalibus potentiæ cupido* Hiſt 2

[l] This was *Mucianus*'s Senſe of the Matter, when he ſaid to *Veſpaſian*, I call you to the Empire, 'tis in your own Option, and you can-not without Indolence and Cowardice ſuffer another to be raiſed to it, under whom beſides you will neither be free nor ſafe *Ego te ad imperium voco, in tua manu poſitum eſt —Torpere ultra, & perdendam rempub relin-quere, ſopor & ignavia vide-retur, etiamſi tibi, quàm in-honeſtè, tam tuta ſervitus eſſet.* Hiſt 2.

to have done it; but if his own Forces were
not sufficient, he ought not to have shared it
with any other Power. And if his consenting
to the Partition of *Lombardy* with the *Venetians*, is excusable, 'tis because he got Footing by that means in *Italy*.   But his dividing
Naples with the King of *Spain* is greatly
to be blamed, because it was done without any such Necessity   *Lewis* therefore
committed five Errors in this Expedition:
He ruin'd the inferior Lords of that Country;
augmented the Dominions of a neighbouring
Prince, called in a Foreigner as powerful as
himself; neglected to continue there in Person, and planted no Colonies.   Nevertheless
all these Errors might have been of no Prejudice, whilst this King lived, had he not
committed a sixth, in depressing the Power
of the *Venetians*. If indeed he had not aggrandized the Church, and brought the *Spaniards* into *Italy*, it would have been prudent and necessary to humble them; but
after taking such Measures, he should never
have suffer'd the *Venetians* to be ruin'd;
because whilst their Strength was entire, they
would have hindered others from making any
Attempts upon *Lombardy*; for they would
never have consented to it, but upon Condition

dition it should be delivered to them; and no Prince would ever have taken it from *France* to give it to the *Venetians*, or have had the Courage to attack them both together. If it is alledged, that King *Lewis* gave up *Romagna* to the Pope, and *Naples* to the King of *Spain*, that he might avoid a War; I answer, as before, that a present Mischief is never to be suffered, in order to prevent a War; for the War is by this means not prevented, but only put off, till the Enemy gathers more Strength, and will break out afterwards with greater Disadvantage. If it is further alledged, that *Lewis*, in order to obtain the Dissolution of his Marriage †, and a Cardinal's Cap for the Archbishop of *Rouen*, had given the Pope his Faith and Promise, that he would undertake this Enterprize for him; I refer to what I shall say hereafter concerning the Faith of Princes, and how far it is binding *.

Lewis therefore lost *Lombardy*, because he did not observe any of those Rules which others

---

† With *Anne* Dutchess of *Bretagne* Upon which *Nardi* pleasantly said, that Pope *Alexander* and King *Lewis* XII both made use of the Spiritual Authority to in-large the Temporals, *Alexander* to get *Romagna* for his Son, and *Lewis* to unite *Bretagne* to his Kingdom Book 4 of his History of *Florence.*
* Chap XVIII.

others have follow'd who conquered Provinces, and kept them.   Nor is it any thing
extraordinary, but what commonly happens,
in such Cases, and ought to be expected.   I
remember I once talked upon this Subject
with the Cardinal of *Rouen* at *Nantes*, just
when *Romagna* was seized by *Valentino*;
for this was the Name commonly given
to *Cæsar Borgia*, Pope *Alexander*'s Son.   In
the Heat of our Conference the Cardinal
told me, *That the* Italians *were ignorant of
the Art of War.* I replied, *That the* French
*were not less ignorant in Affairs of State;
otherwise they would never have made the
Church so powerful.* And it has been found
since by Experience, that the Grandeur of
the Pope, and of the *Spaniards* in *Italy*,
has been owing to *France*; and that in Return the Pope and the *Spaniards* have occasioned the Expulsion of the *French*.

From whence a general Conclusion may
be drawn, and such as seldom or never fails;
*That every Prince, by increasing the Power
of another, lessens his own·* For that Increase proceeds either from his Conduct, or
his Power, and both these make him at length
suspected and odious to the Person he has raised.

CHAP.

CHAP. IV.

Why the Kingdom of Darius, *subdued by* Alexander, *did not rebel against his Successors.*

COnsidering the Difficulties in preserv-ing a new Conquest, one may well admire how it happened, that *Asia*, which was subdued in a few Years by *Alex-ander* the Great, who died not long after, did not shake off the Yoke of his Succes-sors, but was enjoyed by them without any other Disturbances, but such as arose from their own Ambition. I answer, that all So-vereignties whatever, of which we have any Account, were governed after one of these two

OBSERVATIONS.

To make a right Judgment of the Genius of any Nation, we must necessarily compare it with others: *Machiavel* therefore in this Chapter draws a Parallel between the *Turks* and the *French*, whose Manners, Customs and Opinions are so very diffe-rent, he gives the Reasons why the Conquest of the *Turkish* Empire would be difficult, and the keep-ing it, when conquered, easy, and shews, that on the contrary, the intestine Divisions of *France*,

D   which

two different Manners Either by a Prince
and his Servants, whom, out of his mere
Favour and Choice, he constitutes his Ministers, and whose Assistance he takes in the
Administration of his Kingdom; or by a
Prince and his Barons, who hold that Rank,
and share in the Government, not by the
Favour or Concession of the Prince, but by
virtue of their ancient and noble Extraction.
These Barons have States and Subjects of
their own, who acknowledge their Authority, and pay them a natural Respect In
those States that are governed by a Prince
and his Servants, the Prince is more absolute,

which are the continual Disturbance and Danger
of its Sovereign, would make it easy to be conquer'd, but hard to be kept.

Our Author views Things only in one single
Light, and considers nothing but the different
Constitutions of a Government; he seems to believe, that the Power of the *Turkish*, and likewise
of the *Persian* Empire, is solely owing to the general Slavery of these Nations , and that an absolute and despotic Power, well established, is the
surest means for a Prince to govern without Disturbance, and make a vigorous Resistance against his
Enemies.

In *Machiavel's* Time *France* had still its Grandees and Nobles. those petty Sovereigns, who in
some

lute, becaufe there is no other Sovereign in all his Dominions but himfelf; and if any other is obeyed, it is not out of any particular Affection to his Perfon, but only becaufe he is the Minifter and Subftitute of the Prince. We have at this Time Examples of thefe two different Governments, in *Turkey* and *France* The whole *Turkifh* Monarchy is govern'd by a fingle Perfon; the reft are all his Slaves; he divides it into Provinces and Governments, fends thither what Officers he thinks fit, and changes them as often as he pleafes. But the King of *France* is furrounded by a great Number of antient Lords, whofe Sovereignties have been owned, and Families long beloved, by their Subjects, and who enjoy a Pre-eminence, which it is not in the King's Power to take from them, without inevitable Danger to himfelf.

fome meafure fhared with their Prince in Authority and Power : This gave Occafion to continual Divifions, kept up and fomented Faction and Party, and was the Caufe of frequent Rebellions. Neverthelefs, it may be queftioned whether the Grand Signior is not more expofed to be dethroned, than a King of *France* was in thofe Times: There feems to be this Difference between them, that the *Turkifh* Emperor is commonly ftrangled by his Janif-

faries,

himſelf.   So that whoever compares the *Tur-
kyſh* Empire with that of *France*, will find
the former more difficult to be conquered,
but when once conquered, more eaſy to be
kept.   The Reaſon of the Difficulty is, becauſe the Invader cannot be called in by the
Grandees of the Empire, nor expect any Aſſiſtance from the great Officers, to facilitate
his Enterprize   And this proceeds from the
Cauſes above-mentioned ; for being all Slaves,
and under Obligations to their Sovereign,
they are not eaſily corrupted; and even if they
could be corrupted, would be of very little
Service, becauſe, for the Reaſons already
given, they have no Intereſt with the People.
Whence it appears, that whoever invades
the *Turk*, muſt expect to find him intire
and united, and muſt depend more upon his

own

ſaries, whereas the Kings of *France*, who have been
put to Death, were either aſſaſſinated by Monks,
or by the Tools of Monks, and ſuch Monſters as
were of their forming.

But in this Chapter *Machiavel* treats rather of
Revolutions in general, than of any particular
Caſe; and indeed he has pointed out ſome ſecret
Springs of a very complicated Machine ; but does
not ſeem to have examined others, that are not leſs
conſiderable.

The

own Strength, than upon any Divisions
among his Enemies. But when once they
are conquered, and their Armies defeated
beyond the Possibility of a Recruit, the
Danger is at an End; for there is nobody
remaining to be feared, but the Family of
the Emperor, which being once exterminated,
the rest having no Interest with the People,
are as little to be apprehended after the Victory, as they were to be relied upon before.
But in Kingdoms governed after the Model
of *France*, it happens quite otherwise; for
when you have gained some of the Barons,
(and some of them will always be discontent,
and disposed to Innovation) you may readily
enter; they can give you easy Admission,
and

The Diversity of Climates, Food and Education in Men, gives them a quite different Manner
both of Thinking and Acting: This appears by
comparing an *Italian* Monk with a *Chinese* Lite-
rato. But even in Nations that are not very remote from one another, this Difference of Manners
and Genius is remarkable; as between a *German*
and *Italian*; the one blunt and open, the other secret and artful: An *Englishman*, deep and solid,
but melancholy, has but little Resemblance with
the haughty, boasting *Spaniard*; and the Manners
of a *Frenchman* are as different from those of a

Dutchman,

and contribute to your Victory. But in defending and preserving such a Conquest, you will meet with great and numberless Difficulties, occasioned both by those who have assisted you, and by those whom you have conquered. Nor will it suffice to exterminate the Race of the Prince, because other Princes will remain, who will always be disposed to head any Commotion; and as they can neither be contented, nor extinguished, you must of Necessity be expelled upon the first Insurrection.

Now if we consider the Nature of *Darius*'s Government, we shall find it very much resembled that of the *Turks.* Wherefore *Alexander* was forced to attack the *Persian* Empire,

Dutchman, as the Vivacity of a Monkey from the Heaviness of a Tortoise

It has often been observed, that there is in the Genius of the *Eastern* Nations a Spirit of Perseverance in their antient Customs and Usages. This, however, seems rather to secure the Throne than the Monarch, for their Monarchs have often been destroyed, or dethroned, but the Form of their Government is never altered. The Genius of the *French* Nation is intirely different from that of the *Orientals* Its Fickleness and Inconstancy has been if not the sole, at least the principal Cause of the many Revolutions in *France.* But the Cardinals
who

Empire, whole and entire, to give *Darius* a total Defeat, and drive him out of the Field. After this Victory, *Darius* dying, *Alexander* came of course to the peaceable Possession of that Empire, for the Reasons above-mentioned; and his Successors, had they continued united, might have enjoyed it without any Disturbance; for no other Tumults happened but such as were raised by themselves. But Kingdoms that are constituted like *France*, can never be enjoyed with so much Quiet. Hence arose the many Defections of *Spain*, *France* and *Greece* from the *Romans*· For those Countries abounding with Principalities, as long as the Memory of these

who successively governed that Kingdom, and were hated and esteemed by the *French*, made good Use of our Author's Maxims, to humble and depress the Grandees, and took Advantage of the Temper of the Nation, in order to avert those Storms with which the Sovereign was continually threatened.

The single Policy of Cardinal *de Richelieu* was to depress the Grandees, and raise the Prerogative of the Crown, that it might be the sole Basis of the Government: He succeeded so well, that at present there are hardly any Traces remaining in *France* of the Power of the great Lords, a Power

D 4   which

thefe lafted, the Dominion of the *Romans* was always precarious and unfettled; but when, by the Power and Continuance of the Empire, the Memory of them was extinct, the *Romans* were fecure and undifturbed in their Poffeffions. Afterwards, when they quarrelled among themfelves, every Officer, according to the Extent of his Command in thefe Provinces, was able to bring a Party into the Field, and the Reafon was, becaufe the Race of their old Princes being extirpated, there was no other Sovereign left

which was always formidable, and often fatal to the Sovereign.

Cardinal *Mazarin* trod in the Steps of *Richelieu*; he met with great Oppofition, but at length fucceeded; he ftripped the Parliament of its Privileges, and reduced it from a Subftance to a Shadow; fo that in our Days, if at any time a Parliament of *France* miftakes itfelf for a real Being, it is foon made to feel and to repent its Error.

The fame Politics that taught the Minifters of *France* to eftablifh an abfolute Government in that Kingdom, taught them likewife to amufe and employ the Ficklenefs and Inconftancy of the Nation, that it might be no longer dangerous to the Prince. Trifles, Pleafures, and a thoufand frivolous Occupations, put the *French* upon a new Scent: So that the fame People, who had fo long ftruggled with *Julius Cæfar*, who often fhook off the Yoke of

left for them to acknowledge, but the *Romans*. These Things being considered, 'tis not surprising, that *Alexander* so easily kept Possession of the Empire of *Asia*, whilst *Pyrrhus*, and many others, found it so very difficult to preserve their Conquests · It did not proceed from the good or ill Conduct of the Victor, but from the different Forms of the Governments [a].

CHAP.

of Emperors, who called in Foreigners to their Assistance during the Reigns of the Family of *Valois*, who leagued against *Henry* IV. and caballed under Minorities; are in our Days employed in nothing so much as changing Modes, Mistresses, Places, Amusements and Follies. Nor is this all the Security of a King of *France*. Numerous Garisons, and powerful Armies, kept up in Times of Peace, guard him as much against Insurrections at home, as against foreign Invasions.

[a] *Machiavel* gives a beautiful Example of this in Chap 12 Book III of his Discourses If we compare, says he, *the Neighbourhood of the City of* Florence, *with that of* Venice, *we shall not wonder, as many do, that* Florence, *though it has spent more in the Wars, yet has got less by them, than the* Venetians · *For this proceeds from the Difference of their Neighbourhood* Florence *is surrounded with Cities that are free, and therefore harder to be subdued* · *Whereas those which bordered upon the Territories of* Venice, *were for the most part subject to some Prince Now a People that are accustomed to Servitude, have but little Aversion to change their Sovereign, and very often desire it And therefore, though the Cities upon the Frontiers of* Venice *were stronger than those upon the Frontiers of* Florence, *yet they were more easily reduced*

CHAP. V.

How Cities and Principalities are to be governed, which enjoyed their own Laws, before they were subdued.

IF States that are newly conquered, were accustomed to Liberty, and their own Laws, there are three ways of preserving them· The first is, utterly to ruin them *; the second, to reside there in Person; the third, to permit them to enjoy their Laws, making them pay a Tribute, and putting them under the Government of a few Persons,

OBSERVATIONS.

According to our Author, there is no sure way of preserving a free State, newly conquered, but by destroying it. Certainly this is the most effectual way to prevent a Rebellion. Not many Years ago, a Lunatic killed himself in *London*; upon his Table he left a Paper, wherein he justified the Action, and pretended he had done it to prevent Sickness. The Lunatic is in the same Case with the

* This is the Maxim of the *Turks.*

fons, who may keep the People in Obedience and Allegiance[a]; which they will always be careful to do, as being appointed by the Prince, and solely depending upon his Protection and Power. And certainly a Town that has been formerly free, cannot more easily be kept in Subjection, than by employing its own Citizens. We have Examples of this in the *Spartans* and *Romans*. The *Spartans*, having made themselves Masters of *Athens* and *Thebes*, settled an Oligarchy

the Prince, who destroys a Conquest in order to keep it. I will not reason with *Machiavel* upon the Principles of Humanity, which indeed are foreign to his Writings; but upon those of Interest, the sole Basis of his wicked Politics.

You say then, that a Prince ought to destroy a City or Country newly conquered, in order to secure the Possession of them. I ask, For what End he conquer'd them? You will answer, To augment his Power, and make himself more formidable But by following these Maxims, he does the very reverse. For the Conquest must needs have

---

[a] This is what *Arfaces*, King of the *Parthians*, did in *Seleucia*, he changed its popular Government into an Oligarchy, as more resembling the Government of a single Person Quia plebem primoribus tradidit, ex suo usu (as his Interest required, says *Tacitus*) Nam populi imperium juxta libertatem, paucorum dominatio regiæ libidini propior est Ann 6

garchy in both thefe Cities, and yet they loft
them. The *Romans*, to keep Poffeffion of
Capua, Carthage and *Numantia,* ordered
them to be deftroyed, and by that means preferved their Conquefts. Thinking afterwards to keep Poffeffion of *Greece,* as the
Spartans had done, by declaring it free, and
fuffering it to enjoy its own Laws, they did
not fucceed; fo that they were forced to
deftroy many Cities in that Province, before
they could keep it: For indeed there is no
other fure way of preferving fuch Conquefts,
but by deftroying them. And whoever conquers

have put him to great Expences; and he ruins the
only Country that fhould have defrayed them, and
compenfated his Loffes For it muft needs be
granted, that the Poffeffion of a Country laid wafte
and difpeopled, cannot add either to the Riches or
Power of the Conqueror. The Defarts of *Libya*
and *Barca* would never make a Prince more formidable than he was before; unlefs Panthers,
Lions and Crocodiles, could be compared with
Cities and Citizens, Harbours and Ships, Cattle,
and all the Produce of a well-inhabited Country.
There is no Folly greater, or more pernicious to
Mankind, than that of making Conquefts. 'Tis
univerfally agreed, that the real Strength and
Greatnefs of a State does not confift in the Extent
of its Territories, but in the Number of its Inhabitants

quers a free City, and does not demolish it,
may expect it will demolish him; for the
Name of Liberty, and the Laws of their Ancestors, which no Length of Time, nor Obligation whatever, will be able to root out of
their Memory, will always furnish the Citizens with a Pretence for Rebellion, to which
they will have recourse upon the very first
and slightest Occasion, if they are not either
dis-

bitants. This appears by comparing *Holland* with
Russia. *Holland*, inhabited by an infinite Number
of People, industrious, vigorous, powerful and
rich, consists of a small marshy Territory, about
48 Leagues in Length, and 40 in Breadth, and of
a few barren Islands rising in the neighbouring Sea;
and yet it was able to shake off the Yoke of *Spain*,
at a time when the *Spanish* Monarchy was the most
formidable and powerful in *Europe*; its Commerce extends at present over the whole Earth; it
ranks immediately after Kings; and in Times of
War, besides its numerous and strong Fleets, can
send into the Field and maintain an Army of Fifty
thousand effective Men.

Russia, on the other hand, resembles the World
newly brought out of Chaos; it is bounded on
one Side by *Great Tartary* and *India*, and on the
other by *Hungary* and the *Black-Sea*; and extends
to *Poland*, *Lithuania*, *Courland* and *Sweden*, it is
above 500 *German* Miles in Length, and 300 in
Breadth; produces all sorts of Corn, and furnishes
all

disunited [b] or dispersed. This was the Case of *Pisa*, after it had continued many Years in Subjection to the *Florentines*. But it happens quite otherwise in Cities or Provinces that have been used to a Prince whose Race is extinct. For, on the one hand, accustomed to obey, and on the other, having lost the antient Family, they can never agree among themselves about setting up another; and

all the Necessaries of Life, at least in the Neighbourhood of *Moscow*, and towards *Little Tartary*: But this immense Country hardly contains fifteen Millions of Inhabitants; and the *Russians*, who now begin to make so considerable a Figure in *Europe*, are but little stronger than the *Dutch* by Land,

---

[b] *Quoties concordes agunt,* says *Tacitus,* Ann. 6 *sperni Parthus, ubi dissensere, dum sibi quisque contra æmulos subsidium vocat accitus in partem, adversus omnes valescit* " When the " *Seleucians* act with Unanimity, they despise the " *Parthians,* but when Discord reigns, while each " Side calls in a foreign Aid " against their Competitors, " the Person invited prevails " against the whole " And in the eleventh Book of his Annals, *Deditur Seleucia, sep-* *timo post defectionem anno, non sine dedecore Parthorum, quos una civitas tamdiu elu- serat* " *Seleucia* surren- " dered in the seventh Year " of its Siege, so long had " that single City maintain- " ed its Independency, and " baffled the Power of *Par-* " *thia,* to the signal Dis- " grace of the *Parthian* " Monarchy " A single City held out seven Years against the whole Power of the *Parthians,* merely be- cause its Inhabitants were united

and as they know not what it is to be free, they are flow to take Arms, and the Prince may eafily gain and fecure them. But as to Republics, their Hatred is more inveterate, their Revenge more infatiable; and the Remembrance of their Liberty continually fpurs them on to Rebellion, and can never fuffer them to reft. So that the fecureft way is either to deftroy them, or to refide among them.

Land, and much lefs formidable by Sea, have fewer Refources in Times of Danger, and cannot compare with them in Riches.

Since therefore it is not the Extent of Territory, but the Number and Wealth of the Inhabitants, that conftitutes the real Strength and Greatnefs of a State, a Prince ought, for his own Intereft, to people his Conquefts, and render them flourifhing, inftead of deftroying and laying them wafte; and *Machiavel*'s Reafoning in this Cafe is as bad, as his Politics are inhuman and barbarous.

His third Maxim is, That a Prince ought to fix his Refidence in a free City or Country newly conquered. This Maxim is not fo cruel as the other, but I have already fhewn, Chapter III. that it cannot be followed, without many Inconveniencies.

A Prince who conquers a free Country, in a War undertaken upon juft Grounds, might be content, methinks, with inflicting fome Punifhment upon it, and afterwards reftore its Freedom and

and Laws. But if this should be thought insufficient, he might secure it, by placing strong Garisons in the principal Towns, and suffer the People in all other respects to enjoy their Liberty.

CHAP. VI.

Of Principalities which a Prince acquires by his own Conduct and Arms.

LET no one be surprised, if in speaking of Principalities wholly new, and of Princes and States, I should here bring in the greatest Examples; for as Men commonly follow Ways that are beaten, and are guided in their Actions by Imitation, but cannot always hold on in the Foot-steps of others.

OBSERVATIONS.

If Men were not sufficiently supplied with Passions, it would be at least excusable in *Machiavel* to make up the Defect; this would be imitating *Prometheus*, who robbed Heaven of its Fire, to animate *Automata*. But Things are quite otherwise; and as the Passions, when moderate and subject to Reason, are the very Life and Soul of Society, so, when unbridled, they are the Destruction of it.

Of

others, and come up to the Perfection they imitate; so a wise Man ought to set out in the Steps of those who have most excelled, and copy after the best Models; that if he cannot equal them, he may at least resemble them: like a good Archer, who knowing the Strength and Reach of his Bow, takes his Aim a little higher than the Mark, when it is at great Distance, not with Design to hit above it, but only to reach it.

I say then, that Principalities wholly new, and subject to a new Prince, are more or less difficult to be kept, as the Prince has fewer or more great Qualities: And as the Happiness of rising from a private Man to be a Prince, presupposes either great Qualities or great Fortune, so, when both concur, they help

---

Of all the Passions that tyrannize over the Mind of Man, there is none more repugnant to Humanity, or more unhappy to those who feel its Impulses, than an unbridled Ambition, or an immoderate Desire of false Glory. A Man born with such a Disposition, has no Enjoyment of the present Time, and only exists in Futurity. Nothing can satisfy his Desires, and these imbitter all his Pleasures. If he is a Prince, his Misery is great in proportion to his Elevation. Honours and Preferments might possibly content the Passions of

E   private

help to remove many Difficulties: Neverthelefs the Prince maintains himfelf longeft,
who has been leaft indeb.ed to Fortune. It
likewife prevents much Trouble, if he is
obliged, for want of other Dominions, to
live perfonally among his new Subjects.

But to fpeak of thofe who have rifen to
fupreme Power rather by their own Virtues
than by Fortune, I fay the moft eminent are
Mofes, Cyrus, Romulus, Thefeus, &c *Mofes*
indeed ought to be fet afide, as having only
executed the Orders which God had given
him : neverthelefs he deferves to be admired,
was it only for that Grace which rendered
him worthy of converfing with God. But if
we confider *Cyrus* and others, who either
conquered or founded Monarchics, we fhall
find

private Men, whereas Provinces and Kingdoms,
which are ftill harder to be attained, can fcarce fate
the Ambition of Monarchs.

Machiavel fets before them the Examples of
Mofes, Romulus, Thefeus and *Nero*: This Cata-
logue might be increafed by feveral Authors of
Sects, as of *Mohammed* in *Afia, Mango Kapac* in
America, Odin in the North, and many others: I
hope the *Jefuit* will give me leave to add their
Sect to the reft, and it muft needs do them great
Honour to rank them with Legiflators.

Ma-

find they were Persons of great and uncommon Abilities, and that their particular Actions and Institutions were but little different from those of *Moses*, notwithstanding *Moses* had so great an Instructor. Upon examining their Lives it will appear, that they were beholden to Fortune for nothing but Opportunity, which enabled them to establish such Forms of Government as they thought proper : Without Opportunity, their great Abilities would never have appeared ; and without these, Opportunity would have been lost.

It was necessary therefore, *Moses* should find the People of *Israel* Captives in *Egypt*, and oppressed by the *Egyptians*, that to free themselves from Bondage, they might be disposed to follow him   It was necessary, that

---

Machiavel shews Ambition only in its best Light ; he only speaks of such Lawgivers and Conquerors as have been successful and happy ; but is quite silent about those who have been the Victims of their Passions.   This is imposing upon the World, and handling his Subject with Artifice and Cunning   When he spoke of the Legislator of the *Jews*, of the *Athenian* Monarch, of the Conqueror of the *Medes*, and of the Founder of *Rome*, whose Successes were great and

re-

that *Romulus* should be driven out of *Alba*, and exposed to the wild Beasts, when he was young, that he might afterwards be King of *Rome*, and Founder of the *Roman* Empire. It was necessary, that *Cyrus* should find the *Persians* discontented under the Domination of the *Medes*, and the *Medes* degenerate, and enervated by a long Peace. Nor would the great Abilities of *Theseus* have ever appeared, unless the *Athenians* had been dispersed [a]. These Opportunities therefore made those Men successful, and their excellent Qualities made the Opportunities known; and thus they aggrandised and ennobled their Country.   Those

remarkable, why did he not add Examples of those who have been unsuccessful? Because it would have shewn, that if a few Men succeed in their Ambition, the greatest Number miscarry, and are undone by it. Was not *John* of *Leyden*, Chief of the *Anabaptists*, tortured, burnt, and hung in an iron Cage at *Munster*? If *Cromwell* was successful, was not his Son dethroned, and his own Body dug out of his Grave, and hung up in a Gibbet? Were not two or three *Jews*, who pre-

---

[a] Military Discipline was corrupted, says the younger *Pliny* to *Trajan*, that you might have the Glory of reforming it. *Corrupta est disciplina castrorum, ut tu corrector emendatorque contingeres.* In his Panegyric

Thofe who rife to Sovereignty by the like
Virtues, attain it with great Difficulty, but
keep it with Eafe: The Difficulty in attaining it arifes, in fome meafure, from the new
Laws and Cuftoms which they are forced to
introduce for eftablifhing their Dominion,
and fecuring their Perfons For it muft be
confidered, that there is no Enterprize more
difficult in itfelf, more dangerous in conducting, or more doubtful in the Succefs,
than that of fetting up for a Chief, and introducing new Laws, becaufe the Perfon
who introduces them will be hated by thofe
to whom the old Laws are beneficial, and
but ill fupported by others, who find their
Account in the new And this laft arifes
partly from their ftanding in Awe of their
Adverfaries, who have the old Laws on
their

pretended each to be the *Meffias*, put to Death;
and was not another forced to turn *Mohammedan*,
and fpend the reft of his Days as a Scullion in the
great *Turk's* Kitchen? If *Pepin* dethroned his
Sovereign with the Pope's Approbation, was not
'*Guife* affaffinated, who attempted to dethrone his
King with the fame Approbation? Are there not
above thirty Chiefs of Sects, and about a thoufand
others, who loft their Lives by the Ambition that
is here talked of?

E 3   Befides,

their Side, partly from a natural Incredulity
in Man, which makes him averfe to all new
Eftablifhments, unlefs they are recommended
by Experience and Succefs. From hence it
proceeds, that as often as the Enemies of the
new Prince have an Opportunity of attacking, they do it with great Briskness and Vigour, while his Friends make but a faint and
weak Defence; fo that he is in Danger on
both Sides.

'Tis therefore neceffary, for difcuffing this
Point, to examine whether Legiflators depend
upon themfelves, or upon the Favour of others;
that is, whether they are obliged to make
ufe of Intreaties, for effecting their Defigns,
or have a Power to compel. In the firft
Cafe, they never fucceed in any thing, but
in

Befides, it is methinks very inconfiderate in *Machiavel* to rank *Mofes* with *Romulus*, *Cyrus* and
Thefeus. Either *Mofes* was infpired, or he was
not. If *Mofes* was not infpired, he can only be
looked upon as an Impoftor, who made ufe of the
Name of God much in the fame manner as it is
ufed in the Machinery of a Poem. And, in this
Cafe, *Mofes* muft have been a Man of very little
Ability, fince he took forty Years to carry the
People of *Ifrael* through a Country which they
might have eafily paffed in fix Weeks, he muft
have

in the second, when they have the Power
in their own Hands to make themselves
obeyed, they very rarely miscarry, or run
any Hazard. Thus it happened, that all the
Prophets succeeded who were armed, and
that all who were unarmed miscarried and
were undone. For, besides the Reasons already given, the People are naturally changeable; 'tis an easy matter to persuade them,
that a new Doctrine is true, but extremely
difficult to settle them in that Persuasion:
So that it is always necessary to have such a
Power,

have made but little Improvement by his Studies
in *Egypt*, and must have been much inferior to
Romulus, *Theseus*, and the like Heroes. If *Mo-*
ses was inspired, as is evident he was, he can
only be considered as the blind Instrument of the
Wisdom and Power of God; and in this Case Likewise the Conductor of the *Jews* was, setting aside
his Inspiration, every way inferior to the Founder
of the *Roman* Empire. to the *Persian* Monarch,
and those other Heroes, who by their own Valour
and Ability executed greater Enterprizes, than *Mo-*
ses did with the immediate Assistance of God

It must be owned indeed, that great Genius,
Courage, Address and Conduct, are necessary in or-
der to equal those Lawgivers and Conquerors, but
I know not whether the Epithet of Virtue pro-
perly belongs to *Machiavel*'s Heroes. Valour and
Address are common to Heroes, and Highway-

men:

Power, as, when their Faith begins to stagger, may compel them to believe. *Moses* [b], *Cyrus*, *Theseus* and *Romulus* could never have made their Laws to be long observed, had they been unarmed: This appears from what happened in our own Times to Frier *Jerom Savonarola*, who was ruined by his new Institutions, when the People of *Florence* deserted him; the Reason was, that he had not a Power either

men: The only Difference is that the Hero acts in a greater, the Highwayman in a lesser Sphere, and that the one is rewarded with a Laurel, the other with a Rope.

It must likewise be granted, that whoever introduces Innovations, must expect to meet with a thousand Obstacles: and that a Prophet at the Head

[b] *Whoever reads the Bible with Coolness and Attention, says Machiavel* Chap 30 Book III *of his Discourses, will find that* Moses, *for the promoting and establishing his Laws, was forced to put to Death an infinite Number of People, for no other Reason but because they opposed his Designs* We read in *Exodus,* Ch 32 *that he put to Death above Three thousand in one Day* Moses *called the People to him, and spoke after the following manner,* v 25, &c " Thus saith the " Lord God of *Israel*, Put " every Man his Sword by " his Side, and go in and " out from Gate to Gate, " throughout the Camp, and " slay every Man his Brother, and every Man his " Companion, and every " Man his Neighbour And " the Children of *Levi* did " according to the Word of " *Moses*, and there fell of " the People that Day above " Three thousand Men "

either to secure himself of his Proselytes, or
to compel others, who had no Faith in him [c].
Such Persons have many Difficulties to struggle
with, in the Pursuit of their Designs, and are
continually exposed to great Dangers; which
they can only overcome by their own Abilities: But when that is done, when they begin
to be held in Veneration, and have taken
off those who envied and opposed them, then
they are powerful, safe, honoured and happy.

To

Head of an Army, will make more Proselytes, than
if he fought with no other Weapons but Syllogisms.
It must be granted, that the *Christian* Religion,
when only supported by Arguments and Disputa-
tion, was in a languishing Condition, and very
much oppressed; and that it was not propagated
in *Europe* without a great deal of Bloodshed.

Yet it cannot be denied, but that new Opinions
have commonly some Run in the Beginning. How
many Religions, how many Sects, have been introduced without the least Difficulty! For there is
nothing more proper to bring them into Credit
than Enthusiasm, and therefore *Machiavel* has
spoken too positively on this Head.

I shall

---

[c] *Machiavel* says, he had
persuaded the People of *Florence*, that he held Confer-en-
ces with God (Disc Book I
Chap. 11). *Savonarola*'s
Party were called *Piagnoni*,
that is, the Mourners, or the
Hypocrites, and his Ene-
mies *Arrabiati*, or the Furious and Untractable *Nardi*'s History of *Florence*,
Book II

To thefe great Examples I fhall add one, which indeed is of an inferior Nature, but has neverthelefs a great Refemblance with the former, and it fhall fatisfy me for all others of the fame Kind. It is that of *Hiero*, who from a private Man rofe to be King of *Syracufe*, without being indebted to Fortune for any thing but Opportunity. The *Syracufians*, being opprefled, chofe *Hiero* their General; and in this Station he acted with fo great Ability, that he was thought worthy to be their Sovereign: It is obferved by thofe who have made mention of him, that he had, when a private Man, all the Qualities that could intitle him to a Crown He dif-banded the old Troops, and raifed new ones; he forfook his old Friends, and betook him-felf to others; and thus, having fecured him-felf

I fhall now make fome Remarks on the Ex-ample of *Hiero* King of *Syracufe*, which *Machia-vel* propofes to thofe who would raife themfelves by the Affiftance of their Friends, and of an Army. *Hiero* turned off his old Friends and Soldiers who had affifted him in effecting his De-figns, and afterwards raifed new Troops, and made new Friends. Now I affirm, that *Hiero's* Policy was not only full of Ingratitude, but likewife very dangerous, and that it is always fafeft and moft

felf by an Army and by Friends, who were devoted to his Intereſt, he muſt have found it an eaſy matter to build any Superſtructure upon ſuch a Foundation: So that he met with many Difficulties in acquiring, but with very few in preſerving his new Kingdom.

moſt prudent to rely upon Troops and Friends whoſe Valour and Fidelity have been tried and experienced. This indeed is too evident, to need any Proof: No Man can be at a Loſs to prove it to himſelf, who abhors Ingratitude, and is ſo happy as to have felt the Pleaſures and Contentment of Friendſhip.

Without Opportunity, ſays *Machiavel*, the great Abilities of thoſe Men would not have appeared. This muſt certainly be granted; and we may add, that without Opportunity, that is, without favourable Circumſtances, Villains and Madmen could never have made uſe of their Talents.

To conclude, the only Opportunity when a private Man may raiſe himſelf to a Crown, without Guilt, is, either when he is born in an elective Kingdom, or when he delivers his Country. *Sobieski* in *Poland*. *Guſtavus Vaſa* in *Sweden*, the *Antoninus's* at *Rome*, are Examples of both theſe Kinds. Let *Cæſar Borgia* be the Pattern of *Machiavel's* Hero, that of all virtuous Princes will be *Marcus Aurelius*.

CHAP. VII.

Of new Principalities acquired by the Arms of other Princes, and by Fortune.

THOSE who rife from a private Condition to that of a Prince merely by the Indulgence of Fortune, attain their Dignity without much Trouble, but find great Trouble in preferving it; they meet with no Obftruction in their Advancement, and feem, as it were, to fly to the Throne; but when they are feated there, it is then that all the Difficulties break upon them. Princes who rife after this manner, are thofe to whom a Principality is granted either for Money,

OBSERVATIONS.

Compare the Archbifhop of *Cambray's* Prince with that of *Machiavel*. In the Character of the one you will find Goodnefs, Juftice, Equity, and in fhort every Virtue, carried to its greateft Height: He feems to be one of thofe pure, ethereal Beings, who for the Good of Mankind prefide and watch over the Government of the Word. The Character of the other is a Complication of Villainy,

Money, or by the Favour of the Donor; as happened to many Persons in *Greece*, in the Cities of *Ionia*, and upon the *Hellespont*, where they were created Princes by *Darius*, for his greater Security and Glory; and to those Emperors of *Rome* who obtained the Empire by corrupting the Army.

As such Persons have their sole Dependence upon the Fortune and Pleasure of those who have advanced them, which are two Things very changeable and unsettled, so they have neither Ability nor Power enough to hold their Dignity; not Ability, because

it

lainy, Craftiness, Perfidy, Treachery, and of all manner of Crimes: He seems to be such a Monster as Hell itself could hardly produce, to scourge and destroy the World. And if in reading *Telemachus* we imagine that our Nature comes up to that of the Angels; it seems to resemble that of infernal Beings, when we read *Machiavel's* Prince.

Cæsar Borgia is the Model by which our Author would form his Prince, and which he has the Boldness to propose, for the Imitation of those who rise to Principalities by the Assistance or Arms of their Friends. It is therefore necessary to examine the Character of this Hero, in order to form an Idea of our Author's Maxims and Politics.

There is scarce any Crime of which *Cæsar Borgia* was not guilty: His Brother, who was his Rival

both

it is not to be expected, that a Man who has always lived in a private Station, unless he has uncommon Parts, can know how to command; not Power, because they have no Forces, upon whose Allegiance and Fidelity they can depend.

Besides, it is with Principalities suddenly acquired, as with all other Things in Nature whose Rise and Progress are sudden; they can have no Root or Foundation, but what will be torn up by the very first Blast of Adversity. This must always happen, unless those who are so suddenly advanced have Skill enough to prepare in Time for preserving what Fortune has so luckily thrown into their Lap, and to lay such Foundations after their Advancement,

23

both in Glory and Love, he caused to be assassinated almost in the Sight of his own Sister: Some of the Pope's Guards having offended his Mother, he ordered them to be murdered. He plundered several Cardinals, and rich Men, to satiate his Avarice; the Duke of *Urbin* he deprived of *Romagna*, put *d'Orco* his Minister to Death, not for his Cruelties, but merely to content the Populace; he was guilty of the most horrible Treachery at *Sinigalia*, where he ordered some Princes to be murdered, because he thought their Lives inconsistent

as others have done before they were advanced.

I will give two Examples, within my own Memory, of the two Ways of attaining a Principality, either by Ability, or by Fortune; the one *Francis Sforza*, the other *Cæsar Borgia*. *Sforza* by juſt Means, and his own great Abilities, roſe from a private Man to be Duke of *Milan*, and enjoyed in great Peace what he had gained with much Trouble. *Borgia*, commonly called Duke *Valentine*, at ained a Principality by the Fortune of his Father Pope *Alexander*, and loſt it upon his Father's Death, notwithſtanding he uſed all the Induſtry, and all the Arts, which a wiſe Man ought to do, in order to faſten and to root himſelf in a Principality which he owes to the Fortune and Arms of another.

For,

ſiſtent with his Intereſt: He deflowered a *Venetian* Lady, and then drowned her. But it would be needleſs to number up his Crimes and Barbarities. And ſuch is the Man, whom *Machiavel* prefers to all the great Genius's of his Time, and to all the Heroes of Antiquity, and whoſe Life and Actions he thinks a fit Pattern for thoſe Princes who owe their Advancement merely to Fortune! But to be more particular.

Cæſar

For, as was hinted already, he who does not lay the Foundations of his Security before his Advancement, may by his great Abilities do it afterwards, though with much Trouble to the Architect, and Danger to the Building. If we confider all the Steps and Meafures taken by Duke *Valentine*, it will appear, that he laid the ftrongeft Foundation for his future Security and Power And therefore I think it may not be fuperfluous to inlarge a little upon this Example, as I know nothing that can be more properly fet before a new Prince for his Imitation, than the Conduct of this Duke; for if his Meafures were at laft unfuccefsful, it cannot be imputed to himfelf, but to a ftrange and uncommon Malignity of Fortune.

Pope

Cefar Borgia formed the Defign of raifing himfelf by embroiling the Princes and States of *Italy*. Wherefore he that would raife himfelf, muft ufurp the Poffeffions of his Neighbours; for this End he muft weaken them, and in order to weaken them, he muft embroil them: Such was the Practice of *Borgia*, and fuch is the Doctrine of *Machiavel!*

Borgia wanted foreign Affiftance: It was therefore neceffary, that Pope *Alexander* his Father fhould diffolve the Marriage of *Lewis* XII. in order to procure him that Affiftance. Thus has the World been

Pope *Alexander* VI. had a mind to aggrandize his Son Duke *Valentine*, but found several immediate Difficulties, and foresaw others that would follow. First, he could see no Way of giving him any Territory, which did not belong to the Church; and he knew, that if he dismembered any of the Ecclesiastical Dominions, it would be opposed by the Duke of *Milan* and the *Venetians*; for *Faenza* and *Rimini* had already put themselves under the Protection of the latter: He was likewise sensible, that the Forces of *Italy*, especially such as were capable of assisting him, were in the Hands of those who ought to apprehend the Greatness of the Pope; as the *Ursini, Colonnesi*, and their Followers; and therefore he could

been often deluded by many Politicians, who whilst they were seemingly zealous for the Interest of Heaven, meant nothing at bottom but their own. If *Lewis's* Marriage ought in Justice to have been dissolved, the Pope should have done it without any Equivalent: If it could not be with Justice dissolved, nothing should have prevailed with the Head of the Church to sacrifice Religion to his Interest.

It was necessary that *Borgia* should gain Dependents and Adherents, and therefore that he should

F   bribe

could put no Truſt in them. For theſe
Reaſons it was neceſſary to embroil the
States of *Italy*, before he could make himſelf Maſter of any Part of it: And this was
no hard Matter to accompliſh, becauſe the
Venetians had, for Reaſons of their own,
called back the *French* into *Italy*. The
Pope therefore was ſo far from hindering
this new Expedition of the *French*, that he
promoted it by diſſolving King *Lewis*'s former Marriage. *Lewis* therefore paſſed the
Alps, by the Aſſiſtance of the *Venetians*,
and with Pope *Alexander*'s Conſent; and was
no ſooner in *Milan*, but he ſent Forces to
aſſiſt him in his Enterprize againſt *Romagna*,
which, becauſe of the King's Reputation,
was preſently ſurrendered

The

bribe over the Duke of *Urbin*'s Party: But Bri-
bery was the leaſt of *Borgia*'s Crimes, and had
ſome Reſemblance of Generoſity, and therefore
we ſhall paſs it over. He had a mind to rid himſelf of ſome Princes of the *Urſini* Family, of *Vitellozzo Vitelli*, *Olivoretto da Fermo*, and others;
wherefore *Machiavel* affirms, that he had the Prudence to make them come to *Sinigaglia*, where he
cut them all off by Treachery. Diſſimulation,
Trick, Treachery, Perjury, Murder, are the infamous Arts which *Borgia* employed, and *Machiavel* here recommends. But even granting
theſe

The Duke having thus reduced *Romagna*, and defeated the *Colonnesi*, was willing not only to keep what he had got, but to inlarge his Territories. In this he met with two Obstructions; one from his own Army, whose Fidelity he suspected, the other from the *French*: He was afraid, that the *Ursini*, whose Forces he had employed, would supplant him, and not only hinder him from gaining more Territories, but deprive him of those he had already acquired: And the same Fears he had of the *French*. As for the *Ursini*, he had observed that when he led them on to the Attack of *Bologna*, after making himself Master of *Faenza*, they had advanced with Coldness and Reluctance. And the Inclination of King *Lewis* he discovered, when having

possessed

these horrible Expedients were lawful, I ask whether it is Prudence in a Prince to make use of them? I ask whether he can deceive, betray, and assassinate others, without setting others an Example, nay giving them a Right, by the Law of Retaliation, to deceive, betray and assassinate himself?

Nevertheless, in others *Borgia* punished with Barbarity, Crimes which were much inferior to his own. He who himself was guilty of Usurpation, Perjury, Cruelty, Poisoning and Murder, condemned to the most inhuman Punishments Rogues,

Sharpers

poſſeſſed himſelf of the Dutchy of *Urbin*; he invaded *Tuſcany*, and was by him re-queſted to deſiſt.

Whereupon the Duke reſolved to depend no longer upon Fortune, and foreign Arms. The firſt Courſe he took was to weaken the Party of the *Urſini* and *Colonneſi* at *Rome*, which he did by gaining ſuch of their Adherents as were Gentlemen, taking them into his own Service, giving them large Penſions, and honouring them with Governments and Commands,

Sharpers and Rioters, who copied his Character, and were ſo many *Borgia's* in Miniature.

That King of *Poland*, whoſe Death of late em-broiled *Europe*, acted more conſiſtently and with more Generoſity towards his *Saxon* Subjects. By one of the Laws of *Saxony* all Adulterers were condemned to be beheaded. I ſhall not inquire into the Riſe of ſo barbarous a Law, which ſeems more ſuitable to the Jealouſy of the *Italians*, than the Patience of the *Germans*. An unhap-py Tranſgreſſor was accordingly condemned to Death, and *Auguſtus* was to ſign the Sentence. But being ſuſceptible of Love, and moved by Hu-manity, he pardoned the Criminal, and abrogated a Law which tacitly condemned himſelf.

Such a Conduct was both prudent and humane. *Cæſar Borgia*, on the contrary, having made the cruel *d'Orco* Governor of *Romagna*, with Deſign to ſuppreſs ſome Diſturbances, and puniſh thoſe

who

Commands, according to their respective Qualities; so that in a few Months their Zeal for that Faction evaporated, and they came all over to the Duke: Having thus dispersed the *Colonnesi*, he waited for an Opportunity to ruin the *Ursini*; the Opportunity soon offered, and he made good Use of it.

The *Ursini* perceiving too late that the Greatness of the Duke and the Church tended to their Ruin, held a Council at a Place called *Magione* in the Territory of *Perugia*. This Council occasioned the Revolt of *Urbin*, and the Tumults of *Romagna*, and exposed the Duke to infinite Dangers: Though he overcame them all, by the Assistance of the *French*, and recovered his Reputation, yet he would no longer trust to *France* or any other foreign Allies, as having no Opportunity to secure them in his Interest: He

who had raised them, afterwards ordered him to be cut in Pieces merely for accomplishing his own Designs; and thus sacrificed the Instrument of his Barbarity, to ingratiate himself with the People. The Load of Tyranny is never so grievously felt, as when the Tyrant puts on the Appearance of Innocence.

Borgia,

He betook himself therefore to fraudulent
Means, and so well diffembled his Intentions, that the *Urfini* were reconciled with
him, by the Mediation of Signor *Paulo*,
whom the Duke had lulled into Security, by
fhewing him all manner of Civilities, and
prefenting him with Money, Horfes, and rich
Cloaths; infomuch that the *Urfini* were
fimple enough to come to *Sinigaglia*, and
put themfelves in the Duke's Power. Having thus cut off the Chiefs of his Adverfaries*, and reduced their Friends, the Duke
had laid a fecure Foundation for his Greatnefs; he was now in Poffeffion of all *Romagna*, with the Dutchy of *Urbin*; and the
People, who already began to tafte their
future Peace and Happinefs, were wholly
in his Intereft   As this Part of the Duke's
Story

Borgia, carrying his Forefight even beyond the
Death of the Pope his Father, exterminated the
whole Race of thofe Lords whom he had ftripped
of their Poffeffions. Thus you fee how one Crime
draws on another. In order to be powerful, a
Man

Vitellozzo Vitelli, Olive-   of *Piene* by Duke *Valentine's*
rotto da Fermo, the Duke *de*   Order See *Machiavel's* Ac-
Gravina, and Signor *Paulo*,   count of this Murder. *De-*
were all ftrangled in theCaftle   *fcriptione del modo, &c*

Story well deserves to be known and to be imitated by others, I will not pass it over in Silence.

When Duke *Valentine* had possessed himself of *Romagna*, finding it had been governed by poor and inferior Lords, who had rather plundered than corrected their Subjects, and been the Occasion of Discord rather than of Union, insomuch that the whole Country was over-run with Robberies, Murders, and all manner of Riots; to reduce them to Order and Subjection to Monarchy, he thought it necessary to provide them with a good Governor. This Post he conferred on *Remiro d'Orco*, a Man of great Dispatch and Cruelty, and to him he gave an unlimited Power. It was not long before *d'Orco* settled the whole Country in Peace and Concord, and gained great Reputation Afterwards the Duke suspecting that his delegating such an absolute Authority would make him odious to the People[a], he erected

in

Man must have large Possessions; for this Purpose, he must turn out the lawful Possessors: And to enjoy with Safety what he has got with Injustice, these

F 4

Pos-

[a] *Nec unquam, satis fida potentia, ubi nimia est,* says *Tacitus,* Hist 2.

in the Middle of the Province a Court of Justice, in which each City had its Advocate; and a Man of great Worth was appointed to preside. But knowing that his past Severity had created him several Enemies, in order to disculpate himself, and to recover the Affections of the People, he one Morning caused the Governor to be apprehended, his Head to be struck off in the Market-place at *Cefena*, and his Members exposed upon a Stake, with a bloody Dagger by them; having a mind to shew the People, that if any Cruelties had been committed, they had not proceeded from himself, but from the Arrogance of his Minister[b]. And in effect this cruel Spectacle pacified and stunned the People for some time.

But to resume our Discourse; I say the Duke now found himself very powerful, and

Poffeffors, and their whole Race, must needs be exterminated. This is *Machiavel's* Doctrine, and the Practice of Highwaymen and Banditti.

Borgia

[b] Nothing is more common than for Princes to sacrifice sooner or later the Instruments of their Cruelty. *Scelerum ministros*, says *Tacitus* of *Tiberius, ut perverti ab aliis nolebat, ita plerumque fatiatus, veteres et prægraves afflixit* Ann 4 *Levi post admiſſum ſcelus gratia, dein graviore odio.* Ann. 14

and in some measure secure against present Danger; he was now armed in the manner he had chosen, and had reduced most of his Neighbours to an Incapacity of hurting him; insomuch that he had nothing to fear from any Power but *France*. But he knew that *Lewis*, who had at length perceived his Error, would not suffer him to inlarge his Dominions: He began therefore to look abroad for new Allies, and to hesitate and waver with regard to *France*; as appeared when the *French* Army advanced into the Kingdom of *Naples* against the *Spaniards*, who besieged *Caeta* · His main Design was to secure himself against the *French*, which he would have quickly done, had the Pope his Father lived.

"These were the Measures he took, with regard to present Affairs; as to the future, the chief thing he feared was that the next Pope would be his Enemy, and seek to resume all that *Alexander* had given him. To prevent this, he proposed four Expedients: The first was to exterminate the whole Race of those Lords whom he had dispossessed [c], that

---

[c] *Mucianus Vespasian's* Minister put to Death the Son of *Vitellius*, because, as he pretended, civil Discord would

that the Pope might have no Opportunity of restoring them: The second, to ingratiate himself with all the Nobility at *Rome*, that by their means he might keep the Pope in Awe: The third, to gain, if possible, the College of Cardinals to his Interest ; and the fourth, to inlarge his Territories, and thus make himself so powerful before the Death of his Father, that he might be able with his own Forces to repel the first Attacks of his Enemies.

Three of these four Designs he effected before his Father's Death, and had very near

ac-

Borgia invited some of the Cardinals to sup with his Father, in order to poison them · The Pope and he having drank, by Mistake, of the Liquor that was poisoned, the former died of it, and the other recovered, to linger out in Misery and Pain. Such is the due Reward of Poisoners and Assassins.

These

would never cease, unless the Seeds of War were crushed and destroyed *Mucianus Vitellii filium interfici jubet, marsuram discordiam obtendens, ni semina bella restinxisset* Hist 4 It is dangerous for a Prince not to put those to Death whom he has robbed of their Possessions *Periculum ex misericordia----Ubi Vespasianus imperium invaserit, non ipsi, non amicis ejus, non exercitibus securitatem, nisi extincta æmulatu, reddituram.* Hist 3

accomplished the fourth. Of the dispossessed Lords, he had cut off as many as he could come at, and very few had escaped: The Nobility of *Rome* he had brought over to his Interest, and had made a strong Party in the College of Cardinals. As for inlarging his Territories, he designed to make himself Master of *Tuscany*: He had already got Possession of *Perugia* and *Piombino*, and taken *Pisa* into his Protection; so that by this Time he had no need of keeping Measures with the *French*, especially as the *Spaniards* had just dispossessed them of the Kingdom of *Naples*, and both *French* and *Spaniards* were under a Necessity of courting his Alliance:

These are the Arts of Policy which *Machiavel* recommends and extols. The Bishop of *Meaux*, the Bishop of *Nimes*, the eloquent Panegyrist of *Trajan*, could not have celebrated their Heroes more than our Author celebrates *Borgia*. Had he done this in a Poem, or in some rhetorical Piece, his Subtlety might have been applauded and his Choice abhorred. But in a grave and serious Work, in a political Treatise, designed for the Instruction of Posterity, it is impossible for an Author to recommend the Example of the most abandoned Ruffian that ever infested the World, without coolly and deliberately exposing himself to the Contempt and Hatred of Mankind.

ance: He propofed therefore to fall fuddenly upon *Pifa*; after which *Lucca* and *Siena* muft have quickly furrendered, partly out of Hatred to the *Florentines*, partly through Fear: and the *Florentines* could have expected no Relief.

Had the Duke fucceeded in thefe Views, as doubtlefs he would have done in the very fame Year the Pope died, he muft have gained fo much Reputation and Strength, as to have ftood afterwards upon his own Bottom, without depending upon Fortune, or foreign Supplies, or any thing except his own Power and good Conduct. But five Years after he took Arms, Pope *Alexander* died, leaving him fecure in none of his Poffeffions except *Romagna*; the reft were all in a hovering Condition, whilft the Duke himfelf was hemmed in between two formidable Armies, and mortally fick. Neverthelefs he was a Man of fo great Abilities, had fuch a Ferocity of Spirit, knew fo perfectly how his Enemies were to be gained, or duped, or deftroyed, and in a few Years had laid fo fure a Foundation for his Greatnefs, that if two powerful Armies had not been upon his Borders, and himfelf at the fame time afflicted with a dangerous

Dif-

Diſtemper, he would have triumphed over all Oppoſition, and perfected his Deſigns.

That the Foundations he had laid were ſtrong, appears from the Patience of his Subjects in *Romagna*, who held out for him a whole Month; from the ill Succeſs of the *Baglioni, Vitelli* and *Urſini*, who though they came to *Rome* when the Duke lay there at the Point of Death, yet could make no Party againſt him; and from the Influence he kept in the College of Cardinals; for though poſſibly he could not get any Man whom he pleaſed elected Pope, yet he was able to exclude all thoſe whom he thought his Enemies. But had he been well when his Father died, every thing would have gone according to his Wiſhes. He told me himſelf, about the Time that *Julius* II. was elected, *That he had well conſidered all the Accidents which might befal him upon his Father's Death, and provided againſt them; but had not imagined that he ſhould be in ſo great Danger of dying himſelf, at the time his Father died.*

Upon conſidering the whole of Duke *Valentine's* Conduct, I find nothing in it that deſerves to be blamed. On the contrary,

me-

methinks, it ought to be propofed as an Example for all Princes to imitate, who fuddenly rife to fupreme Power by Fortune, and foreign Arms: For as the Duke had a high Spirit, and vaft Defigns, he could not act otherwife than he did; nor can his ill Succefs be afcribed to any thing, but his Sicknefs, and the fhort Reign of Pope *Alexander*. So that whoever attains a new Principality, and thinks fit to fecure himfelf againft his Enemies, to gain Friends, to conquer either by Force or Fraud, to make himfelf loved and feared by his Subjects, and obeyed and honoured by his Army; to deftroy and exterminate fuch as either may or fhould do him Injury, to repeal and fupprefs old Laws, and introduce new, to be fevere, and yet agreeable, magnanimous and liberal, to cut off fuch of his Guards as are unfaithful, and fupply their Place with others; to preferve the Friendfhip of Kings and Princes, fo as to make them either ready to oblige, or afraid to offend him· Such a Perfon, I fay, cannot find a frefher or better Model, than the Actions of this Duke.

If in any thing he is to be blamed, it is in fuffering the Election of *Julius* II, which was much to his Prejudice; for though, as was

said

said before, he could not make a Pope to his mind, yet he was able to exclude any one from being chosen; and therefore he should never have consented to the Election of any of those Cardinals whom he had formerly offended, or who after their Promotion were likely to be jealous of him: for Men are as mischievous through Fear as through Hatred d. Those Cardinals whom he had disobliged were, among others, the Cardinals *St. Peter ad vincula* e, *Colonna* f, *Saint George* g, and *Ascanius* h. The rest, if any of them were advanced to the Popedom, might well be afraid of him, except the *Spanish* Cardinals, and the Cardinal of *Rouen*; the *Spaniards*, because

---

d *Nero* displaced four Tribunes, only because he was afraid of them *Exuti tribunatu, quasi Principem non quidem odissent, sed tamen extimerentur* Ann 15 He put to Death *Ostorius*, because he feared the great Strength of his Body, and his Reputation *Causa festinandi (cædem) ex eo oriebatur, quod Ostorius ingenti corporis robore, armorumque scientia, metum Neroni fecerat, neinvaderet pavidum semper* Ann 16 For *Satis clarus est apud timentem, quisquis timetur.*

e *Alexandro Pontifice, quicum veteres & privatas simultates habebat, perpetuis decem annis urbe abfuit* Onuphr in Vita Julii II "The "Cardinal of *St Peter ad* "*vincula* had been ten Years "absent from the City, in the "Pontificate of *Alexander* "VI with whom he had "several old and private "Quarrels

f *John*

g *Raphael Riarii*, the Pope's Great Chamberlain

h *Ascanius Sforza*, Son of *Galeas*, Duke of *Milan*.

cause of their Connexion with him, arising either from Alliance or Obligations; the other, by reason of the Interest he had in the Kingdom of *France*. The Duke therefore ought, above all things, to have made a *Spanish* Cardinal Pope: If this could not have been done, he should rather have consented to the Election of *Rouën*, than of St] *Peter ad vincula*: For it is Folly to believe that new Obligations make great Men forget old Injuries [1]. The Duke therefore, in this Election of Pope *Julius* II. committed an Error, that was the Cause of his utter Ruin.

[1] *Quarum apud præpotentes in longum memoria est Tacit.* Ann 5 For Favours never penetrate so deep into the Heart as Injuries Besides, Gratitude is expensive to ourselves, Revenge to those who are the Objects of it *Tanto proclivis est injuriæ, quam beneficio vicem exsolvere, quia gratia oneri, ultio in quæstu habetur.* Hist 4

CHAP. VIII.

Of those who have acquired Principalities by wicked and unjustifiable Means.

AS there are two other Ways of rising from a private Condition to a Sovereignty, which are not intirely the same either with good Fortune or good Conduct, methinks I ought not to pass them over. One of these Ways is, when a Sovereignty is attained by wicked and infamous Means: The other, when a private Citizen, by the
Fa-

OBSERVATIONS.

In the preceding Chapter, *Machiavel* had recommended to new Princes the Example of *Cæsar Borgia*, who was raised to Sovereignty by means of his Father Pope *Alexander*, and maintained it by deceiving, poisoning and destroying all those who either did or might oppose his Ambition. In this Chapter, he seems to go a Step farther, and to shew how sovereign Power may not only be maintained, but acquired, by Dissimulation, Perfidy, Murder, and the other Arts of Policy, which he had celebrated in *Cæsar Borgia.*

Such

Favour of his Fellow-citizens, is made Prince of his Country. Of this last I shall treat more fully when I come to speak of Commonwealths: What I design to say here of the other, I shall illustrate by two Examples, one antient, the other modern; without entering into the Merits of the Cause, which, I think, are sufficient, when there is a Necessity of following such Examples.

Agathocles, the *Sicilian*, rose not only from a private, but from a mean and abject Condition, to be King of *Syracuse*. This Man, the Son of a Potter, led a criminal and profligate Life throughout all the Degrees of his Fortune. Nevertheless, his Vices were accompanied with such Courage and Activity, that having betaken himself to the Army, he came, by the several Steps, to be

Prætor

Such Doctrines are so absurd in themselves, so glaringly inconsistent with the Peace and Good of Society, so repugnant to all the Sentiments of Humanity, as well as of Justice; that the bare mentioning them seems to be a sufficient Confutation. Nor do I see how any Man, as a Writer, can be more obnoxious to Society, or make himself more infamous and abhorred, than he who recommends and inculcates Dissimulation, Breach of Faith, Cruelty, and Murder; recommends them in a

serious

Prætor of *Syracuse*. He was no sooner settled in that Post, but he resolved to make himself Sovereign of the City, and to hold by Violence, without Obligation to any Man, what had been conferred upon him by Consent. For this Purpose he entered into a Correspondence with *Hamilcar*, who then headed the *Carthaginian* Army in *Sicily*. Having one Morning assembled the People and Senate of *Syracuse*, as if it had been to consult them about public and important Affairs, he gave his Soldiers a Signal which he had before appointed; whereupon they immediately flew all the Senators, and the richest of the Citizens. After their Death, he usurped the Sovereignty of *Syracuse*, and possessed it without any Molestation from his Subjects. And though he lost two great Battles to the *Carthaginians*, and was afterwards besieged, yet he not only defended the City,

serious Performance designed for the Perusal and Instruction of Posterity, and of those in particular upon whom the Good of Mankind so eminently depends. And it were to be wished, that such Examples of superior Villany, as our Author singles out, for illustrating his Precepts, were for ever buried in Oblivion.

The

City, but leaving part of his Forces to maintain it, he invaded *Africa* with the reft, and by that means quickly raifed the Siege, and brought the *Carthaginians* fo low, that they were fain to make Peace with him, and content themfelves with *Africa,* leaving *Sicily* to *Agathocles*

If therefore we examine the Conduct and Exploits of *Agathocles,* we fhall fcaice find that Fortune was at all concerned in them : For, as we faid before, he did not attain the Sovereignty by the Favour of any Man, but rofe to it by Degrees, through all the Steps of the Army, with great Difficulty and Danger; and preferved it afterwards by executing the boldeft Enterprizes Indeed it cannot be called Virtue * in *Agathocles* to murder his

Fellow-

The Life of an *Agathocles,* or of an *Oliverotto da Fermo,* can only tend to quicken and to feed every thing in our Inftinct that is vicious, and to call up all thofe Seeds of Vice that may lie hid in the Mind, and would otherwife be neglected and die away How many young People have been

fpoiled

* In this Paffage, Machiavel feems to put a new Senfe upon the Word Virtue, which he commonly makes ufe of to fignify a y Quality whatever, good or bad, that gains Efteem and Applaufe He had juft faid, a few Lines before, *le azzione eminenti d. Agatocle.*

Fellow-citizens, betray his Friends, and act without any Regard to Faith, Pity or Religion: This may be the means of attaining supreme Power, but can never purchase true Glory. Nevertheless, when I consider his Courage and Conduct in facing and overcoming Dangers, and his Greatness of Mind in supporting and mastering his Misfortunes; though he cannot be ranked with the most excellent Men, on account of his horrible Cruelties and numberless other Crimes; yet I see no Reason why he may not be deemed equal to the greatest Commanders. Wherefore we cannot ascribe to Fortune or Virtue, what *Agathocles* effected without the help of either.

In our own Times, under the Popedom of *Alexander* VI. *Oliverotto da Fermo*, having been left an Orphan, was brought up by his Uncle on the Mother's side, whose Name was *John Fogliani* †, and in his Youth was

listed

spoiled by reading Romances; insomuch that *Gandalin* or *Medor*, or some other Hero in Romance, has been the sole Pattern of their Thoughts and Actions? Certainly there is something epidemical and infectious in our manner of Thinking,

G 3

some-

---

† *Guicciardin* calls him *Fiangiani*.

lifted a Soldier under *Paul Vitelli*, to learn the Art of War, and thereby attain some confiderable Command in the Army *Vitelli* dying, he ferved afterwards under that General's Brother *Vitellozzo* ; and being a Man of Parts, Courage, and good Appearance, he quickly rofe to be one of *Vitellozzo*'s principal Officers But thinking it beneath him, and fervile, to be longer under any Superior, he refolved, with the Affiftance of the *Vitelli*, to make himfelf Mafter of *Fermo*, and for this purpofe entered into a Confpiracy with fome of the Inhabitants of that City, who preferred Slavery to Liberty Whereupon he wrote to *Fogliani* his Uncle, that after fo many Years Abfence, he intended to come and vifit him and his native Country, and take a View of his Inheritance And that, as he had long ferved in the Wars merely to pur-

fomething that communicates itfelf from Mind to Mind with Eafe and Rapidity

Charles XII that wandering Hero, that King-Errant, worthy of old Chivalry, whofe Virtues were pufhed to fuch an Excefs, that they degenerated into Vices, always carried about him from his Youth the Life of *Alexander* the Great, and copied after it fo that many who particularly knew him, affirm that it was *Quintus Curtius* who ra-

purchase Reputation and Honour, he proposed to make such a Figure at his Entry, as
might shew his Fellow-citizens that his Time
had not been ill spent. He therefore desired
Admittance for a hundred Horse of his
Friends and Equipage, and begged he would
be pleased to procure them an honourable
Reception, both for his own Reputation,
and for his Uncle's, who had brought him
up. *Fogliani* was wanting in no good Office on behalf of his Nephew; so that he was
received in *Fermo* with great Distinction, and
lodged in *Fogliani*'s House. A few Days
after, when he had made the necessary Dis-
positions for perpetrating his Design, he prepared a magnificent Entertainment, to which
he invited his Uncle, and all the principal
Ci-

ravaged *Poland* and *Saxony*, that *Stanislaus* owed
his Crown to the Promotion of *Abdolonymus* [*], and
that the Battle of *Arbela* occasioned the Defeat at
Pultowa.

As I am now speaking only of the Mind of
Man in general, and of the Impressions and Mo-
difications that may be produced in it by external
Causes, without considering the Difference of

[*] *Abdolonymus*, a Gardener, was made King of *Sydon*
by *Alexander*

Rank

Citizens. The Feaft was over, with the other Diverfions which are ufual upon fuch Occafions, when *Oliverotto* purpofely brought in fome ferious Difcourfe concerning the Pope and his Son *Cæfar Borgia,* their Grandeur and their Enterprizes. His Uncle and the other Guefts partaking of the Difcourfe, he ftarted up on a fudden, and faid thefe were Affairs of too great Moment not to be difcourfed of in a more private Place. Accordingly he retired into a Chamber, whither he was followed by the whole Company No fooner were they fat down, but fome Soldiers, who were concealed about the Chamber, rufhed in and murdered them all. *Foglianι* and the principal Citizens being thus difpatched, *Oliverotto* mounted on Horfeback, rode up and down the City, cleared it of all his fufpected Enemies, and

be-

Rank or Fortune, methinks I may be allowed to pafs from this great Example to another of a meaner fort —— Not many Years ago, a mock Opera was acted in *London,* and met with uncommon Applaufe, infomuch that it has been often reprefented fince · The Subject of it was the Feats, Adventures and Intrigues of Highwaymen, Pickpockets, *&c.* What was the Confequence? The Heroes of the Piece were admired and imitated,

and

besieged the chief Magistrate in his Palace.
Whereupon the rest of the Citizens, through
Fear, submitted, and settled a Government of which *Oliverotto* assumed the Sovereignty. After dispatching all the Malecontents, who had any Power to hurt him,
he so well secured himself by several new
Laws, both Civil and Military, that in the
Space of one Year, he was not only fixed in
the Sovereignty of *Fermo*, but grown formidable to all his Neighbours. Insomuch
that he might have enjoyed his Principality
as long as *Agathocles* did that of *Syracuse*,
had he not suffered himself to be circumvent-
ed by *Cæsar Borgia*, who, as we said before,

fur-

and the Roads and Streets more infested with Robbers than they were before. So dangerous it is to
proclaim and dwell upon Examples of Vice !

   Machiavel here produces two Examples of successful Villains, takes in just as much of their Story
as would serve his Purpose, and passes over every
thing that might tend to shew their Misery. But
it is not true, that *Agathocles* enjoyed his Usurpation
in Peace. *Agathocles* was almost continually at
War with the *Carthaginians* ; he was forced, in
Africa, to fly from his own Army, who afterwards
murdered his Children ; and he was at length
poisoned by his own Grandson.

Oli-

furprifed the *Urfini* and *Vitelli* at *Sinigalia;* where *Oliverotto* being likewife taken a Year after the Parricide he had committed, was ftrangled with his Mafter *Vitellozzo,* from whom he had learned his Skill both in War and Villany.

Confidering how many Sovereigns, becaufe of the Cruelties they had acted, were unable to defend their Government even in Times of Peace, much lefs when they were intangled in War; one may wonder how it happened that *Agathocles,* and a few more, after numberlefs Acts of Treachery and Inhumanity, reigned fo long and fo peaceably over thofe who had formerly been their Fellow-citizens, and were not deftroyed either by Confpiracies at home, or Invafions from abroad   The Succefs or Mifcarriage of fuch Princes

Oliverotto, the other Example, foon met with the Reward due to his Crimes ; he was deftroyed by the Treachery of *Cæfar Borgia,* in lefs than a Year after his Ufurpation, and thus feems to have been fnatched from the Vengeance of his injured Fellow-citizens: So that this Example proves nothing ; and the other can only fhew that Mifery is infeparable from Greatnefs, when Greatnefs is attained by Perfidy and Inhumanity.

Our

Princes does, I believe, depend upon their Cruelty being well or ill applied. Cruelty may be said to be well applied, (if it is allowable to give any Commendation to ill Actions) when it is committed but once, out of Necessity, and for Self-preservation, and never repeated afterwards, but converted as much as possible to the Benefit of the Subject. Cruelty is ill applied, when it is but little at first, and is afterwards rather increased than abated. Those who are cruel in the first manner, sometimes receive Assistance afterwards both from God and Man, as *Agathocles* did. But those whose Cruelty lingers, and comes on by degrees, cannot possibly subsist long.

Whence

Our Author's Remark upon these Examples is That *Agathocles* and *Oliverotto* maintained their Usurpations by committing all their Cruelties at once, without being reduced to the Necessity of repeating them. From whence he infers, that an Usurper, to maintain his Government, must suddenly assassinate all those whom he suspects and distrusts, as well as his Enemies, and beware of using a slow Revenge, which would always disturb his Subjects, and endanger himself. *Machiavel* seems to feel no Horror at the naming of these Crimes, but talks of them coolly, as stanch political Maxims: He must therefore have approved

of

Whence it may be concluded, that he who usurps the Government of a State, ought to make great Dispatch in his Cruelties, and commit them all at once; that there may be no Need of renewing them from time to time, and that by their Discontinuance, his Subjects may trust in him, and be disposed to adhere to him, upon his obliging them. Whoever acts otherwise either through Fear or Imprudence, is always forced to be ready with his Knife in his Hand, and can never rely

of the Massacre on St. *Bartholomew*'s Day, of the *Sicilian* Vespers, and such-like Barbarities, as being necessary for the Security and Interest of the Sovereign.

But granting Usurpers and Tyrants sometimes escape with Impunity, that is, are not disturbed or destroyed by those whom they oppress; yet still their Conscience is their Tormentor, they can never extinguish the Testimony it bears against them, they can never be free from the most pungent

---

a This was the Conduct of *Augustus*, *Qui post tr-emuti nomine militem dovis, populum annora, cunctos dulcedine otis pellexit* Ann 1 " He laid aside the Name of " Triumvir, gained the Ar- " my by Liberality and Do- " nations, and the People

" by Store of Provisions. " and charmed all by the " Blessings and Sweetness of " public Peace." And Ann 2 *Quæ tribunatu gesserat, abolevit* " He abolished " the Laws he had enacted. " in his Tribuneship "

rely upon his Subjects, because the fresh and repeated Injuries they receive will always make them dread and distrust him. Injuries therefore must be done all at once, that those who suffer may have the less Time to feel, and therefore be the less disposed to revenge them. Whereas Favours ought to be bestowed by little and little, that there may be the more Time to relish them. And above all things, a Prince ought so to behave himself to his Subjects, that no Accident, good or bad, may be able to make any Alteration in his Conduct. For when Misfortunes bring him to a Necessity either of hurting or obliging them, his Injuries will be unseasonable, and dangerous to himself, and his Favours will be looked upon as forced, and consequently have no Effect [b].

gent Remorses, and their Minds are always overwhelmed and blackened with Melancholy. If we read the Lives of *Dionysius, Tiberius, Nero, Lewis* XI. *Basilowitz*, or other Tyrants, we shall find these Monsters had no true Contentment and Peace, and generally ended their Days in the utmost

[b] In this Sense it was that *Otho* said to his Nephew, That *Vitellius* would not be so implacable, as either to murder or dispossess the Nephew of an Emperor who had preserved all his Family, and surrendered the Empire to him, when he was able to keep it, and when his whole Army

most Wretchednefs. So that if there were no Juftice either in this World or the next, Virtue would ftill be the Intereft of Mankind, becaufe it unites, cements and preferves them; whereas Vice is the true Caufe of their Difcord, Mifery and Deftruction.

Army were extremely defirous to engage with that of *Vitellius An Vitellium tam immitis anim. fore, ut pro sæcolans tota domo, ne hanc quidem sibi gratiam redderet? Non enim ultima desperatiбте, fed pofcente prælium exercitu remisisse Reip noviffimam casam* He had juft before faid to the Army, *Quanto plus spei oftenditis, si vivere placeret, tanto pulchrior mors erit* " The " more Zeal you fhew to " fight for me, if I cared to " live, and the more confi- " dent voi are of Succefs, the " more honourable will be " my Death " *Tacit Hift* 1

CHAP. IX.

Of Civil Principalities.

I SHALL now fpeak of the other Way by which a Principality is attained, to-wit, when a chief Citizen is made Sovereign of his Country, not by wicked Means, or intolerable Violence, but by the Favour of his Fellow-citizens; this may be called a Civil Principality. To attain it, there is no need of extraordinary Merit or Fortune, but only of a lucky Sort of Cunning, which may gain the Favour and Intereft either of the

the People, or the Nobility: For there is no
City but is divided into thefe two Factions;
becaufe the Nobles always feek to command
and opprefs the People [a], and the People to
fave themfelves from Obedience and Oppreffion. This Strife never fails to produce one
of thefe three Effects, either a Principality,
or Liberty, or Licentioufnefs [b].

A Prin-

OBSERVATIONS.

There is no Sentiment more infeparable from
our Being, than that of Liberty; nor is there any
that is more equally, or more univerfally felt. As
we are born without Fetters, fo we defire and we
claim to live without them 'Tis this noble Spirit
of Independence that has produced fo many illuftrious Men, fo many free Governments, and fo
many Republicks wherein a Sort of Equality is
fettled that brings us back, as it were, to the State
of Nature.

In this Chapter *Machiavel* gives fome excellent
Political Rules for thofe who rife to the Sovereignty
of a Republick by the Suffrages of their Fellow-
citizens. And indeed this is almoft the only Cafe
wherein

[a] *Naturalem nobilitatis fu-*
perbiam, fays *Paterculus,* Hift
2 " That Pride and Arro-
" gance which is natural to
" the Nobility" *Avariti-*
am et arrogantiam præcipua
validorum vitia Tacit Hift.
2 " Avarice and Infolence
" are the common Vices of
" the Great "
[b] *Poftquam exigi æqual-*
tas, et pro modeft.a ac pu-
dore

A Principality is introduced either by the Nobility, or the People, according as either of the two Parties has need of it: For when the Grandees find themselves in no Condition to resist the People, they cast their Eyes upon some one of their Number, and make him Sovereign, that under his Name they may vent

wherein he would suffer a Prince to be virtuous: But unfortunately, 'tis a Case that very rarely happens. The Republican Spirit is so excessively jealous of its Liberty, that it startles at the very Name

dore ambitio et vis incedebat, provenere dominationes Tacit Ann 3 "As soon as "Equality was destroyed, "and instead of Modesty "and Moderation, Pride, "Ambition and Violence "prevailed, a Principality "was settled '——*Postquam Regum pertæsum, leges maluerunt* Ibid "When they "were surfeited with the "Kingly Government, they "preferred and assumed the r "Liberty "——*Tribunis reddita licentia, quoquo vellent populum agitandi:--Exin continua per viginti annos discordia, non mos, non jus deterrima quæque impure* Ibid "The Tribunes were re- "stored to their licentious "Authority of throwing the "People into Combustions "at Pleasure ——Henceforward for twenty Years "civil Discord raged, and "there was neither Law, "nor Settlement, the most "Wicked found Impunity "in the Excess of their "Crimes "——*Inter Patres plebemq, certamina exarsere, modo turbulenti Tribuni, modo Consules prævalidi* Hist 2 "Contentions were raised, "and fomented between the "Senate and the People, "sometimes by the Turbu- "lence of the Tribunes, and "at other times by the too "great Power of the Con- "suls ' These are the Accounts which *Tacitus* gives of Principality, Liberty, Licentiousness, and Contention between the Nobles and the People

vent their Animosity c. In the same manner the People, when they are not able to resist their Adversaries, transfer their Power to a single Person, and create him their Prince, to be protected by his Authority d.

The

Name of a Master. We know some Nations in *Europe* that have shook off the Yoke of their Tyrants, and established a Sort of natural Independence; but we know of none, who from being free have subjected themselves to a voluntary Servitude: For the *Danes* in surrendering their Liberties did no more than prefer one Master to many; they made their Sovereign absolute with no other View but to deliver themselves from the Tyranny and Oppression of the Nobles.

Many Republicks have with Length of Time fallen back into despotick Governments. This seems to be a Calamity that inevitably happens to every free Government, sooner or later. And indeed how can it perpetually resist every thing that

H saps

c Thus the Grandees of *Heraclea*, to be revenged on the People, who overmatched them, recalled *Clearchus* from Exile, and made him their Sovereign, notwithstanding the Opposition of the People See *Machiavel*, Chap 16 Book I of his Discourses

d Thus the Constitution of *Denmark* was changed, not many Years ago, from a limited to an absolute Monarchy For in the Reign of *Frederick* III the Commons and Clergy of that Kingdom, to free themselves from the Oppression of the Nobles, made a formal and voluntary Surrender of their Liberties and Privileges to the King and his Heirs for ever, and compelled the Nobles to join with them, in putting on the Yoke.

The Prince who is raised to his Sovereignty by the Nobles, finds greater Difficulty in maintaining it, than he who rises by the Favour of the People: For the former is surrounded by many who look upon themselves as his Equals, and whom therefore he cannot govern and command as he would [e]; whereas the latter has no Rival in Power, and is surrounded

saps and supplants it? How can it always check the Ambition of those greatMenwhom it produces, and harbours in its Bosom? How can it always watch against the dark and secret Practices and Machinations of its Neighbours, or against the Corruption of its own Members; while Interest prevails in the World, over every other Motive? How should it expect always to come off with Success in the Wars it must needs undertake and support for its Security? or prevent those dangerous Conjunctures, those critical and decisive Moments, when its Liberty is at stake, or those unforeseen Accidents that animate and favour the Wicked and Audacious? [2]

[e] According to *Clearchus* was forced to exterminate all the Grandees of *Heraclea*, in order to deliver himself from their Insolence, and to content the People, by avenging them upon those who had deprived them of their Liberty. From whence *Machiavel* infers, Chap. 16. Book I. of his Discourses, that whichever way a Prince attains his Sovereignty, the Good-will of the People must always be gained, sooner or later, because 'tis otherwise impossible he should be safe. Besides, the more a Prince destroys the People, the more he weakens himself.

rounded by few or none who are not dif-
pofed and ready to obey f. Befides, the Grandees cannot, with Honour, be contented, or
without doing Injury to others; but it is not
fo with the People, who are more reafonable
in their Expectations; and would only be fecure againft Oppreffion; whereas the Grandees want to opprefs. Add to this, that a
Prince can never be fafe, when the People
are his Enemies, becaufe of their Number;
on the contrary the Nobles are but few, and
therefore eafily fecured. The worft a Prince
may expect from an injured People, is to be
forfaken; but when the Grandees are his
Enemies, he ought to fear that they will not
only

eious? If any Armies are commanded by timid
and unfkilful Generals, it fails a Prey to any Enemies; if they are headed by bold and fuccefsful
Commanders, thefe will be as dangerous in Times
of Peace, as they were ufeful and beneficial during
the War.

There are few, if any Republicks, but have rifen
from the very Abyfs of Tyranny to Freedom, and
from thence have funk again into the Dregs of Ser-
H 2 vitude.

f *Cofmo* of *Medicis* prevailed over the Nobles of
Florence, becaufe, (fays *Nardi*, Book I of his Hiftory)
the Nobles being all equal,
did not fo well agree among
themfelves, as *Cofmo's* Adherents, who dazzled with the
Splendor and Reputation of
his Family, thought it no
Difhonour to depend upon,
or obey him.

only forsake, but attack him; for having more Penetration and Cunning, they anticipate their Dangers, and court the Favour of the Person who is like to overcome. Besides, the Prince is obliged to live always with one and the same People, but not always with the same Set of Grandees; for these he may make and unmake, advance and remove as he pleases

But for the better explaining of this Subject, we must consider the Conduct of the Nobles with regard to their Prince. They are either wholly attached to his Fortune and Interest; and in this Case, they ought to be valued and preferred, unless they are rapacious. Or they are not. This again proceeds either from Fear, and a natural Want of Courage; or from Design and Ambition. In the first Case, they may be employed, especially if they are Men of Prudence, and fit for giving Counsel; because they will do

Honour

vitude. The same *Athenians,* who in the Times of *Demosthenes* provoked and insulted *Philip of Macedon,* crouched to *Alexander* The *Romans,* who abhorred Royalty, and expelled their Kings, suffered, some Ages after, the most horrible Oppression and Cruelties from their Emperors. And the same *Englishmen* who rebelled against, imprisoned,

Honour to the Prince in his Prosperity, and are not to be feared in his Misfortunes. But when the Nobles are acted by Ambition and Self-designs, which shew that their Thoughts are more intent upon their own Advantage than the Prince's, he ought to be as much upon his Guard against them, as against his open Enemies§; for in his Misfortunes, they will always help to bring on his Ruin.

The Prince who owes his Advancement to the People, ought always to keep them his

foned, and beheaded *Charles* I. submissively bore the galling Yoke of a Protector.

In the same manner as Men are born, grow up, live for some Years, and if not cut off by some Disease or Accident, die of old Age; Republicks are formed and settled, flourish for some Ages, and if not destroyed either by foreign Arms, or by some of their own Citizens, perish by the Length

H 3 of

§ We have an Instance of this in *Valerius Festus* ——*Legatus studia provincialium cum fide juvit, mox nutabat, palam epistolis edictisque Vitellium, occultis nuncius Vespasianum fovens, & hæc illave defensurus, prout invaluissent Tacit* Hist 2 "Valerius Festus, Governor of the Province, promoted the Zeal and Inclinations of the People, with exemplary Fidelity, in the Beginning In a short time he began to halt, and whilst in Letters and Edicts he asserted the Cause of *Vitellius*, he gave secret Intelligence and Encouragement to *Vespasian*, being resolved, whichever Party prevailed, to maintain the Justice of it."

his Friends; and this is easily done, the People only desiring to be saved from Oppression. But he who is advanced by the Grandees, against the Inclinations of the People, should make it his chief Endeavour to ingratiate himself with the latter; which may be easily done, by granting them his Protection. For when Men receive good Offices where they expected Injuries, the Obligation is doubled; and therefore the People grow better affected to such a Prince, when he is their Benefactor, than they would have been, had he owed his Principality to them. Now the Affections of a People are to be gained many ways, for which no certain Rules can be given,

of their Duration. As every thing in Nature has its Period, so all Governments, and the greatest Monarchies, have but their limited Time. Republicks are sensible of this; and therefore look upon every Family that is grown too powerful, as the Beginning and Root of a Distemper by which they must perish. But tho' many Revolutions in States and Kingdoms must needs happen, yet Governments that are truly free will never be perfuaded to put themselves under a Master; at least a better Master: For they will always alledge that it is safer to be subject to the Laws, than to the Caprice of any single Man.

given, because they vary according to the Times; and therefore I shall pass them over. I will only conclude, that it is always necessary a Prince should be well with his People; for otherwise he has no Resources in Times of Danger and Distress. *Nabis* Prince of *Sparta*, attacked and besieged by all *Greece*, and by a victorious Army of *Romans*, was able to defend his Government and his Country against their united Strength, by securing a few of the Nobles. But had the People been his Enemies, this would not have been sufficient.

Let no Man here object the trite Proverb, *That he who builds upon the People, builds upon Sand.* This indeed may be true, when a private Citizen rests upon the People, and persuades himself, that they will protect or deliver him from the Oppression of his Enemies or of the Magistrates: Such a Man will often find himself deceived; as happened to the *Gracchi* in *Rome* [h], and to *George Scali* in *Florence* [i]. But if the Prince, who relies upon them,

H 4

---

[h] *Tiberius Gracchus* was attacked and killed by the People, upon *Scipio Nasica's* calling out, *Qui salvam velint Remp. me sequantur* " Let all those who would " maintain the Liberty of " the Commonwealth, fol- " low me" *Paterc.* Hist 2. His Brother *Caius* was killed afterwards

[i] *Machiavel* relates, Book III of his History of *Florence*.

them, knows how to command, is courageous, and neither dejected in his Distress, nor wanting in the necessary Preparations; if by his own Valour and Conduct he keeps alive the Courage of a whole People, he will never be deserted by them, nor find that he rests upon a tottering Foundation.

Principalities that are suddenly raised from a limited to an absolute Government, are for the most part in a dangerous and unsettled Condition: For either the Sovereign governs by himself, or delegates his Power to the Magistrates: In this last Case, the Danger is greatest; for he solely depends upon the Affection of his Delegates; who may with great Ease deprive him of his Authority, especially in Times of Danger, either by acting against him, or by withdrawing their Obedience. Nor can such a Prince, when his Affairs are perplexed, resume and exert his whole Authority; because his Subjects, accustomed to receive their Orders from their Magistrates and Fellow-citizens, will refuse Obe-

rence, that *George Scali* was beheaded in Presence of a People, who but a little before had adored him Whence proceeded the Proverb at *Florence, Fondarsi come Messer Giorgio Scala* The Affection of the People, he adds, is as easily lost as it is gained

Obedience to those of their Prince, besides, it always happens in such pressing Exigencies, that there are but few upon whose Fidelity he can rely. Wherefore a Prince, in such a Situation, ought not to take his Measures according to what he sees in Times of Peace; for then the Citizens have need of the State, and his Subjects of his Protection; and every one runs, and promises, and dies to serve him, when Death is at a Distance: But in Times of Distress, when the State and the Prince have need of their Service, most of them fly off[k]. And this Trial is the more dangerous, as it can be made but once.

Upon the Whole, a wise Prince ought to find some Means of making his People, at all Times and upon all Occasions, have need of his Government, and in this Case they will ever be faithful and true to him.

CHAP.

---

[k] *Prosperis Vitellii rebus certaturi ad obsequium, adversam ejus fortunam ex æquo detectabant,* says Tacitus, Hist 2 "Those who " during the Prosperity of " *Vitellius,* would contend " with one another in Acts " of Submission and Duty, " equally concurred to de- " sert his falling Fortune" ---*Languentibus omnium studiis, qui primo alacres fidem atque animum ostentaverant* Hist 1. "The Zeal of all " those Men decaying, who " had at first appeared con- " fident, faithful and coura- " geous."

CHAP. X.

How the Strength of all Principalities ought to be computed.

IN examining the Nature of these Principalities, it must further be considered, whether the Prince has Power and Territory enough to subsist by himself, or whether he has need of foreign Assistance: To clear this Point, I say that as I think those Princes capable of subsisting by themselves,
who

OBSERVATIONS.

Since the Time that *Machiavel* wrote his political Prince, the Face of *Europe* is so much altered, that it would be no longer known to be the same. If some great General in the Age of *Lewis* XII. was to come back into the World, he would find himself much at a Loss; he would see War now carried on by such numberless Bodies of Men, as can hardly be subsisted in the Field, and yet are kept up in Times of Peace, as well as of War; whereas in his Age, to execute great Enterprizes, and strike decisive Blows, a Handful of Men was sufficient, and these were disbanded as soon as the War was over. Instead of Coats of Mail, Lances, and Harquebusses with Matches, he would find the Army furnished with common Cloathing,
with

who either by the Numbers of their Men,
or the Greatneſs of their Wealth, can raiſe
a complete Army, and give Battle to thoſe
who attack them; ſo thoſe I think depend
upon others, who not being ſtrong enough
to meet the Enemy in the Field, are forced
to keep within the Walls of their Towns.
Of the firſt Caſe we have ſpoken already,
and ſhall ſay more as Occaſion offers. As
to the other, we can only adviſe ſuch Princes
to ſtrengthen and fortify the Capital Towns
in their Dominions, and to have no Dependence upon the Country: For if the Prince
has fortified his Capital, and behaved himſelf

with Firelocks and Bayonets; he would ſee new
Methods of Encamping, Beſieging, and giving
Battle; and find the Art of ſubſiſting the Troops
as neceſſary now, as that of Conquering was before.

But what would *Machiavel* ſay himſelf, upon
ſeeing this new political Face of *Europe*, and ſo
many Princes ſcarce known in his Days, who are
now ranked with the greateſt Monarchs? upon
ſeeing the Power and Authority of Sovereigns
firmly eſtabliſhed; the preſent Manner of Nego-
tiating; and that Balance which is ſettled in *Europe* by the Alliance of many Princes and States
againſt the Over-powerful and Ambitious, a Balance which is ſolely deſigned for ſecuring the Peace
and Tranquillity of Mankind?

All

felf to his Subjects fo as I have deſcribed, and ſhall deſcribe hereafter, he will never be wantonly attacked [a]; for Men are always affraid of embarking in difficult Enterprizes [b]; and there

All theſe Things have produced ſuch an univerſal Change, as renders our Author's Maxims inapplicable in Modern Politicks As appears chiefly from this Chapter. I ſhall here give a few Examples.

Machiavel ſuppoſes that a Prince who has a large Territory, a numerous Army, and full Coffers, may defend himſelf againſt his Enemies by his own Strength without foreign Supplies. As I will venture to contradict, nay I affirm, that let a Sovereign be ever ſo formidable, he cannot defend himſelf againſt powerful Enemies without the Aſſiſtance

[a] Upon this Account *Tacitus* cenſures *Bardanes* for laying Siege to *Seleucia* ---- *Solis Seleucenſibus domitationem ejus abnuentibus, & quos, ut patris ſui quoque defectores, ita magis, quam ex uſu præſenti, accenſus, implorabatur obſidione urbis validæ, & munitionibus objecti amnis, muroq, & commeatibus firmatæ Ann 11 "Seleucia was the only "City that diſowned his "Sway So that, more "tranſported with Wrath "againſt the *Seleucians*, as "a People who had likewiſe "revolted from his Father, "than conſulting his preſent "Intereſt, *Bardanes* entangled himſelf in the Siege "of a Town, ſtrongly forti-"fied, fenced by a River, "and repleniſhed with "Stores"

[b] *Omnes qui magnarum rerum conſilia ſuſcipiunt, æſtimare debent, an quod inchoarunt promptum effectu, aut certe non arduum ſit Hiſt 2 "Thoſe who undertake "ſome great Enterprize, ſays "*Tacitus*, ought to examine "well, whether the effect-"ing it is eaſy or difficult."

there is always great Difficulty in attacking a Prince who keeps his Capital in a good State of Defence, and is not hated by his People.

The Towns in *Germany* are many of them free, have but little Territory, obey the Emperor only when they pleafe, and are in no Awe either of him, or of any other Prince of the Empire: The Reafon is, they are all fo well fortified, that the taking any one of them is looked upon as a Work of great Difficulty and Time; their Walls are ftrong, their Ditches deep, their Fortifications fufficiently provided with Cannon; and their Stores and Magazines furnifhed for a Twelvemonth. Befides, that the lower People may be no Burden to them, but maintain themfelves by their own Labour, they have Workhoufes,

---

Affiftance of fome Allies. If the moft formidable Prince in *Europe*, *Lewis* XIV. was reduced to the greateft Diftrefs, and had like to have been ruined by the War about the *Spanifh* Monarchy; if for want of foreign Affiftance, he was unable to defend himfelf againft the Alliance of fo many Kings and Princes; how fhould a Sovereign, lefs powerful, be able without Allies to refift the joint Attacks of his Neighbours, to which he may often be expofed?

'Tis

houfes, where, for a whole Year, the Poor may be employed in fuch Manufactures as are the Nerves and Subfiftence of thofe Towns: Military Difcipline and Exercifes are likewife much in Requeft among them, for fupporting which they have many good Laws and Cuftoms.

A Prince therefore who poffeffes a City well fortified, and has the Affections of his People, cannot be attacked; or if he is attacked, his Enemies will come off with Difhonour For Affairs of this World are fo changeable, that it is fcarce poffible for an Army to lie a whole Year before a Town. Some may object, that if the People have

Houfes

'Tis often faid, and often repeated without much Reflection, that Treaties are ufelefs, becaufe they are never obferved in all Points; and that the prefent Age is not more fcrupulous in keeping them than any other I anfwer, that though many Examples may be produced, both ancient and modern, and fome very late, of Princes who have not fulfilled all their Engagements, yet it is always prudent and neceffary to make Alliances. For your Allies will otherwife be fo many Enemies; and if they refufe to fend you Supplies, when you have need of them, you may at leaft expect they will obferve an exact Neutrality.

Machiavel

Houfes and Poffeffions in the Country, they will not have Patience to fee them plundered and deftroyed, and that Charity to themfelves will make them forget their Prince. I anfwer, that a Prince who is not wanting in Courage or Authority, will always overcome thefe Difficulties, either by giving his People Hopes that their Troubles will foon be over, or by prepoffeffing them with the Cruelty of the Enemy, or by ufing his Addrefs in correcting thofe who are turbulent and audacious. Befides, it is the common Practice of the Enemy to burn and deftroy the Country at their firft coming, when

Machiavel fpeaks afterwards of the *Principini,* thofe diminutive Sovereigns, who having but fmall Dominions, cannot fend an Army to the Field. He advifes them chiefly to fortify their Capitals, in order to fecure themfelves and their Troops in time of War. Thofe *Italian* Princes, whom *Machiavel* treats of, are properly a fort of Mongrels, half Sovereigns, half Subjects: They only appear as Sovereigns by the Number of their Domefticks: The beft Advice that can be given them, would be, methinks, to leffen a little the Opinion they entertain of their own Grandeur, the extreme Veneration they have for their antient and illuftrious Pedigree, and their inviolable Zeal for the Scutchions. Men of Senfe pretend, that they had better affume

when every Man's Spirit is high, and bent upon Defence; so that the Prince need be in no Fear at first; and in a few Days, when the People begin to cool, and to consider that the Mischief is already done, and that there is no longer any Remedy; they join the more chearfully with their Prince, as they think they have done him an Obligation, by sacrifising their Houses and Possessions in his Defence. And such is the Nature of Man, that he is just as much pleased with confering Obligations as receiving them. If all these things are fairly considered, it will not appear difficult for a Prince not only to gain, but

assume no other Rank in the World than is due to Noblemen of easy Fortunes; that they ought to descend from the Scaffold of their Pride, to maintain at most no more Troops than would be necessary to guard their Palaces against Robbers, if any Robbers could be reduced to the starving Condition of seeking a Subsistence in those Palaces; that they ought to raze and demolish their Ramparts and Walls, and every thing that gives the Place of their Residence the Appearance of Strength. The Reasons are these . Most of those petty Princes, and especially in *Germany*, ruin themselves by the excessive Sums they expend in maintaining that Grandeur with which they are intoxicated, and to support the Honour of their Family,

but to retain the Affections of his People, and to make them endure a long Siege; if he is wife and provident, and has fupplied them with every thing neceffary for their Suftenance and Defence [c].

mily, they reduce themfelves to Beggary and Want: There is fcarce a fecond Son of a fecond Son of a younger Brother, who does not believe himfelf to be fomething like *Lewis* XIV. he builds his *Verfailles*, keeps his Miftreffes, and maintains his Armies.

There is, at this Day, a certain Prince, defcended from the younger Son of a great Family, who maintains all that Variety of Guards which compofe the Houfhold of a great King; but fo much in Miniature, that each Corps can fcaice be feen without the Help of a Microfcope. His Army would perhaps be numerous enough to reprefent a Battle in the Play-houfe of *Verona*.

The Reafon why thefe diminutive Monarchs have no need of fortifying their Capitals, is very plain: They can hardly be befieged at any time by their Equals; for their fuperior Neighbours would prefently interpofe, and offer a Mediation, which they are not at Liberty to refufe: Thus, inftead of Bloodfhed, two or three Dafhes of a Pen are fufficient to terminate their Quarrels.

[c] *Tacitus*, in his Life of *Agricola*, obferves, that he annually renewed the Garifons of his Towns, and fent them frefh Supplies of Ammunition and Provifions, that they might be able to hold out a long Siege

What

What can be the Ufe of their fortified Towns?
Were they ftrong enough to endure a Siege as long
as that of *Troy*, againft their Equals, they would
not be able to hold out as long as *Jericho* againft
a powerful Prince. Befides, if they lie between
two mighty Neighbours, who are at War, it is
not in their Option to obferve a Neutrality; unlefs
they would be totally ruined: And if they join
with either of them, their Capitals become the
Frontier-Towns of that Prince's Dominions.

The Defcription which *Machiavel* gives of the
Imperial Towns in *Germany*, is quite different
from what they are at prefent. A Petard or two,
nay the Emperor's bare Mandate, would be fufficient to put him in Poffeffion of any of them.
They are all ill fortified, moft of them have old
Walls, flanked here and there with huge Towers,
and furrounded with Ditches filled up almoft to
the Top, with the Earth that has tumbled down
from time to time: They have very few Troops,
and thefe ill-difciplined; their Officers are either
the Refufe of the *German* Army, or fuperannuated
and unfit for Service. Some of the Imperial
Towns, indeed, are pretty well fupplied with Ar-
tillery; but this would by no means be fufficient
for withftanding the Emperor, who often ufes to
make them feel their Weaknefs. In fhort, to
make War, give Battle, attack and defend fortified Places, is only the Bufinefs of powerful Sovereigns; and thofe who affect to imitate them, are
no wifer than the Man who counterfeited the Noife
of Thunder, and believed himfelf to be *Jupiter*.

CHAP.

CHAP. XI.

Of Ecclesiastical Principalities.

IT only now remains that we should treat of Ecclesiastical Principalities; which indeed it is hard to acquire, but herein the whole Difficulty lies; for though they are acquired by Merit or Fortune, they are maintained without the Help of either; being founded on old religious Customs, which have such Weight and Influence, that in whatever manner such Princes govern and live, they are sure of preserving their Dignity. These alone have Dominions which they defend not, and Subjects whom they do not govern; and neither for this Cause are their Dominions

nions

OBSERVATIONS.

Antiquity scarce furnishes us with any Examples of Sovereign Priests. Among the Nations of which we have the least Knowledge, the *Jews* only, methinks, had a Succession of priestly Monarchs. It is not surprising, that in the most superstitious as well as the most ignorant of all barbarous Nations, those who were at the Head of Religion did at length usurp the Management of

Affairs;

nions taken from them, nor have their Subjects any Inclination, Design or Power to
withdraw their Allegiance, so that only such
Principalities are safe and happy. But as
these are governed by supernatural Causes,
which the Mind of Man comprehends not, I
shall forbear to speak of them For since they
are raised and maintained by God alone, it
would be Rashness and Presumption in any
Man to account for them.   Nevertheless, if it
should be asked, whence it proceeds that the
Temporal Power of the Church is now arrived at such a Height, as to become formidable to the King of *France*, to drive him
out of *Italy*, and to ruin the *Venetians*;
whereas before the Time of Pope *Alexander*
it was but little regarded by the *Italian*
Princes, I mean, not only by such as are properly

Affairs ; but every-where else, I am of Opinion
the Priests meddled only with the Duties of
their own Function.   They offered Sacrifices, received a certain Allowance, and had some Privileges , but neither Instruction nor Government was
any part of their Business. And if there were no
religious Wars among them, I believe it was
owing to this , they had no Tenets calculated
to sow Division in the Minds of Men, nor any
Power to oppress.
When

perly fo ftyled, but likewife by every Baron and petty Lord · Though this be well enough known, yet I think it will not be fuperfluous to make fome Mention of it here.

Before the Expedition of *Charles* VIII. King of *France*, into *Italy*, that Country was fubject to the Pope, the *Venetians*, the King of *Naples*, the Duke of *Milan*, and the *Florentines*. Thefe Powers had two things chiefly to mind. One was, to prevent a foreign Invafion; and the other, to take care that not any one of themfelves fhould inlarge his Dominions. Thofe over whom they kept the ftricteft Eye, were the Pope and the *Venetians*. To reftrain the latter, it was neceffary that all the reft fhould join in a Confederacy; as it happened in the Defence

of

When *Europe*, in the Decline of the *Roman* Empire, was under an Anarchy of Barbarians, it was parcelled out into a thoufand petty Principalities. Many Bifhops became Sovereign Princes, and the Bifhop of *Rome* fet an Example to the reft. One would think that under thefe Ecclefiaftical Governments, the Subjects fhould have been in a tolerable Situation; fince elective Princes, Princes raifed to the Supreme Power at an advanced Age, fuch, in fhort,

I 3

whofe

of *Ferrara* · And in order to check the Pope,
they made ufe of the *Roman* Barons, who
being divided into two Factions, the *Urfini*
and the *Colonnefi*, were eternally quar-
relling with one another; and as they were
conftantly in Arms under the very Eye of the
Pope, his Power was thereby kept in a low
Condition: Though now and then there
arofe a Pope of Spirit, fuch as *Sixtus* IV.
yet either his Fortune or Wifdom was not
fufficient to extricate him from thefe Difficulties. The Shortnefs of their Lives was
the Occafion of this; becaufe ten Years, more
than which few Popes lived, could hardly
give them an Opportunity fo much as to
humble one of the Factions. And if, for Example, one Pope had in a manner quite deftroyed

whofe Dominions, like thofe of Churchmen, are
of a very fmall Extent, ought to keep Meafures
with their Subjects, if not from a Principle of Religion, at leaft from a Principle of Policy.

It is neverthelefs certain, that no Country
fwarms fo much with Beggars, as that of Priefts.
'Tis there one may fee a moving Picture of
all the Miferies of human Nature; not in thofe
Wretches whom the Liberality and Alms of Sovereign Princes draw thither, in thofe Infects
which faften upon the Rich, and crawl in the
Train

stroyed the *Colonnesi*, presently up sprung another, an Enemy to the *Ursini*, who made it his Business to set them up again, so that there was never Time enough to destroy them utterly. Hence it proceeded, that the Temporal Power of the Pope was but little regarded in *Italy*. Afterwards arose *Alexander* VI. who more than all his Predecessors, shewed what a Pope could do by the Force of Money and Arms · Taking Advantage of the *French* Expedition, he performed, by the means of Duke *Valentine*, all those things which I have touched upon elsewhere, in speaking of the said Duke's Actions. Although his Design was not to aggrandize the Church, but the Duke; the Church, after

their

Train of Wealth; but in those Starvelings, whom the Charity of their Prince deprives of the Necessaries of Life, in order to prevent Corruption, and the wrong Use which People commonly make of too great Abundance.

It is no Doubt upon the Laws of *Sparta*, where the Use of Money was forbidden, that the Principles of the greatest Part of these Ecclesiastical Governments are founded; with this only Difference, that the Prelates reserve to themselves the Enjoyment of those Goods of which they deprive their Subjects. Happy, say they, are the Poor;

I 4

for

their Death, reaped the Benefit of all that he had done

Pope *Julius* II. who succeeded *Alexander*, found the Church in a flourishing Condition, all *Romagna* being in Subjection to it, and the Factions of the Barons having been intirely rooted out by the Severities of his Predecessor. Having likewise found a way opened for filling his Coffers, (a way not practised before the Time of Pope *Alexander*) he not only pursued the same Track, but also extended his Views farther, and formed Schemes for making himself Master of *Bologna*, for humbling the *Venetians*, and driving the *French* out of *Italy* All which he atchieved with the more Honour to him-

for they shall inherit the Kingdom of Heaven; and as they are willing that all should be saved, they take particular Care that all shall be indigent.

Nothing ought to be more edifying than the History of the Heads of the Church, those Vicars of *Jesus Christ*. One would expect to find there Examples of a blameless and holy Life, but it is quite the reverse. We meet with nothing but Obscenities, Abominations, and scandalous Proceedings In short, it is impossible to read the Lives of the Popes. without being frequently shocked at their cruel and perfidious Actions.

himfelf, as he did every thing for the
Service of the Church, and not for that of
any particular Perfon. He kept, befides, the
Factions of the *Urfini* and *Colonnefi* in the
fame Situation wherein he found them; and
though there were fome Seeds of Difcord
remaining, neverthelefs two things obliged
them to be quiet; the Grandeur of the
Church, which keeps them in Awe, and their
having no Cardinals *, who, in general, have
been the Authors of their Broils· Nor will
thefe two Factions ever be at Reft, fhould they

at

In general, we find their Ambition bent to increafe their Temporal and Spiritual Power, their
Avarice bufied in conveying the Subftance of the
People to their own Families, to enrich their Ne-
phews, their Miftreffes, or their Baftards.

Thofe who make but little Ufe of Reflection,
are furprifed to find that People fhould bear with
fo much Tractability and Patience the Oppreffion
of fuch Sovereigns ; that they do not open their
Eyes to behold the Vices and Exceffes of their
Ecclefiaftical Governors, and that they fhould endure from a fhaved Crown, a Treatment which
they would not bear from a Head girt with

Laurels.

* The *Urfini* and *Colonnefi* and thus raifed up fo many
were ftill more depreffed by Rivals and Enemies to both
Pope *Sixtus* V who created thefe Families.
feveral Dukes and Princes,

at any time have Cardinals belonging to them; becaufe thefe, both within and without the City, promote Quarrels, which the Barons are obliged to efpoufe; and thus to the Ambition of Prelates are owing the Diffentions and Broils of the Barons.

His prefent Holinefs Pope *Leo* X. having, for thefe Reafons, found the Church in a very powerful Condition, there is room to hope, that as his two immediate Predeceffors aggrandized it by the Force of Arms, he, by his Goodnefs, and a thoufand other Virtues, will make it ftill greater and more venerable.

Laurels. This *Phænomenon* feems lefs ftrange to thofe who know what Influence Superftition has upon weak Minds, and Bigotry upon the Mind of Man in general. They know that Religion is an old State Engine, which will never wear out, and has always been employed to fecure the Allegiance of the Subject, and to curb the Intractability of human Reafon: They know that Error may blind the moft Difcerning; and that nothing is more fuccefsful than the Policy of thofe who fet Heaven and Hell, God and the Devil, at work, in order to compafs their Ends. So true it is that Religion itfelf, the Source of all our Happinefs, is often rendered, by the fatal Abufe of it, the true Caufe of our Mifery and Deftruction!

The

The Author judiciously points out what contributed most to the aggrandizing of the Holy See: The principal Cause, he thinks, was the skilful Conduct of *Alexander* VI. a Pope who carried his Cruelty and Ambition to the utmost Excess, and who knew no Principle but that of Interest. Now if it is true that *Alexander* was one of the most wicked and profligate Men that ever wore the triple Crown, what must we think of our Author's Heroes?

This Chapter concludes with an Encomium on *Leo* X. whose Ambition, Debauches, and Impiety, are sufficiently known. These, indeed, are not the Qualities which *Machiavel* celebrates; but he makes his Court to Pope *Leo*: Such Princes deserve such Courtiers. If *Machiavel* praised him only as a magnificent Prince, as the Restorer of Arts and Sciences, he could not be blamed; but he commends him for his wise and political Management.

CHAP. XII.

Of the several Sorts of Military Discipline, and of mercenary Troops.

HAving spoken particularly of the several Sorts of Principalities, as I proposed in the Beginning, considered most of the Causes of their good or ill Constitution, and shewn the Ways which many have taken to acquire and preserve them, it now

now remains that I difcourfe in general of fuch things as conduce to the Defence or Offence of either of them.

We have already mentioned how necef-fary it is for a Prince to take care his Foun-dations be good; otherwife his whole Fabrick will be fure to fall. The principal Founda-tions of all States, new, old, or mixt, are

good

OBSERVATIONS.

There is nothing in the Univerfe but Variety: Nature feems to have made the fame Diverfity in the Conftitution of States, as in that of particular Men. By the Conftitution of a State, I mean its Situation and Extent, the Number and Genius of its People, its Commerce, Cuftoms, Laws, Strength, Weaknefs, Riches and Refources. This Diverfity in Governments is very perceptible, and if, nicely examined, will be found infinite. As in Phyfick there is no univerfal Remedy, no Catholicon for all Diftempers and all Complexions; fo in Politicks there is no general Rule that can be alike applied to all Forms of Government. This leads me to examine our Author's Opinion concerning foreign and mercenary Troops, to wit, that they are not to be relied upon, and therefore are of no Ufe. He brings fome Examples to fhew that they are not only ufelefs, but prejudicial, to the Prince or State by whom they are employed.

It muft be owned, Experience has fhewn that the national Troops of a State are always the moft

ferviceable;

good Laws, and good Arms [a]; and becaufe there cannot be good Laws where there are not good Arms, and where there are good Arms, the Laws muft needs be good, I fhall pafs by the latter, and only fpeak of the former.

I fay then, That the Arms with which a Prince defends his Dominions, are either his own, or mercenary, or auxiliary, or mixt: Thofe that are mercenary and auxiliary are unprofitable and dangerous; and the Prince who refts upon them will never be fecure nor fafe, for they are difunited, ambitious, undifciplined, treacherous, infolent to their Friends,

ferviceable, as appears from feveral Examples, particularly from the Valour of *Leonidas* at *Thermopylæ*, and from the amazing Progrefs of the Arms of the *Romans* and *Arabians*. Our Author's Maxim therefore may juftly be applied to all Countries, that are enriched with fuch a Number of Inhabitants as to be able to fend out a complete Army for their Defence. I agree with *Machiavel*, that a State is generally

[a] *Imperatorium majeftatem,* fays *Juftinian* in his Preface to his Inftitutes, *non folum armis decoratam, fed etiam legibus oportet effe armatam, ut utrumque tempus, et bellorum & pacis, recte poffit gubernari* " The Majefty " of an Emperor muft not " only be adorned with " Arms, but armed with " Laws, that he may be able " to govern well in Times " both of Peace and War."

Friends, abject to their Enemies, without Fear of God, or Faith to Man; and the Ruin of such a Prince is no longer deferred than till he is attacked: He is plundered, as by his Enemies in Time of War, so by his Mercenaries in Time of Peace. The Reason is, because it is not Affection for him that keeps them in the Field, they have no Attachment but to their Pay; and this is not a Motive strong enough to make them willing to die for him They are glad to serve him when there is no need of their Service, but when War

generally but ill served by mercenary Troops, because they can never act with so much Fidelity and Courage as Men who fight for their Possessions and Families. It is particularly dangerous for a Prince to suffer the People to languish in a State of Inaction, and grow soft and effeminate, at a Time when the Fatigues of War harden and discipline their Neighbours

It has often been observed, that a Nation newly come out of a Civil War, is far superior in Valour to its Neighbours: For in a Civil War all the People are Soldiers; there is more room for Merit, and less for Favour; and every Man has more frequent Opportunities of discovering and improving his military Talents.

There are some particular Cases, however, that must be excepted from our Author's general Rule. If a Country does not produce a sufficient Number

of

War comes on, they either disband before, or run away in the Battle [b].

To prove this would require no great Pains: The Ruin of *Italy* at this Time proceeds from nothing but its having depended for many Years together upon mercenary Troops: These indeed may have formerly been of Service to some particular Person, and behaved well enough among themselves; but as soon as a foreign Enemy appeared, they quickly shewed what they were. Hence it was that *Charles* VIII.

of Men for raising a complete Army, and recruiting it from time to time, according to the Consumption of the War, mercenary Troops are absolutely necessary for supplying the Wants of the State. In this Case several Expedients are found for removing the Difficulties and Dangers to which a State is exposed by employing Mercenaries; these are mixt with the national Troops, that the former may not make a separate and independent Body; both are used to the same Discipline, that both may be equally

[b] He makes the same Remark, Chap 43 Book I of his Discourses, and then adds, That Troops which have no Affection for the Prince or State who employs them, will never have Courage enough to resist their Enemies, if these have but the least Affection for their Masters And as there can be no Affection or Emulation but among a Prince's own Subjects, it is necessary he should employ none but them, if he would preserve his Dominions.

VIII. King of *France* was suffered to chalk
out his Way into *Italy* [c]. The Man who
affirmed that our own Errors were the Cause
of our Distress, spoke the Truth; though
they were not the Errors he meant, but
those I have mentioned [d], the Ambition and
Avarice of our Princes; and these have likewise shared in the Punishment [e].

But to shew more fully the Infelicities
which mercenary Troops occasion; I say,
their

equally faithful. and particular Care is taken that
the Number of foreign Troops do not exceed that
of the National.

There is a *Northern* Prince whose Army is composed after this Manner, and who nevertheless is
very powerful and formidable. Most of the *Eu-
ropean* Armies consist of National and mercenary
Troops;

[c] This alludes to a Saying
of Pope *Alexander* VI who
compared King *Charles* to a
Quarter-master, to denote
that *Charles* had over-run
Italy with as much Ease and
Expedition, as a Man who
had no more to do but measure out the Ground, and as-
sign Quarters to his Army
[d] Chap 2
[e] *Guichardin*, Book 3d of
his History of *Italy*, relates,
That *Peter* of *Medicis* said to
Lewis Sforza Duke of *Milan*, That *Lewis* had been be-
fore-hand with him, but to
no purpose, because he had
missed the right way. The
Duke answered, '*Tis true,
one of us two has missed it,
but possibly 'tis yourself*, re-
proaching him indirectly
with having entered into
wrong Engagements with
France But Time has shewn,
con-

their Commanders are either Men of Courage and Ability, or not · If they are, you
can never rely upon them, becaufe they will
always afpire at aggrandizing themfelves,
either by fupplanting you their Mafter, or
oppreffing thofe whom you would protect:
And if they are not Men of Capacity and
Courage, you muft expect to be undone.

Should it be objected, that every Man at the
Head of an Army, whether a Foreigner or
a Native, will act in the fame manner; I
anfwer,

Troops; thofe who inhabit Cities, or who till the
Ground, are exempted from the War, upon pay-
ing a certain Tax for maintaining the Soldiers who
defend them: So that our Armies, for the moft
part,

continues *Guichardin*, that
they had both miffed their
way, and the Duke efpe-
cially, who prided himfelf
in being the Guide and Di-
rector of others, where-
upon his Flatterers were not
afhamed to tell him, nor he
to hear, *That there were none
in Heaven, except Jefus Chrift,
nor upon Earth, except* Lewis
the Moor, *who knew what
would be the Iffue of the War
with* France *Nard.,* Book 3d
of his Hiftory of *Florence,*
where he adds, That the Duke
one Day rallying a Gentleman
of *Florence,* and fhewing him
a large Map of *Italy,* where a
Moor was reprefented with a
Broom in his Hand, driving
away a great many Cocks and
Chickens of all Sorts, he asked
his Opinion of the Defign.
Your Moor, faid the *Florentine,
in cleanfing and fweeping*
Italy, *feems to cover himfelf
with Duft and Filth* Thus
he foretold the Duke what
happened to him foon after

K

anſwer, That War is undertaken either by a Prince, or a Republick: The Prince ſhould go to the War in Perſon, and take upon him the Office of General: The Republick ought to confer it upon one of its own Citizens; to change him, if he is not an able Commander; and if he is, to limit him by the Laws, and keep him in a State of Dependence   And indeed it appears by Experience, that Princes and Republicks, with their own Forces alone, execute great Enterprizes, and that Mercenaries are always prejudicial.   Beſides, a martial Commonwealth, that reſts upon its own Valour, is not ſo eaſily inthralled by any of its Citizens, as one that depends upon foreign Troops *Rome* and *Sparta* maintained their Freedom for many Ages by their own Forces and Arms.   The *Swiſs* are more martial than their Neighbours, and conſequently more free.

As

part, are compoſed of the Dregs of the People, of Sluggards, Rakes, Debauchees, Rioters, undutiful Sons, and the like, who have as little Attachment to their Maſters, or Concern about them, as Foreigners. How different are theſe Armies from thoſe of the *Romans*, who conquered the World? Deſertions, which are now ſo frequent in

all

As to the Danger of mercenary Arms, we have an old Example in *Carthage*, which, after the Conclusion of the first War with the *Romans*, had like to have been oppressed by its Mercenaries, though these were under the Command of *Carthaginians*. After the Death of *Epaminondas*, the *Thebans* chose *Philip* of *Macedon* their General; who, after defeating their Enemies, enslaved the *Thebans*. Upon the Death of Duke *Philip*, the People of *Milan* employed *Francis Sforza* in their War with the *Venetians*: *Francis* defeated the Enemy at *Coravaggio*, and then joined with them, to oppress the People of

all Armies, were unknown among the *Romans*; those who fought for their Families, their Houshold Gods, their Fellow-citizens, and every thing that was dear to them, never betrayed so many Interests by their Cowardice and Desertion. 'Tis the Security of the Sovereign Princes of *Europe* at present, that their Troops are much alike, so that in this respect they have no Advantage over one another. There are none but the *Swedes*, who are Citizens, Peasants and Soldiers at the same time; but on the other hand, when they go to War, there are too few Inhabitants left at home to till the Ground. So that their Power is by no means formidable; they can execute nothing without ruining themselves at length, as well as their Enemies.

K 2   As

of *Milan*, his Masters. *Sforza* his Father, being employed by *Joan* Queen of *Naples*, suddenly withdrew his Army, and left her disarmed and defenceless: insomuch that to save her Kingdom she was forced to throw herself under the Protection of the King of *Arragon*[f]. If lately the *Venetians* and *Florentines* enlarged their Dominions by employing mercenary Troops, and if their Generals have always been their Defenders, without aspiring to be their Sovereigns; the *Florentines* have been in this Case the particular Favourites of Fortune: For of those Commanders, whom they might have justly feared, some gained no Victories, some met with

As for the Manner in which a Prince ought to make War, I entirely agree with *Machiavel*. Indeed a great King ought always to take upon him the Command of his Troops, and to look upon the Camp as the Place of his Residence. This is what his Interest, his Duty and Glory require: As he is the chief Magistrate in distributing Justice to his People, in Times of Peace, so he ought to be their chief Protector and Defender in War. When a Prince is his own General, and present

[f] *Alphonso*, whom she adopted her Son, and afterwards rejected, to adopt *Lewis* Duke of *Anjou*.

with Opposition, and others turned their Ambition another way. The General who did not conquer was *John Acute* s, whose Fidelity could not be known, because he had no Temptation to depart from it: But had he been victorious, every one must own, that the *Florentines* had lain at his Mercy. *Sforza*, the Father, was continually opposed by the *Braccefchi*, insomuch that they were a mutual Check upon one another. *Francis* his Son turned his Ambition towards *Lombardy* h; and *Braccio* against the Church i, and the Kingdom of *Naples*. But let us come to later Occurrences.

The *Florentines* made *Paul Vitelli* their General; this was a Man of great Prudence, and

present in the Field, his Orders are more easily suited to all sudden Emergencies, and are executed with more Dispatch; his Presence prevents that Misunderstanding among the Generals, which is so often prejudicial to the Interests of the Sovereign, and fatal to the Army. more Care is taken of the Magazines, Ammunitions and Provisions, without

---

s An *English* General, who commanded 4000 *English*, in the Service of the *Gibelins* in *Tuscany* *Mach* B. I. of his History of *Florence*

h He became Duke of *Milan*

i He made himself Master of *Perorse* and *Mantua*.

which

and had raised himself from a private Fortune to the highest Reputation · Had *Vitelli*
taken *Pisa*, it cannot be doubted but that
the *Florentines* would not have been at Liberty to break with him; for if he had quitted
their Service, and engaged with their Enemy, they must have been lost without Remedy; and to continue him in so much
Power, would in time have made him their
Master. If we consider the Progress of the
Venetians, it will appear that they acted
with great Security, Success and Reputation,
whilst they made War with their own Forces;
that is, whilst they fought only by Sea, where
they employed their own Gentlemen and
common People, and performed great Actions:
But as soon as they made a Land War, they
degenerated

which *Cæsar* himself at the Head of 100,000 Men
would never be able to effect any thing. As it is
the Prince himself who gives Orders for the Battle,
it seems to be his Province to direct the Execution
of them, and by his Presence and Example to
inspire his Troops with Valour and Confidence.

But it may be objected, that every Man is not
born to be a Soldier, and that many Princes have
not the Talents, Experience, or Courage, that are
necessary for commanding an Army. This Objection may be easily removed: A Prince will
always find Generals skilful enough to advise him,

and

degenerated from their former Valour, and adopted the Manners and Customs of *Italy*. When they first began to conquer upon the Continent, as they had but a small Territory, and were in great Reputation, they had little Occasion to fear their Generals: But as soon as they had inlarged their Dominions, and defeated the Duke of *Milan*, under the Conduct of *Carmignola*, they quickly perceived their Error. For on the one hand, the *Venetians* knew that *Carmignola* was an able and successful General: On the other, they observed that he grew cool and remiss in their Service, and protracted the War; insomuch that no great Success was to be further expected under his Command. Wherefore, as they were neither willing nor able to lay him aside, for fear of losing what they had got, they were obliged, for their own Security, to put him to Death. After him, they employed *Bar-*

and it is sufficient for him, in this Case, to be directed by their Advice. Besides, no War can be carried on with great Success, if the General is under the Direction of a Ministry who are not present in the Camp, and consequently not able to judge of sudden Occurrences, and

give

Bartholomew of *Bergamo*, *Robert* of *St.
Severin*, Count *Pitigliano*[k], and others,
whose Losses they had more Occasion to
fear, than their Victories; as happened not
long after at *Vaila*, where in one Battle the
Venetians were stripped of all they had been
acquiring, with incredible Labour and Difficulty, for Eight hundred Years: Nor is this
surprising; for the Conquests that are made
by mercenary Troops are slow, tedious and
weak, but their Losses are rapid and amazing.

These Examples having led me to discourse
of *Italy*, where for these many Years every
thing has been managed by mercenary
Troops, I will begin a little higher, and
point out their Rise and Progress, that it
may the better appear how they are to re-
formed.

give Orders accordingly; this often reduces the
General to an Incapacity of improving great Advantages.

I shall conclude this Chapter with animadvert-
ing upon that Passage of *Machiavel*, where he
says, That the *Venetians* distrusting the Duke of
Carmignola, who commanded their Troops, were
obliged for their own Security to put him to Death.
For my own part, I don't conceive what he means;
unless

k Of the *Ursini* Family.

formed. When the *Roman* Empire began to decline in *Italy*, and the Pope to take upon him Authority in Temporal Affairs, *Italy* was divided into feveral States: Many of the great Cities took Arms againft their Nobility, who having been formerly favoured by the Emperors, kept them under Oppreffion; and the Church affifted thefe Cities, in order to gain a Temporal Power. Other Cities were fubdued by fome of their own Inhabitants, who became their Princes. Thus *Italy* fell into the Hands of the Pope, and a few Commonwealths Thefe Priefts and Citizens, having no Skill themfelves in the Art of War, began to take Foreigners into their Pay. The firft Man who gave any Reputation to this Sort of Troops was *Alberigo da Como*[1], a Native of *Romagna*. Under his Difcipline were brought up, among

unlefs it be that the *Venetians* either betrayed, or poifoned, or affaffinated a General who had ferved them long and fuccefsfully Thus *Machiavel* endeavours to varnifh over the bafeft Actions, by repre-

---

[1] Another *Da Como*, whom *Machiavel* calls *Lewis*, brought the Troops of *Italy* into Credit, by introducing a Body of *Italian* Soldiers, which he called *St George's* League History, Book I.

among others, *Braccio* and *Sforza*, who in their Times were the Arbiters of *Italy*. These were succeeded by all the rest who commanded the Armies of *Italy* down to the present Times. Their Valour and Conduct has ended in this: *Italy* has been over-run by *Charles*, ravaged by *Lewis*, violated by *Ferdinand*, and insulted by the *Swiss*. The Method they took was first to depreciate the Infantry, and transfer their Reputation to themselves. This they did, because having no Dominions, and subsisting only by their own Industry, a few Foot could give them no Reputation, and a great Body they were not able to maintain: Whereupon the Foot were changed into Horse, a small Number of which was sufficient to make them live with Ease and Honour. And by Degrees this Sort of Cavalry grew so much in Fashion, that in an Army of Twenty thousand Men, there were scarce Two thousand Foot. Besides, they used all Endeavours to exempt themselves

representing them as necessary for Self-preservation and Interest The *Greeks* commonly made use of Periphrases when they spoke of Death, because they could not think of it without Horror: In the

felves and their Men from Fatigues and Dangers. They brought in the Custom of not killing one another in Skirmishes, but of taking Prisoners on both Sides, and afterwards dismissing them without Prejudice or Ransom. In the Night, they never disturbed the Besieged in their Towns, nor did these ever disturb the Besiegers in their Tents: They made no Palisado or Trench about their Camp; and never encamped in the Winter. All this was permitted as Part of their Discipline, and invented, as I said before, to free the Soldiers from Labour and Danger; by which Practices they have brought *Italy* into Slavery and Contempt.

the fame manner our Author uses Periphrases, when he mentions Crimes, not perhaps for the same Reason, but that his Doctrines might go down the better with his Readers.

CHAP.

CHAP. XIII.

Of Auxiliary, Mixt, and National Forces.

AUxiliaries, another Sort of unservice-able Arms, are the Forces of some powerful Neighbour, which a Prince calls in for his own Defence and Assistance. Thus not many Years ago, Pope *Julius*, having made an unhappy Trial of his mercenary Troops, in the Enterprize upon *Ferrara*, had recourse to Auxiliaries, and made an Agreement with *Ferdinand* King of *Spain*, to be assisted by his Arms This Sort of Forces

OBSERVATIONS.

Machiavel uses a very strange Hyperbole, when he affirms, that a prudent Prince would chuse rather to perish with his own Troops, than to conquer with foreign Assistance. A Man in Danger of Drowning would, methinks, give but little Ear to those who should tell him, That it ought to be beneath him to owe his Life to any but himself, and therefore that he should rather perish than lay hold of the Rope or the Stick that is offered him. We know by Experience, that the first Care of Man is his own Preservation, and the next his Hap-

Forces may be useful enough in themselves; but are always prejudicial to the Prince who employs them [a]. For if they are defeated, he is left at the Mercy of his Enemies; and if they conquer, he must expect to be the Prisoner of his Auxiliaries [b]. Though ancient Histories are full of Examples of this Kind; yet I shall keep to that of Pope *Julius* II. as being still fresh in every one's Memory: Nor indeed could that Pope have acted more inconsiderately, in his Design upon *Ferrara*, than he did by putting himself wholly in the Power of a Foreigner. But his good Fortune saved him from feeling the Effects of his

Happiness. And this entirely destroys our Author's sophistical Hyperbole

Upon examining this Maxim, we shall find, perhaps, that it is only meant to inspire Sovereigns with an extreme Jealousy of one another. It is nevertheless this Jealousy of Princes, either with regard

---

[a] *Ambiguus auxilio, am animis*, says *Tacitus*, Hist "The Attachment of Auxiliaries is always divided between two Masters" A little below he calls them *Militia sine affectu* "A Sort of Forces that are void of all Affection for those whom they serve"

[b] *Et acciti auxilio Germani*, says *Tacit* ibid *focus pariter atque hostibus servitutem imposuerunt* "The Germans, being called in as Auxiliaries, oppressed and enslaved their Friends and their Allies, as well as their Enemies"

his Imprudence; for his Auxiliaries being broken at *Ravenna,* and the *Swifs* coming in, and beating off the Victors, beyond his own Expectation, or that of any other Man; he escaped being a Prisoner to his Enemies, because they were defeated, and to his Auxiliaries, because he had not conquered with their Arms. The *Florentines,* being quite destitute of Soldiers, hired Ten thousand *French* in order to reduce the City of *Pisa;* and thus brought themselves into greater Danger than they had ever been exposed to in all their Troubles. The Emperor of *Constantinople,* to withstand his Neighbours, sent Ten thousand *Turks* into *Greece,* who when the War was ended, refused to depart*. And this was

regard to their Generals, or to their Auxiliaries, whom they would not suffer to share in their Success and Glory, which has at all times been prejudicial to their Interests. This has occasioned the Loss of a great many Battles; and such petty Jealousies have often been more hurtful than either the superior Number, or any other Advantage, of the Enemy.

I*

---

* *Andronicus Paleologus* was forced to give up *Threfband* to the *Turks,* whom he had called in for the Defence of *Constantinople,* and *John Paleologus* lost all *Thrace,* which *Amurat* I demanded in Return for the Succours he had sent him against the *Servians.*

was the Beginning of the Servitude into which that Country was brought by the Infidels.

Let every Prince therefore, who would reduce himself to an Incapacity of conquering, employ auxiliary Arms; for they are far more dangerous than Mercenaries; the Ruin they bring on is sudden, they are all united, and at all times obedient to the Commands of another Master: Whereas mercenary Troops, when they have gained a Victory, require longer Time and more Opportunities, before they can do Mischief. They are not all the same Body, but made up of different Nations, assembled and maintained by the Prince or State who employs them, and if they are put under the Command of a Native, he cannot suddenly gain so much Power and Authority, as to do any Injury by their Means.

It must be owned, that a King ought not to make War solely with foreign Troops, and to depend, if possible, upon none but his own; and rather to send than receive Auxiliaries. Prudence will teach him, that he must put himself in a Condition of fearing neither his Enemies nor his Friends; and that when he has made a Treaty, he ought to observe it inviolably. Whilst *Germany*, *England* and *Holland* acted in Concert against *Lewis* XIV. under the Conduct of Prince *Eugene* and the Duke
of

Means. In short, it is Cowardice and Sloth that are to be feared in Mercenaries, but in Auxiliaries Courage and Activity.

Wise Princes therefore have always rejected this Sort of Forces, and depended upon their own; chusing rather to be defeated with these, than to conquer with the others, and looking upon that as no Victory which is obtained by borrowed Arms. I shall never make any Difficulty to produce *Cæsar Borgia* for an Example. This Duke invaded *Romagna* with an Army of Auxiliaries consisting wholly of *French*, and with them he took *Imola* and *Furli:* But afterwards finding these Forces were not to be relied upon, he betook himself to Mercenaries, as the less dangerous of the two, and hired the *Ursini* and *Vitelli·* Finding them also irresolute, unfaithful and dangerous, he discharged

of *Marlborough*, they were always victorious, but as soon as *England* abandoned its Allies, *Lewis* recovered his Courage and Strength. Such Powers as have no need of mixt or auxiliary Troops, ought certainly not to employ them; but as few Princes of *Europe* are in such a Situation, I believe they are in no Danger from their Auxiliaries, as long as the Number of these is not superior to that of their own Troops.

Machiavel

difcharged them, and employed none for the future but his own Forces. How great a Difference there is between thefe two Sorts of Arms will appear, if we confider the Difference between the Duke's Reputation, when the *Urfini* and *Vitelli* were in his Service, and when he depended upon none but his own Soldiers; for when he ftood upon his own Bottom, his Reputation was always growing; nor indeed was it confiderable, till every one knew that he was abfolute Mafter of his own Army.

I thought to have confined myfelf to late Examples in *Italy:* But I cannot pafs by *Hiero* of *Syracufe*, whom I have mentioned before. *Hiero*, being made General of the *Syracufian* Army, quickly perceived that his mercenary Forces were not to be relied upon;

for

Machiavel wrote only for the petty Sovereigns of *Italy*, and indeed his Rules are fcarce applicable to any others: Every Prince that makes War only for another, muft indeed be weak himfelf; but if he makes War in Conjunction with other Powers, he muft always be formidable, if not fuccefsful. To fay nothing of the War of 1701, carried on by the Allies againft *France*; that Enterprize againft *Charles* XII. whereby he was ftripped of Part of his Dominions in *Germany*, was

L executed

for their Officers were much the fame with ours of late in *Italy*. And as he found he could neither retain nor difmifs them, he caufed them all to be cut to pieces; and afterwards profecuted the War with his own Forces only, without any foreign Affiftance. The Old Teftament affords us a Figure that may be applied to the prefent Subject. *David* having prefented himfelf to *Saul*, and offered his Service againft *Goliah* the Champion of the *Philiftines*, *Saul*, to encourage him, clad him with his own Armour: But when *David* had tried them on, he declined to make ufe of them, alledging that with them he fhould not be able to exert his own Strength;

executed by an Army fubject to three different Mafters, the Czar, the King of *Denmark*, and the King of *Pruffia*, and the late War begun by *France*, under Pretence of fupporting the Rights of a Prince fo often elected, and fo often dethroned, was carried on by the united Forces of *France*, *Spain* and *Sardinia*.

As for the Allegory concerning *Saul*'s Armour, which *David* refufed when he went to fight with *Goliah*, 'tis mere Ornament, and proves nothing. It muft be granted, that Auxiliaries are often cumberfome to thofe who employ them; but who would not put up with this Inconvenience in order to conquer Cities and Provinces? As for the *Swifs* Troops

Strength; and therefore he chose to meet the Enemy with his Sling and his Sword d. Upon the Whole, borrowed Arms are commonly unfit; they are either too wide, or too strait, or too cumbersome.

Charles

Troops in the Service of *France*, whom *Machiavel* endeavours to vilify, 'tis certain the *French* have owed many Victories to their Valour and Conduct, and reaped signal Advantages from their Service; insomuch that if the *Swiss* and *Germans* employed in the *French* Infantry were to be dismissed, their Army would be much less formidable than it is at present.

This

---

d " And *Saul* armed *David* " with his Armour, and he " put an Helmet of Brass " upon his Head, also he " armed him with a Coat of " Mail And *David* girded " his Sword upon his Ar- " mour, and he essayed to " go, for he had not proved " it And *David* said unto " *Saul, I cannot go with* " *these, for I have not* " *proved them*, and *David* " put them off him And " he took his Staff in his " Hand, and chose him five " smooth Stones out of the " Brook, and put them in a " Shepherd's Bag which he " had, and his Sling was in " his Hand 1 *Sam* 17 *Ma-* *chiavel* calls it *la sua fromba, et il suo coltello* But *Da-* *vid* carried no Sword with him, and made use of *Go-* *liah*'s to cut off his Head, as is expresly said, Verse 50, &c. " So *David* prevailed over " the *Philistine* with a Sling " and with a Stone, and " smote the *Philistine* and " slew him, but there was " no Sword in the Hand of " *David* Therefore *David* " ran and stood upon the " *Philistine*, and took his " Sword, and drew it out " of the Sheath thereof, and " cut off his Head there- " with "

Charles VII Father of *Lewis* XI. having by his own Fortune and Valour delivered his Country from the Power of the *English*, quickly perceived the Neceflity of having Soldiers of his own, and therefore raifed feveral Regiments of Horfe and Foot, confifting of none but Natives. Afterwards his Son *Lewis* disbanded the Foot, and took the *Swifs* into his Pay. This Error, purfued by his Succeffors, is the Source of the many Dangers to which *France* is expofed, as appears at this Day by Experience. For thofe Kings having advanced the Reputation of the *Swifs*, by depreciating all their own Troops, and disbanding the Foot, fo much accuftomed the Horfe to fight in Conjunction with the *Swifs*, that at length they believed they could

do

This may fuffice, as to our Author's Errors in Reafoning. As for thofe in Morality, he produces the very worft Examples, thofe of *Cæfar Borgia*, and *Hiero* of *Syracufe* The latter, finding he could neither retain nor difcharge his Auxiliaries, without equal Danger to himfelf, ordered them all to be cut in pieces. It would be fhocking to read fuch a Fact in Hiftory, but an Author is unpardonable, who fingles out fuch Examples, to illuftrate and enforce his Doctrines, and recommends them to the Imitation of Sovereigns.

do nothing without them. Hence it proceeds, that the *French* Troops are not able to cope with the *Swiss*, and without them will venture upon nothing. The *French* Army therefore is mixt, consisting of Mercenaries and Natives, and is much preferable to an Army either of Mercenaries, or Auxiliaries only, but much inferior to an Army of national Troops, as sufficiently appears from the Example I have already given [e]. *France* would have been unconquerable, had the Establishment begun by *Charles*, been preserved and improved by his Successors. But for want of Prudence, many Innovations are made, which at first appear beneficial, and conceal the Calamities they produce: Wherefore, as I said before of hectick

reigns. Cruelty and Barbarity are often fatal to private Men, who therefore feel a sufficient Horror at the bare naming them. But those whom Providence has raised above common Disasters, have less Pity, as they think they have less Need of it. Wherefore an honest Writer ought to take all Opportunities of inspiring Princes with an Aversion to every thing that has the least Appearance of Inhumanity, or any other Abuse of Power.

[e] That of *Cæsar Borgia*.

L 3

hectick Fevers, a Prince who cannot difcover
Evils, till they begin to grow up, is not
truly wife; and to difcover them in time,
is the Talent but of few.   If we confider the
Decline of the *Roman* Empire, we fhall find
it firft proceeded from employing the *Goths*
as Mercenaries, by which means the Forces
of the Empire were enervated, and all their
Valour transferred, as it were, to thofe
Gothick Troops.

I conclude, therefore, that a Prince is fo
far from being fafe, who refts upon foreign
Arms, that he lies intirely at the Mercy of
Fortune, becaufe he has neither Valour nor
Strength enough to defend himfelf in Adverfity.   And it has been the declared Opinion of wife Men in all Ages, that nothing
is fo unfettled and tranfitory as a Reputation
of Power, when it ftands not upon its own
native Vigour and Bafis [f].   National Troops
confift of Citizens, or Subjects, or Servants;
all others are either Mercenary or Auxiliary.
The Manner of difciplining thofe national
Troops will be eafily difcovered, if the Obfervations

---

[f] *Nihil rerum mortalium   quam fama potentiæ, non fua*
tam inftabile ac fluxum eft,   vi nixæ   Tacit Ann 13.

fervations I have already made, and the Methods taken by *Philip*, the Father of *Alexander*, and by feveral Republicks and Princes, are fufficiently attended to: And to thefe I refer.

CHAP. XIV.

The Duty of a Prince, with regard to Military Discipline.

FROM what has been faid it follows, that every Prince ought to devote all his Care and Attention to War and Military Difcipline, and to make nothing his Profeffion but Arms, as there is no other Art or Knowledge which it concerns him to pof-

OBSERVATIONS.

There is a fort of Pedantry common to all Profeffions, which proceeds from the Avarice and Intemperance of thofe who practife them. A Soldier is a Pedant, if he is too careful about Trifles, if he is a Bully, or infected with *Quixotifm*. *Machiavel's* Enthufiafm makes his Prince ridiculous: He carries things to fuch a ftrange Extravagance, that he would have him be nothing but a mere Soldier; he makes him a complete *Don Quixote*, who has his Imagination

L 4 filled

poſſeſs ᵃ. The Art of War is of ſo great Importance, that it is alone ſufficient, not only
to maintain a Prince in the Dominions he
inherits ᵇ, but often to raiſe Men of private
Fortunes to Regal Authority On the other
hand,

filled with nothing but Engagements, Retrench-
ments, Sieges, Fortifications, and Attacks.

A Prince who applies only to Arms, diſ-
charges but one Half of his Duty. It is evi-
dently falſe, that he ought to be a mere Soldier ;
and

ᵃ It was the Saying of a
King of *Thrace*, That he
was nothing better than his
Groom, but when he made
War. *Nero*, giving a Plan
of his future Government,
affirmed that he would concern himſelf in nothing ſo
much as commanding his
Armies *Tacit Ann* 13
Domitian hated *Agricola*, becauſe *Agricola* was the better General, being enraged
that a Subject ſhould exceed
him in what he looked upon
as the peculiar and diſtinguiſhing Talent of a Sovereign *Id ſibi maxime for-
midoloſum, ſi militarem gloriam alius occuparet, cætera
utcunque facilius diſſimula-
ri, ducis boni Imperato-
rum virtutem eſſe* In *Agricola* Who are the Princes,
ſays *Gratian*, whoſe Names

are written in the Book of
Fame, except Warriors? To
theſe the Epithet of *Great* is
peculiar Hiſtories are full
of their Exploits, and the
World of their Reputation
and Applauſe, for in the
Arts of War there is more
Glory and Grandeur, than in
thoſe of Peace *Chap* 8 *of his
Hero*

ᵇ *Tiridates*, King of *Armenia*, ſaid, That Dominions were to be maintained
not by Indolence and Sloth,
but Arms, that it was the
Virtue of a private Man to
preſerve his own Poſſeſſions,
but the Commendation of a
Prince to conquer thoſe of
others. *Non ignaviâ magna
imperia contineri, & ſua re-
tinere, privatæ domus, de
alienis certare, regiam lau-
dem eſſe* Tacit Ann 15.

hand, the Prince is often reduced to a private Condition, and ſtripped of all his Poſſeſſions, who, inſtead of applying to Arms, gives himſelf up to ſoft and indolent Amuſements: Inſomuch that the chief Cauſe of the Loſs or Acquiſition of a Sovereignty, is the being ſkilled or ignorant in the Art of War.

Francis Sforza, by his Arms alone, roſe from a private Fortune to be Duke of *Milan*; and his Deſcendants, by declining the Fatigues and Hardſhips of War, fell from being Dukes of *Milan* to a private Condition. For of the many Evils that befal a Prince who

IS

and the Reader may be pleaſed to remember what I have obſerved before, concerning the Riſe of Supreme Power, in the firſt Chapter of this Work. Princes are but Judges by their Inſtitution; and their being Generals is only an acceſſory Quality. *Machiavel's* Prince is like *Homer's* Gods, who are deſcribed as very robuſt and ſtrong, but never equitable. Our Author ſeems not to know ſo much as the Catechiſm of Juſtice; he builds upon no other Principles but thoſe of Intereſt and Violence. He fills our Minds with little diminutive Notions: His narrow Genius embraces no other Subjects, but ſuch as relate to the Politicks of petty Princes.

Nothing can be weaker than the Reaſons he makes uſe of to recommend Hunting to his Prince,

is difarmed, one is Contempt, and this is a kind of Infamy which he muft ufe all Endeavours to prevent, for Reafons which I fhall mention below. As there is no Proportion between a Man who is armed, and one who is defencelefs; fo it is not reafonable to expect that the armed Man fhould voluntarily obey the other; or that Sovereigns who are difarmed, fhould be fafe and fecure among their armed Subjects and Vaf-

Prince, which he believes to be the means of knowing the Situation and Avenues of the Country. If a King of *France*, or an Emperor, pretended by this means to make himfelf acquainted with his Dominions, he would need as much Time for Hunting, as the whole Univerfe takes in the great Revolution of the Stars.

My

* *Tacitus* gives two Examples of this in *Tiberius* One of a Governor of a Province, who prefumed in a Letter to threaten the Emperor with an Infurrection, unlefs he prolonged his Government *Quia res Tiberii magis famá, quam vi ftabant*, fays *Tacitus*, Ann 6 "Becaufe *Tiberius*'s Government depended more "upon Reputation than "Strength" The other of a King of the *Parthians*, who fent Embaffadors to make infolent Demands upon the Emperor, and threaten him with a War, unlefs he complied with them And the Reafon which *Tacitus* gives, is, That the *Parthian* defpifed *Tiberius*, on account of his old Age, and voluptuous Life, which rendered him incapable of applying to War *Senectutem Tiberii ut inermem defpiciens* Ibid

Vaffals [d]: For thefe being arrogant and dif-
dainful, and the others fufpicious, it is impoffible they fhould ever unite and co-ope-
rate: So that a Prince unexperienced in
War, befides other Misfortunes that attend
him, cannot gain the Efteem of his Soldiers,
nor depend upon their Fidelity.

Wherefore a Prince muft never lay afide
the Exercifes of War; nay, he fhould be
em-

My Reader, I hope, will allow me to make a
fmall Digreffion upon this Subject; as Hunting is
almoft the fole Pleafure and Diverfion of the Nobility and Sovereign Princes, efpecially in *Germany*, and therefore will admit of a farther Inquiry.
Hunting is one of thofe fenfual Pleafures which
exercife the Body, without affecting the Mind: It
is

---

[d] *Inter impotentes & va-
lidos falfo quiefcas Ubi manu agitur, modeftia, pro-
bitas, nomina fuperioris funt
Tacit in Germ* "There is
"never true Peace between
"Neighbours that are pow-
"erful and ambitious, and
"thofe that are weak and dif-
"armed When Recourfe
"is once had to the Sword,
"Modefty and fair Dealing
"are Names that belong to
"the ftronger Party" *Ma-
roboduus*, King of the *Marco-
manni*, to make himfelf abfolute, and independent of the
Romans, hardened his Troops
by conftant Exercife, and by
making War continually upon his Neighbours, and thus
enured his Subjects fo much
to the Fatigues of War, that
he grew formidable to the *Roman* Empire *Certum impe-
rium vimque regiam com-
plexus animo—— imperium perpetuis exercitiis brevi in emi-
nens & nofiro quoque imperio
timendum perduxit faftigium
——exercitumque affiduis ad-
verfus fin t mos bellis exer-
cendo, majori operi præpara-
bat* Paterculus Hift 8.

employed in them more in Times of Peace, than of War itself [e]: And this may be done two ways, either by the Application of the Body, or that of the Mind. As to the former, he ought principally to train up his Subjects to military Discipline and Exercises, and to be continually employed in Hunting [f], that he may not only inure himself to Hardships and Fatigues, but learn the Situation and

is an ardent Desire of pursuing some wild Beast, for the cruel Satisfaction of destroying it; an Amusement which renders the Body robust and active, and leaves the Mind fallow and uncultivated

Sportsmen, perhaps, will reproach me here with Gravity and Preaching, and alledge, that I assume

---

[e] As was done by *Cassius*, Governor of *Syria*, who never ceased, even in Times of Peace, to exercise his Legions and to re-establish antient Discipline, with as much Care, as if he had been at open War *Quantum sine bello dabatur, revocare priscum morem, exercitare legiones, cura, provisa, perinde agere, ac si hostis ingrueret* Ann 12 *Seneca* observes, that the Army, during Peace, marched in Battle-order, threw up Ditches, and fatigued itself with Exercises which were then unnecessary, that they might be the more accustomed to them, when they were needful *Ep* 18

[f] This was the Practice of the *Romans*. *Romanis solenni viris opus, utile famæ, Vitæque & membris,* says *Horace, Ep* 18 Book 1 *Vonones* was despised by the *Parthians*, who were great Warriors, because he did not love Hunting. *Accendebat dedignantes & ipse, diversus à Majorum institutis, raro venatu* Tacit. Ann. 2.

and Coasts of the Country, the Height and Ascent of the Mountains, the Largeness and Avenues of the Valleys, the Extent of the Plains, and the Nature of Rivers and Fens; all which he should examine with great Exactness. From this Knowledge he will reap two Advantages: First, he will be the better able to guard and defend his own Country; and

assume the Prerogative of a Priest in his Pulpit, who may affert whatever he pleafes, without being afraid of Contradiction. Hunting, fay they, is the nobleft and moft antient of all Amufements; the Patriarchs and many other eminent Men were Hunters, and by this we continue to exercife that Dominion over the Beafts, which God vouchfafed to give *Adam*.

But

This Knowledge, fays *Machiavel*, Chap 29 Book 3 of his Difcourfes, is more eafily acquired by Hunting, than by any other Exercife Befides, Hunting teaches many other things which are neceffary in War And *Cyrus*, as *Xenophon* relates, faid to his People, when he went to the War againft the King of *Armenia*, That the Enterprize was no more than one of thofe Chafes, to which he had led them fo often before, comparing thofe whom he placed in Ambufh among the Mountains, to fuch as rouzed the wild Beafts fiom their Dens, in order to catch them in the Nets This fhews, agreeably to *Xenophon*'s Opinion, that Hunting is a Reprefentation of War, for which Reafon it is commonly faid, that good Soldiers ought to have the Spring and Swiftnefs of the Hare, the Flight of the Wolf, who retires grinning and gnafhing at his Enemy, and the Defence of the wild Boar.

and in the next place he will acquire a Facility and Exactneſs in judging of any new Situation, which it may be neceſſary for him to view : For the Hills, Valleys, Plains, Rivers, and Marſhes, for Example, in *Tuſcany*, differ but little from thoſe in other Provinces ; ſo that a Man acquainted with the Situation of one Country, may eaſily come to know that of any other   The Prince who is not Maſter of this Art, is wanting in the firſt Qualification of a General : For by knowing the Situations of a Country, he learns where to obſerve the Enemy, where to attack them, where to encamp, how to regulate

his

But no Folly is the better for being antient, eſpecially if it is carried to Extravagance . Many great Men, I own, have been paſſionately fond of this Diverſion , but theſe had their Weakneſſes as well as Perfections · Let us imitate their great Qualities, without copying after their little and idle Occupations   The ſame Patriarchs were not only given to Hunting, but to Polygamy ; nay, would marry their own Siſters ; and had many other Cuſtoms, which favoured of the barbarous Ages wherein they lived.   They were rude, ignorant, and uncultivated, idle Men, who, to kill Time, employed it in Hunting, and threw away thoſe Moments in uſeleſs Amuſements, which they had no Capacity to employ in the

Com-

his Marches [h], draw up his Men for Battle, and befiege Towns with moft Advantage. *Philopemenes*, Prince of *Achaia*, is celebrated by antient Writers, among other Qualities, for this, that in times of Peace he applied to nothing fo much as Military Affairs: When he travelled with his Friends, he would often ftop, and ask them, *If the Enemy were upon that Eminence, and our Army*

Company and Converfation of Men of Underftanding. Let me now ask whether thefe are Examples to be imitated, whether thefe barbarous Ages, or others that were more refined, ought to be the Model of the prefent?

To inquire whether *Adam* received Dominion over the Beafts, would be foreign to my Subject; but it is well known, that Men have been always more cruel and ravenous than the Beafts themfelves, and

[h] Thefe are the Qualities which *Tacitus* afcribes to his Father-in-law *Loca caftris ipfe capere, aftuaria ac fylvas ipfo prætentare, difjectos coercere* " *Agricola* " himfelf always chofe the " Ground for encamping, " the falt Marfhes, Friths, " and Woods, he himfelf " always firft examined, and " he took the Care of check- " ing thofe who in march- " ing did not obferve their " Duty and Rank, but were " loofe and ftraggling" And a few Lines after, *Adnotabant periti, non alium ducem opportunitates locorum fapientius legiffe* In *Agricola* " It was obferved of " *Agricola* by Men of Experience, that never did " any General more wifely " chufe his Pofts for Com- " modioufnefs and Situa- " tion "

*Army posted here, which of the two would
have the Advantage of Situation? How
could we march up to them with most Security, and without breaking our Ranks?
Which way should we retreat, if it was
necessary? If the Enemy retreated, how
should we pursue them?* And thus, in his
Journey, he proposed to them all the Accidents that could happen to an Army in its
March, listened to each Opinion, gave his
own, and supported it with his Reasons.
Insomuch that when he was at War, no Inconvenience could happen to his Army,
which he had not seen before in Times of
Peace, and knew not how to remove.

As for the Exercise of the Mind, the
Prince ought to be conversant in History, and
therein to consider the Actions of famous
Men,

and make the most tyrannical Use of that Dominion they pretend to. If any thing gives us Advantage over these Animals, it is certainly our
Reason, but professed Hunters, for the most
part, have their Heads furnished with nothing but
Horses, Dogs, Boars, Stags, and the like. They
are sometimes as wild and savage themselves as
the Beasts they pursue; and it may well be feared,
lest they should become as inhuman to their Fel-
low-Creatures as they are to their Fellow-Animals;

or

Men, examine their Conduct in War, and the Caufes of their Victories and Loffes; in order to avoid the one, and imitate the other. But he ought efpecially to follow that Method which has been taken by fome excellent Men, who formed themfelves upon the Models of thofe whofe Lives have been moft celebrated and glorious, and have always fet their Actions before them as the Pattern of their Conduct. Thus it is faid, that *Alexander* copied after *Achilles, Cæfar* after *Alexander*, and *Scipio* after *Cyrus*. For whoever reads the Life of *Cyrus*, written by *Xenophon*, will perceive how much *Scipio*'s Glory was owing to his Imitation of that Hero, and how clofely he copied that Modefty, Affability, Humanity and Liberality,

or at leaft that the cruel Cuftom of perfecuting and deftroying thefe, may take away their Sympathy for the Misfortunes of the others. And is this fo noble an Occupation, fo worthy of a thinking Being?

It may be objected, that Hunting is an healthful Exercife, and that thofe who are given to it, live to a great Age; as appears by Experience; that it is a harmlefs Amufement, and very proper for Sovereigns, as it difplays their Magnificence, diffipates their Cares, and in times

M

of

rality, which *Xenophon* has described in *Cyrus* [i].

These ought to be the Employments of every wife Prince: In Times of Peace and Tranquillity he fhould never be idle or indolent, but make it his chief Endeavour to gather Strength againft War and Adverfity; that when Fortune frowns, fhe may find him prepared to ward off her Blows.

of Peace prefents them with an Image of War. I would be far from condemning a moderate Ufe of this Exercife; but let it be remembered, that Exercife, in general, is hardly neceffary to any but the Intemperate. Never Prince lived longer than Cardinal *Fleury*, Cardinal *Ximenes*, or the late Pope; and yet neither of the three was a Hunter. But is it neceffary to choofe an Employment which has no other Merit but that of promifing long Life? *Monks* commonly live longer than other Men: Muft a Man therefore become a *Monk?*

[i] *Scipio Africanus* ought to be the Model of every Prince According to *Paterculus*, he divided all his Time between the Employments of Peace, and the Fatigues of War, being always engaged either in Arts or Arms; either enuring his Body to Hardfhips and Dangers, or cultivating his Mind by his Application to the Sciences *Neque quifquam hoc Scipione elegantius intervalla negotiorum otio difpunxit, femperque aut belli aut pacis feruit artibus, femper inter arma ac ftudia verfatus, aut corpus periculis, aut animum difciplinis exercuit* Paterc Hift 1. *Scipio* always carried *Cyrus's* Life about him

Monk? There is no need of leading an indolent and ufelefs Life, as long as that of *Methufalem*: The more a Man improves his Underftanding, and the more great and ufeful Actions he performs, the longer he lives.

Hunting, befides, is of all Amufements that which is leaft proper for a Prince: He may difplay his Magnificence a thoufand ways, that are all more ufeful to his Subjects: And if it fhould be found, that the Peafants were ruined by the too great Number of wild Beafts; the Care of deftroying thefe might be committed to profeffed Hunters, hired for that Purpofe. The proper Employment of a Prince is that of improving his own Mind, and governing his People, in order to acquire more Knowledge, and confequently be able to accommodate his Government to their Intereft.

It muft not be omitted, that to be a great General, there is no need of being a Hunter. *Guftavus Adolphus*, Marfhal *Turenne*, the Duke of *Marlborough*, and Prince *Eugene*, whofe Characters, as able Generals and illuftrious Men, will not be queftioned, were not Hunters, nor do we read of the Huntings of *Cæfar*, *Alexander*, or *Scipio*. One may make more judicious and folid Reflections in a Walk, upon the different Situations of a Country with regard to War, than when Partridges and Setting-dogs, Stags and Hounds, and a Multitude of other Animals, with the Keennefs of the Sport, diftract the Attention. A great Prince, who lately made his fecond Campaign in *Hungary*, had like to have been kidnapped by the *Turks*, upon ftraying a little at a Hunting. This is an Exercife which ought to be forbid in all

Armies,

Armies, becaufe of the Diforders it occafions in their Marches.

I conclude therefore, that it is excufable in a Prince to go a Hunting, if it is but feldom, and to refrefh him after his ferious and often melancholy Employments I fay once more, that I object to no honeft Pleafure, but the Care of rendering a State flourifhing and happy, and of protecting and encouraging Arts and Sciences, is unqueftionably a much fuperior Pleafure, and a much fitter Employment for a Prince, and whoever betakes himfelf to any other, neither confults his Pleafure nor his Intereft.

CHAP. XV.

Of the Things for which Men, and particularly Princes, are applauded or cenfured.

IT remains now to be confidered, how a Prince ought to govern with regard to his Subjects and his Friends; and as many have written before upon this Head, I fear I fhall be taxed with Prefumption for departing, as I poffibly may do here, from the Maxims of others But as my only Defign is to write fomething that may be ufeful to Men of Underftanding, I chufe rather to

present

preſent them with the real Truth, than with any fanciful Repreſentation.

Many have formed in their Imaginations ſuch Republicks and Principalities as were never known to exiſt[a] But ſo wide is the Difference between the Manner in which People

OBSERVATIONS.

Painters and Hiſtorians have this in common, that they ought to copy Nature. The former draw the Features and Complexions of Men, the latter

[a] *Cunctas nationes & urbes populus, aut primores, aut ſinguli regunt Delecta ex his & conſtituta Reip forma, laudari facilius quam evenire, vel, ſi evenit, haud diuturna eſſe poteſt Tac Ann 4* "All Nations and Cities " are governed either by " the People, or by the No- " bility, or by ſingle Rulers " The Frame of a State cho- " ſen and compacted out of " all theſe three is eaſier " applauded than accom- " pliſhed, or, if accompliſhed, " cannot be of long Dura- " tion" Machiavel, ſays one of his *French Tranſla- tors, treats only of the Way by which a Man may acquire Dominion, and preſerve it, which he makes the ſole View*

of his Prince, refuſing in this to follow the Tradition of thoſe who wrote before him upon the ſame Subject, and who in their Writings have imagined a ſtrange ſort of Perfection in a Prince, which is not to be copied by Men, conſidering the Frailty of their Nature On the contrary, Machiavel endeavours to ac- commodate his Precepts to Experience, and to the com- mon Method of proceeding among wiſe Princes, eſteem- ing it an egregious Folly to point out a Path which no- body treads, and to paſs over one that all the World uſes. Gaſpar d'Auvergne, in his ſecond Epiſtle Dedicatory to his Tranſlation of the Prince,

People live and that in which they ought to live, that he who leaves the Practice to follow the Duty of Mankind, feeks his Ruin rather than his Prefervation. A Man that makes a Confcience of being ftrictly honeft on all Occafions, muft needs be undone among the many that act upon different Principles *. A Prince therefore muft learn, for his own Security, to be virtuous or vicious according to the Exigence of his Affairs.

To

latter their Actions and Characters. There are fome Painters of fuch a fingular Caft, that they draw nothing but Monfters and Devils. *Machiavel* is of this Stamp; he makes a Hell of the Univerfe, and reprefents all Men as being in the State of the Damned. One would think this Politician had a mind to defame the whole human Race, from a particular Hatred he bore to it; and that he had undertaken to annihilate Virtue, perhaps with a View to make all the Inhabitants of this Continent as bad as the Prince he would form.

Machiavel maintains, that, in this wicked and degenerate World, it is certain Ruin to be ftrictly honeft: For my part, I affirm, that in order to be fafe, it is neceffary to be virtuous. Men are commonly neither wholly good, nor wholly bad, but both good and bad; and fuch as are between the two will unanimoufly revere a powerful Prince, who is juft and virtuous. I had much rather make

War

* See the Example of *Pertinax* in the 19th Chapter.

To wave all imaginary Notions about a
Prince, and to speak only of such as are
well-grounded, I say that all Men, and particularly Princes, as being placed in a more
conspicuous Rank, and therefore more the
Subject of Discourse, are characterized by
some Epithet of Praise or Censure. One is
counted liberal, another penurious; one
munificent, another rapacious, one cruel,
another compassionate; one perfidious, another faithful; one effeminate and pusillanimous, another fierce and courageous; one
humane, another haughty; one lascivious,
another chaste; one sincere, another crafty;
one harsh, another gentle; one grave, another giddy; one religious, another profane,
and the like. Every Man, I know, will
agree that it would be highly commendable
in a Prince to possess all the good Qualities

War upon a Tyrant than upon a good King, upon
a *Lewis* XI. than upon a *Lewis* XII. upon a *Domitian* rather than upon a *Trajan*; for the good
King will be well served, whereas the Tyrant's
Subjects will join my Troops. Let me go into
Italy with Ten thousand Men against an *Alexander* VI. half *Italy* will side with me: But let me
march with Forty thousand against an *Innocent* XI,
and all *Italy* will rise in his Defence. No wise

and

lities above-mentioned, without any Mixture
of the bad [b]; but since the Condition of human Nature will neither suffer him to possess nor to exert them all, he should be
wise enough to shun the Infamy of those
Vices which might occasion the Loss of his
Dominions; and, if possible, he should likewise abstain from others which might not
have so fatal an Effect; but if that is impracticable, he must not be too nice; nor
ought he to make any Scruple of incur-
ring the Reproach of those Vices without
which his Dominions could hardly be preserved: For if we fairly examine this Matter, we shall find that some things have the
Appearance

and good King in *England* was ever dethroned by
great Armies; all their bad Kings have been
ruined by Competitors, who, when they began the
War, could not muster Four thousand regular
Troops. Every wise Prince therefore will look
upon Virtue as his chief Security, and as the
Means of gaining and preserving the Attachment
and Fidelity of his Subjects, and striking Terror
into his Enemies.

---

[b] *Adhuc nemo extitit*, says
Pliny the younger in his Panegyric, *cujus virtutes nullo
vitiorum consortio læderentur.*
" Never yet was there any
" Man whose good Qualities
" had no Allay of bad ones."

Appearance of Virtue, which, if practised, must inevitably ruin him; and that others are seemingly vicious, which, if followed, will render him secure and happy *c*.

c There are some Vices which do not hinder a Prince from reigning well, nor blemish his Character as a Prince. *Solomon* was much given to Women, *Trajan* to Boys and Wine. *Vicio es de hombre, no de Principe* "It is the Vice of the Man, "not of the Prince," said the Count de *Penneranda* to an Emperor's Ambassador, who told him it was much to be lamented that *Philip* IV King of *Spain* should be so much addicted to Women. In Princes we ought to distinguish their domestic from their publick Life, their kingly Virtues from those of a private Nature. In this Sense *Tacitus* must be understood, when he says, *Palam laudares, secreto male audiebant* Hist. 1 "Their publick Character was good, their private bad." It is always commendable to do what is right, but this does not always produce good Consequences. Some things are conformable to Reason, but not to Experience, and consequently a Prince, to discharge his Office well, must accommodate himself to the Exigence of his Affairs, and do for the sake of the State, what he neither would nor should do as a private Man. *Morem accommodari, prout conducat* Ann. 12 It is sufficient for him to be good when it is his Interest to be so *Quoties expedierat, magnæ virtutes* Hist. 1 It is necessary for him to know what is good, but not always expedient for him to do it *Omnia scire, non omnia exequi* Tacit. in the Life of *Agricola. Catharine de Medicis,* Queen of *France,* finding that the Pope and the King of *Spain* blamed her for concluding a Peace with the *Huguenots,* after having in vain endeavoured to reduce them by Fire and Sword, said very properly, that *the Kingdom of France was not to be governed like* Aliffe *and* Torbia (two little desolate Towns in *Italy*), for what succeeds in a small Model, will not always succeed in a great one.

CHAP.

CHAP. XVI.

Of Liberality and Penuriousness.

TO begin with the two firſt Qualities that are obſerved in a Prince; I ſay, the Reputation of being liberal is beneficial to him. Nevertheleſs, when his Liberality is not ſo applied as to make him formidable, it proves hurtful: Now if it is uſed, as it ought to be, with Prudence and Diſcretion, it will not be known, nor will it ſave him from the Infamy of being penurious: For there is no gaining the Reputation of Liberality, without being ſumptuous and expenſive upon all Occaſions: But a Prince who ſhuns no Expence, quickly exhauſts his Treaſure, and is forced at length, if he would ſtill keep up the Reputation of being liberal,

to

OBSERVATIONS.

Two famous Sculptors, *Phidias* and *Alcamenes*, having each made a Statue of *Minerva*, the *Athenians* had a mind to chuſe the moſt beautiful of the two, in order to place it upon a high Pillar: When both were publickly ſhewn, that of *Alcamenes* was immediately preferred; and the other rejected, as

rough

to overload his People with Taxes [a], and betake himself to Confifcations, and all other Means whatever of getting Money: This makes him odious to his Subjects, and but little refpected by others, becaufe of his Poverty: And thus his Liberality having made him a great many Enemies, and but few Friends,

rough and unfinifhed. *Phidias*, not at all difconcerted at the Judgment of the Vulgar, defired that the two Statues might each be placed upon the Pillar. When this was done, the Beauties that had been admired in the Statue made by *Alcamenes* difappeared, and the other carried the Prize.

Phidias owed his Succefs to the Study of Opticks and Proportions. The fame Proportion ought to be obferved in Politicks: A Difference in Elevations occafions a Difference in Maxims; and there is no general Rule but is defective in fome particular Cafes: What would be admired in a great Kingdom, would be very unfuitable in a petty State. Luxury, which is the Effect of Plenty, and caufes Money to circulate, makes a great Kingdom flourifh, fupports Induftry, multiplies the Wants of the Rich, and thus connects them with the Poor. If any Quack-politician fhould banifh Luxury from a great Empire, that Empire would quickly

[a] If by Ambition we exhauft the public Treafury, fays *Tiberius*, we muft replenifh it by unjuft and wicked Means *Si ærarium ambitione exhaufirimus, per fcelera fupplendum erit* Ann 2

Friends b, he is in Danger of being undone by the first and slightest Misfortune that happens. When he becomes sensible of his Danger, he endeavours to prevent it by changing his Conduct. Whereupon he suddenly falls under the Infamy of Penuriousness.

If a Prince therefore cannot exercise this Virtue of Liberality so as to make it known, without Prejudice to himself, he ought not,

if

quickly fall into a languishing Condition. On the contrary, Luxury would undo a little Principality. Money being carried out in greater Abundance than brought in, such a State must needs

b *Cicero* says that a liberal Prince loses the Affections of more of his People than he gains, and that the Hatred of those from whom he takes is much greater than the Gratitude of those on whom he bestows *Nec tanta studia assequuntur eorum quibus dederunt, quanta odia, quibus ademerunt* Off lib 2 Let a Prince never give, says the younger *Pliny*, provided he never takes away *Nihil largiatur Princeps, dum nihil auferat* Paneg *Tacitus*, speaking of *Otho*, says that he knew how to dissipate, but not how to bestow his Treasure *Perdere iste sciet, donare nesciet* Hist 1 *Falluntur*, adds he, *quibus luxuria specie liberalitatis imponit* "They are deceived "who take Luxury and Pro-"fuseness for Liberality" The younger *Pliny* will not allow those to deserve the Epithet of liberal, who deprive others of their Properties, and affirms that it is seeking a Name of Liberality by means of Avarice *Qui quod huic dabant, auferebant illi, famam liberalitatis avaritia petunt,* Ep 30 lib 9

if he is wife, to mind the Scandal of being penurious. For when at length it appears that by his Parfimony his Revenues are made fufficient for all his Expences, that he not only can withstand those who make War upon him, but execute confiderable Enterprizes, without loading his People, he will be counted liberal to the many from whom he takes nothing c, and penurious only by the few whom he difappoints in their Expectations

In our own Times we have feen no great Actions done by any but those who paffed for

being

needs fall into a Confumption, from which it would never recover It is therefore the Duty of a Politician not to confound fmall States with great Empires; and in this *Machiavel* errs moft egregioufly in the prefent Chapter.

Our Author puts too indefinite and loofe a Meaning upon the Word Liberality, he feems to make no Diftinction between this and Prodigality. "A "Prince, fays he, who would execute great En-
"terprizes,

c *David* faid the Lord was his God, becaufe he had no need of any thing that belonged to him All Subjects have the likeDifpofition with regard to their Prince, who fuffers them peaceably to enjoy their Poffeffions They are always well affected, fays *Mezerai* in the Life of *Charles*VI when theyare well ufed, that is, when they are not molefted in their Poffeffions

being penurious; all others have miscarried.
Julius II. sought the Reputation of Liberality, in order to attain the Popedom; but
afterwards neglected it, that he might be
able to make War upon the King of *France*;
and his long OEconomy so well supplied
his extraordinary Expences, that he made a
great many Wars, without laying the smallest
additional Tax upon his People.   The present King of *Spain* d, had he courted the
Reputation of Liberality, could never have
executed so many Enterprizes.   A Prince
therefore who would maintain his Dominions, and shun Poverty, Contempt, and the
Necessity of plundering his Subjects, in order to defend himself against his Enemies,
ought to make little Account of the Reproach of being penurious; for this is one of
those Vices which support his Government.

If

" terprizes, ought to have the Reputation of Li-
" berality, and to be actually liberal."   I know
no Hero who has not had this Virtue.   Say that a
Prince is penurious, and you tell his Friends and
Subjects that their Services will not be rewarded;
and thus you extinguish that natural Zeal which
every Subject has to serve his Prince.

Doubtless

d *Ferdinand* King of *Castile* and *Arragon*.

If any one should object, that *Cæsar* by his Liberality attained the Sovereignty of *Rome*, and that many others have by the same means risen to the highest Dignities; I answer, that you are either a Prince, or aim at being one. In the first Case, Liberality is hurtful [e]; in the second, the Reputation of it is necessary; and *Cæsar* was one of those who aspired at the Sovereignty of *Rome*: But after he attained it, had he lived much longer,

Doubtless it is only the OEconomist who can be liberal, it is only the Man that makes a prudent Use of his own Riches, who can enrich others. We know that the immoderate Expences of *Francis* I. King of *France*, were the principal Cause of his Misfortunes; and that his Pleasures exhausted the Fund of his Glory. As at first he was not liberal, but lavish, so towards the latter End of his Life, he grew covetous and penurious: He hoarded up his Treasures; but the Treasures that are beneficial to a Prince, are those which circulate. Every private Man, as well as every King,

---

[e] *Liberalitas, si adsit modus, in exitium vertitur,* says *Tacitus*, Hist 3 "Liberality, when it is unbounded, is pernicious and destructive" On the other hand, OEconomy, in a Prince, is a kind of Revenue, which supplies all his necessary Expences *Tantas vires habet frugalitas Principis,* says the younger *Pliny, ut tot impendus, tot erogationibus sola sufficiat* In Paneg

longer, and not retrenched his Expences, he would have ruined that Empire. If it should be replied, That many liberal Princes have with their Armies performed great Actions; I answer, either the Prince spends his own Money and that of his Subjects, or that of others. In the first Case, he ought to be frugal[f], but in the other, liberal upon all Occasions And the Prince whose Army is to be maintained with Free-Quarter, Plunder, and

King, who knows only how to heap up and hide Money, impoverishes others without enriching himself. The Family of *Medicis* obtained the Sovereignty of *Florence* by the Wealth as well as Ability of the great *Cosmo*, the Father of his Country, who rose from a private Merchant to be its Sovereign A covetous Man has but a low and narrow Genius; and it was well said by the

[f] Thus *Otho*, when a private Man, was more expensive than a Prince *Luxuria etiam principi onerosa*, says *Tacitus*, Hist 1 Every time that *Galba* feasted with him, he gave a considerable Sum of Money to each Soldier in the Cohort which attended *Galba* as his Guard *Eo progressus est, ut per speciem concordia, quoties Galba apud Othonem epularetur, cohorti excubias agenti, viritim centenos nummos divideret.* ibid But after he became Emperor, he grew so strict an OEconomist, that when he was dying, he distributed his Riches among his Domesticks, like a Man who had a long Time to live and enjoy them *Pecunias distribuit parcè, nec ut peritsurus* Hist. 2.

and Exactions from other People, is obliged to be liberal, otherwise his Army will desert him . And he may well be prodigal, like *Cyrus*, *Cæsar*, and *Alexander*, of what neither belongs to him nor his Subjects; for this rather adds to his Reputation than leſſens it; it is only ſpending of his own that hurts him g. Nor is there any thing that deſtroys itſelf ſo much as Liberality; for in proportion as a Man is liberal, he takes away the Means of continuing ſo h; he becomes either poor and contemptible, or, to avoid Poverty, odious and rapacious. And there

is

the Cardinal *de Retz*, That in Affairs of State, Money muſt never be minded. Let every Sovereign therefore endeavour to enrich himſelf by encouraging Commerce and Manufactures, that he may be able to ſpend much when Occaſion requires. This will be the Way to make him eſteemed and beloved by his Subjects, as well as formidable to his Enemies. Our Author repreſents Liberality, as the Means of rendering a Prince contemptible This is the Remark of an Uſurer. And is it thus a Man ſhould write, who pretends to give Inſtructions to Princes?

---

g *Tacitus* obſerves, that *Galba* was ſaving of his own, and covetous of the publick Money *Pecuniæ ſuæ parcus, publicæ avarus* Hiſt 1 *Henry* IV King of *France*, was of the ſame Character.

h *Liberalitas enim nimia profuſione mareſcit* Plin. Ep. 4 Lib 2

N

is nothing which a Prince ought so carefully to shun, as Hatred and Contempt, both which are the Consequences of Liberality [i]. For these Reasons, it is more prudent to put up with the Scandal of Penuriousness, which does not produce Hatred, than by affecting Liberality, to lay one's self under the Necessity of being rapacious, which produces both Hatred and Infamy.

[i] Thus *Nero*, upon the Hopes of an imaginary Treasure, consumed the Riches of the Empire, brought on publick Poverty, and rendered himself the more ridiculous, as his Flatterers had rung in many Panegyricks the great Felicities of his Reign *Nova ubertate provenire terras, & obvias opes deferre Deos*——*Gliscebat interim luxuria spe inani, consumebanturque veteres opes, quasi oblatis, quas multos per annos prodigeret. Quin & inde jam largiebatur, & divitiarum expectatio inter caussas paupertatis publicæ erat* Ann 16 " The " Earth, said his Poets and Orators, " teemed, in his " Reign, with Productions " altogether new; and to " him the Gods presented " Treasures already stored. ——" In the mean time *Nero* " rioted in Prodigality from " these fantastical Hopes, " and utterly consumed his " antient Treasure, as if " others, in their stead, were " to be poured upon him in " such Abundance, as to " supply him in a Course of " Profusion for many Years. " Nay, out of his imaginary " Fund, he was already dis- " tributing Largesses, and " the vain Expectation of " great Riches became one " of the Causes of publick " Poverty."

CHAP.

CHAP. XVII.

Of Cruelty and Clemency, and whether it is best for a Prince to be feared or beloved.

TO come next to the other Qualities above-mentioned, I say that every Prince should endeavour to be thought merciful; nevertheless, great Care must be taken that his Mercy be not mis-applied. *Cæsar Borgia* was counted cruel; but his Cruelty reduced *Romagna*, settled it in Peace and Concord, and secured the People's Allegiance; so that his Conduct, if well considered, will appear more merciful than that of the People of *Florence*, who, to shun the Imputation of Cruelty, suffered *Pistoia* to

OBSERVATIONS.

The most precious Depositum that is put in the Hands of a Prince, is the Lives of his Subjects: As his Office gives him a Power of condemning to Death, or pardoning Criminals, so it makes him the supreme Arbiter of Justice. Good Princes look upon this Power, which is so much boasted of, as the weightiest Part of their Charge; they

know

to be deftroyed [a]. When a Prince would
keep his Subjects united and faithful, he muft
not heed the Reproach of Cruelty; for if
he makes a few Examples of Juftice, he acts
with lefs Cruelty than thofe who, through
an Excefs of Mercy, fuffer many Diforders to arife, which occafion Rapine and
Murder [b] Now thefe are prejudicial to the
whole Society, whereas particular Executions, which are ordered by the Prince, affect
only

know they are Men themfelves, as well as thofe
whom they judge; they know that Injuftices and
Injuries may be compenfated in this World, but
that the Execution of a Sentence of Death too
haftily paffed, is an Evil that can never be repaired, they are only inclined to Severity, when
they find Severity neceffary, to prevent greater
Evils, which otherwife could not be averted; they
are

---

[a] By neglecting to deftroy
the *Pauriatichi* and *Cancel-
lieri*, two Families which by
their Quarrels and Animofi-
ties, kept up continual Com-
motions in that City *Ma-
chiav.* Chap 27 Book III
of his Difcourfes

[b] This is agreeable to what
Tacitus obferves of *Corbulo*,
That his Severity, by which
he kept up military Difcipline, was more beneficial

than the Lenity and Indulgence of other Generals,
who by pardoning Deferters,
ruined their Armies *Qua
duritatem cœli militiæque
multi abnuebant, deferebant-
que, remedium feveritate
quæfitum eft —Idque ufu fa-
lubre, & mifericordiâ melius
apparuit; quippe pauciores
illa caftra deferuere, quàm
ea in quibus ignofcebantur.
Ann 13*

only particular Men. Besides, all new Governments are exposed to so many Dangers c, that it is impossible for a new Prince to avoid the Scandal of being cruel. Thus *Virgil* makes *Dido* say,

Res

are always merciful, except in desperate Cases, where Mercy to Particulars would be Cruelty to the Whole, and act like a Man, who having a Leg or an Arm gangrened and incurable, is willing to bear the painful Operation of having it cut off, in order to save the rest of his Body.

Ma-

c Every new Prince, says *Tacitus*, is in a tottering Condition, and liable to a thousand Misfortunes, *Novum & nutantem Principem* Ann 1 *Ad omnes principatús novi eventus casusque* Hist 5 He adds, That the People often rise up against a new Prince, for no other Reason, but because many look upon the Beginning of a Government as the fittest Time for embroiling Affairs, and enriching themselves by a Civil War *Seditio incessit, nullis novis caussis, nisi quod mutatus princeps licentiam turbarum, & ex civili bello spem præmiorum ostendebat* Ann 1 It was a Saying of *Lewis* XI That unless he had governed with Rigour in the Beginning of his Reign, he would have been one of those unfortunate Noblemen mentioned in *Boccace* And the Reason why in our Times a Prince, upon his Accession to a Crown, can hardly refrain from Cruelty, is that his Subjects, for the most part, are licentious, thinking that the Government is not yet well enough settled, to punish their Disorders *Usurpatâ statim libertate licentias, ut erga Principem novum* Hist 1 Duke *Valentine* said, That the Maxim *Oderint, dum metuant,* ought to be strictly followed by those who from a private

Res dura, & regni novitas, me talia cogunt
Moliri, & latè fines custode tueri d.

Nevertheless, the Prince ought not to be too credulous, or too hasty in his Motions, nor ought he to alarm himself with groundless Apprehensions, but so to temper his Conduct with Prudence and Humanity, that neither

Machiavel treats this Subject of Executions with too much Levity. With him the Lives of Men pass for nothing; with him Interest, the sole Divinity which he worships, is all in all. For this Reason he prefers Cruelty to Mercy, and advises those who are newly risen to Sovereignty, to despise more than all other Princes, the Imputation of being cruel.

Mur-

Fortune rise to a Principality; witness *Cæsar*, who enjoyed his Sovereignty but five Months, because he had neglected the good Advice that was given him by *Pansa* and *Hirtius*, which was, that by Arms he ought to keep what by Arms he had got. *Laudandum,* says Paterculus, Hist 2 *experientia concilium est Pansæ & Hirtii, qui semper prædixerant Cæsari, ut principatum armis quæsitum, armis tueretur. Ille dictaturis mori se, quam timeri malle, dum clementiam, quam præstiterat, expectat, incautus ab ingratis occupatus est.* We must therefore conclude with *Salust,* that a Sovereignty is maintained by the same Means by which it was acquired *Imperium iisdem artibus retinetur, quibus partum est.*

d *Æneid* Book I

——My cruel Fate,
And Doubts attending an unsettled State,
Force me to guard my Coasts——

Dryden.

ther too much Confidence may make him unwary, nor too much Diffidence untractable. Hence arises a new Question, *Whether it is best to be feared or beloved?* It may be answered, Both are very desirable; but as both can hardly be attained, it is much safer, if one of the two must be wanting, to be feared than beloved: For, in general, Men are ungrateful, inconstant, double, timid and selfish; as long as they receive any Benefit by you, they are wholly yours, their Blood, their Fortunes, their Lives, and Children, (as I said before) are all at your Service, when you have no need of them, and your Danger is remote; but

Murder raises *Machiavel's* Heroes to the Throne, and Murder maintains them in it. When our Author wants Examples to enforce his cruel Precepts, *Cæsar Borgia* never fails to supply him. He quotes two Lines, which *Virgil* puts in the Mouth of *Dido*: But this Passage proves nothing; for *Virgil* represents *Dido* in the same manner as another Poet represents *Jocasta* in *Oedipus*: Both make them express such Sentiments as are most suitable to the Characters they give them. It is not therefore the Authority of *Dido* or *Jocasta*, but that of *Virgil* or *Sophocles*: And they are only the Examples of illustrious and virtuous Men, that can have Weight in a political Treatise

Our

but when it is at hand, and you have prefent Occafion for their Affiftance, they make no Scruple to forfake you[e] The Prince who leaves himfelf deftitute of other Securities, and wholly relies upon their Proteftations, is fure to be ruined For as to thofe whom he has gained by his Bounties, and not by a Greatnefs and Generofity of Mind, he deferves their Friendfhip, but has it not[f]; and there-

Our Author recommends Severity particularly to the General of an Army He compares *Scipio*'s Indulgence with the Severity of *Hannibal*, prefers the *Carthaginian* to the *Roman*, and prefently infers, that Rigour is the firft Mover of Order and Difcipline, and confequently the principal Caufe of

[e] *Profperis Vitellii rebus certatim ad obfequium, adverfam ejus fortunam ex æquo detrectabant* Tacit Hift 2 " Thofe who in " the Profperity of *Vitellius* ' vied with one another in ' Acts of Duty and Obedi- ' ence, concurred to for- ' fake his failing Fortune *Languentibus officiis, qui primo alacres fidem atque animum oftentaverant* Hift 1 " The very fame Men " fell off from their Zeal and ' Attachment, who had at

" firft appeared faithful and " courageous, and confident ' of Succefs' *Ceteris aliena pericula deficientibus* Ann 13 " The other Na- ' tions forfook the *Anfiba- " rians* in Dangers, which ' they looked upon as fo- " reign to themfelves "

[f] *Amicitias, dum magnitudine munerum, non conftantia morum continere putat, meruit magis, quàm habuit.* Tacit Hift 3 " *Vitellius* " thought to fecure his " Friends, not by a fteady " and

therefore to them he can never truft in Times of Danger. Befides, Men are lefs cautious of offending a Prince who makes himfelf loved, than one who makes himfelf feared; for Affection is a fort of Tyes, which Men, becaufe they are wicked, break upon every Temptation of Profit to themfelves [h]; whereas Fear lays them under a Dread of Punifhment, which they can never fhake off.

Never-

of the Succefs and Triumphs of an Army. *Machiavel* in this Cafe acts unfairly; he fingles out *Scipio*, the mildeft and fofteft of all Generals in point of Military Difcipline, to compare him with *Hannibal*, and enforce the Precepts of Severity.

I own that Difcipline in an Army cannot be kept up without fome Examples of Rigour, for how
fhould

" and unblameable Conduct, but by uncommon " Bounties, and therefore " rather deferved their " Friendfhip, than had it " Friendfhips, fays an Antient, which Intereft makes, Intereft will unmake and deftroy

[g] *Infima vincula caritatis* In *Agricola* " The " feeble Ties of Affection " *Timetur a pluribus, quod plerumque fortius amore eft* " He is feared by many, fays

" the younger *Pliny*, Let er " 5 Book I and Fear is a " ftronger Tye than Affec- " tion "

[h] *Amicos tempore, fortuná, cupidinibus aliquando, nimmius, transfert, defmere* Hift 4 " The Number of " our Friends, fays *Titus* to " *Vefpafian*, is leffened with " Time, they have often de- " ferted us to follow For- " tune, and fometimes be- " caufe of Defires which " we could not gratify "

Neverthelefs, the Prince fhould make himfelf feared in fuch a manner, that if he is
not loved, he may at leaft not be hated:
Now, to be feared, and not hated, are con-
fiftent enough: and this will always be his
Cafe, if he neither invades the Poffeffions,
nor offers any Violence to the Wives of his
Subjects, and if, when he has Occafion to
put any of them to Death, he does it at
a time when the Caufe is manifeft, and when
he has fufficient Grounds for his Juftification:
But there is nothing he ought fo much to
avoid as feizing their Eftates; for Men fooner
forget the Death of their Father, than the
Lofs of their Patrimony.   Befides, Occafions
of Confifcation never fail; and the Prince
who begins to fupport himfelf by Rapine,
will always find Temptations enough to feize
the

fhould Rakes, Debauchees, Rogues, Cowards,
giddy Youths, rude and mechanical Beings, be
kept to their Duty, unlefs they were forced to it
in fome meafure by the Fear of Punifhment?
A.l I ask of *Machiavel* upon this Subject is a
little Moderation.   I own that if Clemency inclines
a Man to Acts of Good-nature, Prudence on the
other hand often inclines him to Acts of Severity
and Rigour.   But this Rigour is like that of a
fkilful Pilot, who never cuts away his Mafts or
Tackling,

the Poffeffions of others: Whereas Opportunities of fhedding Blood are not fo frequent [i].

But when a Prince is at the Head of his Army, and has a Multitude of Soldiers to govern, it is abfolutely neceffary that he fhould not regard the Scandal of being cruel [k]; for without that, no Army can be kept united, or in a Condition to execute any Enterprize. Among the feveral Inftances of *Hannibal's* great Conduct, this is reckoned one, that though he had a vaft Army, gathered out of many different Nations, and led to make War in a foreign Country, yet there never happened any Tumult among them, nor any Mutiny againft

Tackling, but to fhun the imminent Danger to which he is expofed in the Storm. 'Tis neceffary on many Occafions to be fevere, but never to be cruel. I had much rather be loved than feared by my Soldiers, in the Day of Battle.

I

---

[i] *When the Prince is not inclined to Rapine, (adds* Machiavel, *Chap 19 Book III of his Difcourfes) for when he is infatiably greedy of Money, he always finds Pretences for putting fome of his Subjects to Death, in order to confifcate their Eftates*

[k] *Efpecially (fays* Machiavel, *Chap 21 Book II of his Difcourfes) if he has a great Reputation, becaufe this deftroys the Remembrance of all thofe Errors which proceed from his Rigour*

against their General, either in his Successes or
Misfortunes[1]. This could proceed from nothing but his enormous Cruelty, which, joined
with his many Virtues, rendered him both
aweful and terrible to his Soldiers, and without which his other Virtues would never
have produced that Effect. Injudicious Writers, however, on the one hand admire his
great Exploits, and on the other condemn
the principal Cause of them. That his other
Qualities would not have been sufficient to
make him aweful to his Soldiers, appears
from what happened to *Scipio*, one of
the most extraordinary Men not only of
his own, but of any Age whatever: Nevertheless his Army mutinied in *Spain*, and
the true Cause of it was his too great Le-
nity,

' I come now to his most captious Argument;
he affirms that a Prince will find his Account
more in making himself feared than loved, because the greatest Part of Mankind are addicted
to Inconstancy, Ingratitude, Dissimulation, Cowardice and Avarice, because Affection is a Tye
which the Baseness of Human Nature has rendered
extremely weak and britle, whereas the Fear of Pu-
' nishment is a sort of Restraint which they rarely
break

[1] He says the same thing, Chap. 19 Book III of his
Discourses

nity[m], which gave his Soldiers more Liberty than the Difcipline of an Army would permit; for which Reafon he was reproached by *Fabius Maximus* in the Senate, as the Corrupter of military Difcipline[n].

The Inhabitants of *Locris* having been plundered and oppreffed by one of *Scipio*'s Lieutenants[o], their Loffes were never made up, nor was the Lieutenant ever punifhed. All this proceeded from the Mildnefs of *Scipio*'s Nature, which was fo remarkable, that one of the

Senators

break through, becaufe Men are Mafters of their Affection, but not of their Fear· And therefore a wife Prince will chufe rather to depend upon himfelf, than upon others.

I grant there are many ungrateful and perfidious Men in the World, and that Severity upon fome particular Occafions is very ufeful, but I affirm that every King, the fole Aim of whofe Policy is to make himfelf feared, will reign over none but Cowards and Slaves, and can never expect that his Subjects will perform any great Action in his Service;

vice;

---

[n] *Which he was afterwards obliged to puniff with a little Cruelty, fays Machiavel, ibid*

[m] *Naturam eun ad corrumpendam difciplinam militarem arguebat* Liv, Dec 3 Book II

[o] *Plutarch* calls him *Plemnis* It was on account of the Complaints made againft this Lieutenant, that fome propofed to deprive *Scipio* of the Government of *Sicily*, and try him for Maleadminiftration

Senators[P] alledged in his Excuse, that there
were some who knew better how to avoid
Errors themselves, than to punish the Errors of
others. Now it is certain that in Time *Scipio*
would have lost his Reputation and Glory,
had he acted with the same Indulgence in a
Principality; whereas his Error not only was
unobserved, but even increased his Fame, because he lived in a Republican Government.

From whence I conclude, that since Men
love only as long as they please, but fear as
long as the Prince would be feared, a wise
Prince

vice: for whatever is done through Fear, always
bears the Marks and Characteristicks of that Paf-
sion: I affirm that a Prince who has the Talent of
making himself beloved, will reign over the Hearts
of his Subjects, that his Subjects will think it their
Interest to obey such a Master, and that History
furnishes us with numberless Examples of great
and memorable Actions, which have been performed
through a Principle of Affection and Attachment.
I affirm that Seditions and Revolutions seem at
present to have fallen into Disuse. We know of
no Kingdom except *England*, where the King has
any Reason to be afraid of his People; nor has
the King of *England* any Reason to fear his Subjects, unless he raises the Storm himself.

Quintus Metellus.

Prince will chuse to depend upon what is solely in his own Power, and not upon what is in the Option of others; but will take great Care withal, as I said before, to govern so as not to be hated[q].

I conclude therefore, that a cruel Prince exposes himself to Treason and Rebellion, much more than one who is indulgent; because Cruelty is insupportable, and Men are quickly tired of Fear, whereas they are never tired of Affection; and Goodness and Mildness are always amiable.

It were therefore to be wished, for the Benefit of Mankind, that all Princes were good, without being too easy and indulgent, that Goodness in them might always be a Virtue, and never a Weakness.

[q] *Plutarch*, in the Life of *Lycurgus*, says, that *Eurytion* King of *Sparta* having a little slackened the Reins of Government, to gratify the People, they quickly grew licentious and insolent, and that some of his Successors were extremely hated by the *Spartans*, for no other Reason, but because they endeavoured to resume that Authority which *Eurytion* had parted with

CHAP.

CHAP. XVIII.

How far Princes ought to fulfil their Engagements.

EVERY one knows how commendable it is in a Prince to fulfil his Engagements, and to act a sincere, not a deceitful Part. It has nevertheless appeared by Experience, in our Times, that those Princes who made light of their Word, and artfully deceived Mankind, have alone done great things, and have at length got the better of such

Machiavel, the Preceptor of Tyrants, has the Boldness to affirm, that Princes may impose upon the World by Dissimulation. This is the first Position which I shall endeavour to refute. The extreme Curiosity of the Publick is well known, it is a Being that sees every thing, hears every thing, and divulges whatever it has heard or seen. If its Curiosity examines the Conduct of particular Men, 'tis only to fill up idle Hours: but if it considers the Characters of Princes, 'tis with an Eye to its own Interest. And indeed Princes are more exposed than all other Men, to the Conjectures, Comments and Judgment of the World; they are a sort of Stars, at which a whole People of Astronomers

ſuch as proceeded upon honourable Principles. We muſt therefore know that there
are two Ways of contending, one by Right
and Equity, the other by Force. The for
mer is that of Men, and the latter that of
Beaſts: But becauſe the former frequently
proves ineffectual, recourſe muſt be had to
the latter. It is therefore neceſſary that Princes
ſhould be well skilled both how to put on
the Man and the Beaſt. This is what the
Ancients have figuratively pointed out to
them, where they relate that the Education
of *Achilles* and of ſeveral other Princes was
committed to *Chiron* the Centaur; to ſigni-

fy,

nomers are continually levelling their Teleſcopes
and Croſs-ſtaves; Courtiers who are near them are
daily taking their Obſervations, a ſingle Geſture,
a ſingle Glance of the Eye, diſcovers them; and
the People who obſerve them at a greater Diſtance,
magnify them by Conjectures, in ſhort, as well
may the Sun hide its Spots, as great Princes their
Vices and their genuine Character, from the Eyes
of ſo many curious Obſervers
If the Mask of Diſſimulation ſhould cover, for
a time, the natural Deformity of a Prince, yet he
could never keep his Mask always on; he would
ſometimes be obliged, was it only for a Breathing,
to throw it off, and one View of his naked Features would be ſufficient to content the Curious. It

O

will

fy, that as the Preceptor was half Man, half Beast, so the Disciples ought to participate of both Natures, the one being of a short Duration without the other. Since therefore a Prince is obliged to assume the Beast, he ought to put on the Fox and the Lion, because the Lion is but ill-provided against Snares, and the Fox against Wolves; so that he must be a Fox to know the Snares, and a Lion to terrify the Wolves. Those who assume the Lion only, do not rightly understand their Office. From hence it follows, that a wise Prince neither can nor should fulfil

will therefore be in vain for Dissimulation to dwell in the Mouths of Princes, Craftiness in their Discourses and Actions will have no Effect. To judge of Men by their Words and Professions, would be the way to be always mistaken, we therefore compare their Actions with one another, and then with their Words, and against this repeated Examination, Falsity and Deceit will find no Refuge: No Man can well act any Part but his own; he must really have the same Character which he would bear in the World: Without this, the Man who thinks to impose upon the Publick, imposes upon none but himself.

Sixtus Quintus, Philip II. passed for Hypocrites, and enterprising Men, but not for being virtuous. Let a Prince be as artful as he would, he will never be

fulfil his Engagements, when the Observance of them would turn to his Prejudice, and when the Causes for which he entered into them no longer subsist.

If Men were all good, this Maxim would be false, but as they are bad, and would not observe their Promises to us, we ought as little to think ourselves bound by our Engagements to them; nor will a Prince ever want justifiable Pretences to colour such a Violation I could cite a thousand Examples; and shew how many Treaties of Peace, and how

be able, even by following all our Author's Maxims, to gain the Character of Virtue which he has not, and avoid the Scandal of Crimes which belong to him.

Machiavel argues no better, in the Reasons he assigns for employing Trick and Hypocrisy. The ingenious, but fallacious Application of the Fable of the Centaur proves nothing; for if that Animal was half Man, half Horse, does it follow from thence, that Princes ought to be crafty and false? A Man must have a strong Inclination to inculcate Crime, who employs Arguments so weak and so far-fetched as this of the Centaur.

But here follows a Reasoning as false as any we have yet met with Our Politician affirms, that a Prince ought to have the Qualities both of the Lion and the Fox; of the Lion, to destroy the

Wolves;

how many Promises, have been rendered
void and of no Effect, through the Perfidy
of Princes, among whom those who have
beft known how to act the Part of the Fox
have been generally the moft fuccefsful. This
Nature of the Fox muft neverthelefs be artfully difguifed, and the Perfon who adopts
it muft be a thorough Mafter in Hypocrify
and Diffimulation So fimple are Men, and
fo tame to their prefent Neceffities, that
he who deceives will always find People
who will fuffer themfelves to be deceived.
I fhall quote one Example, which is ftill frefh

III

Wolves , and of the Fox, to avoid Snares· From
whence he infers, that a wife Prince neither can nor
fhould fulfil his Engagements. Here is a Conclu-
fio without Premifes. Would not any other Man
blufh to throw out fuch impious Sophiftry?

If *Machiavel* s confufed Notions could be ftrained
into good Senfe and found Morality, they might
be reprefented thus. The World refembles a Match
at Gaming, where Sharpers and fair Players are
promifcuoufly engaged: A Prince therefore who
is in the Game, and would not be cheated himfelf,
fhould be well acquainted with all the Ways of
cheating others : not in order to put any of thefe
Leffons in Practice, but only that he may hinder
them from being practifed upon him by Game-
fters.

But

in our Memory. The sole Business and Aim of Pope *Alexander* VI. was to cozen Mankind, yet he always found Matter to work upon, and as no Man dealt in stronger Asseverations, or in more solemn Oaths than he, so no Man minded his Engagements less [a]; notwithstanding which, he succeeded in every Attempt to deceive, because he thoroughly knew how to attack People on their weak Side.

It

But to return to *Machiavel*'s Sophistry. Because all Men, says he, are wicked, and at all times break their Faith and Promise to you, there is no Obligation upon you to keep yours with them. Now here is a manifest Contradiction; for he says a few Lines after, that Dissemblers will always find People simple enough to be imposed upon. How can this be reconciled with the other? All Men are wicked, and yet you find Men simple enough to be imposed upon! But it is not true, that all Men are wicked. One must have a strange misanthropic Turn, not to perceive, that in every Society there are a great many honest Men, and that the major Part are neither good nor bad. But without supposing all

O 3

the

[a] It was said of Pope *Alexander* VI and of Duke *Valentine* his Son, that the Father never did what he said, and the Son never said what he did, and that both went by this fundamental Rule, to give their Faith to every Man, and to keep it with none. When they were reproached with their Insincerity, they would answer, that they had given their Oath indeed, but not their Promise.

It is not therefore necessary that a Prince should have all the above-mentioned Qualities, but it is extremely requisite that he should appear to have them [b] I will even venture to affirm, that his having them, and putting them in Practice, would be to his Prejudice; whereas his putting on the Appearance of them must be for his Interest.

Let

the World to be wicked, how could *Machiavel* have supported his detestable Maxims? Nay, granting that Men are as wicked as he represents them, would it follow that we ought to imitate their Example? If any Man robs, or commits Murder, I conclude that he deserves to be hanged, not that I must act accordingly If Honour and Virtue were to be banished the World, said *Charles* the Wise, they ought to find an Asylum with Princes.

After

[b] A Maxim which amounts to this You must be seemingly an honest Man, and at bottom a V as *Charles* V always swore by the Faith of an honest Man, and always acted the Reverse of what he swore The Truth is, he had read and studied *Machiavel's Prince*, which, according to a modern Historian, was one of the three Books he liked, and caused to be translated for his own Use, *Hess Hist* of the Empire, Book III Chap 4 This I take Notice of here, because a Minister from the Emperor one Day affirmed to me, in good Company, where among others the Pope's Internuntio was present, that the House of *Austria* had always abhorred the Doctrine and Politicks of *Machiavel*

Let him seem, and let him actually be, merciful, true to his Word, humane, religious and sincere: but at the same time let him have so much Command of himself, that if Occasion requires, he may be quite the reverse.

I must observe, that a Prince, and especially a new Prince, cannot practise all those things by which Men acquire the Reputation of Goodness, because for the Safety of

his

After endeavouring to prove the Necessity of Vice, our Author would encourage his Scholars by shewing them the Facility of succeeding in it. Those who are skilled in the Art of Dissimulation, he affirms, will never be at a Loss to find Men simple enough to be duped by them. His Meaning is, Your Neighbour is a Blockhead, and you are a Man of Sense; wherefore you must cheat him.

O 4 These

" " Though his Style seems " too licentious, and not decent and virtuous enough " to authorize in some Pas- " sages what has the Appear- " ance of Vice, yet as he " had a mind to fall in with " the Nature of his Subject, " he could not write other- " wise, without losing what " he aimed at. For it is " very hard for a Prince to

" preserve his Dominions, " when surrounded by " powerful and ambitious " Neighbours, and sup- " ported by wicked and un- " faithful Subjects, unless " sometimes he departs " from the Severity of the " Rules of Conscience. " And it is a certain Rule in " this World, which is na- " turally vicious, that no long

" Such

his Government he will frequently be obliged to act contrary to the Dictates of Humanity, Charity and Religion. He must therefore have a flexible Disposition, so as to turn with the Winds and Variations of Fortune ; and as I observed above, he should be virtuous when he can, but not scruple to be vicious when he must. In short, a

Prince

These are Syllogisms for which some of *Machiavel*'s Scholars have been hanged and broke upon the Wheel.

Not content with attempting to shew the Necessity and Facility of being vicious, our Author endeavours to point out the Felicities that attend Vice But it unfortunately happens, that his Hero, *Cæsar Borgia*, the greatest and most perfidious of all Villains, was in Effect extremely miserable. *Machiavel* takes great Care not to touch upon this Part of his Life, and is forced to have recourse to the History of wicked Popes and Emperors. He maintains, that Pope *Alexander* VI. the most false

and

" Success can be met with, " even in sovereign Dignities, unless a Man knows " how to help himself in " time of Necessity, by " having recourse to Vice, " that when the Necessity " ceases, he may immediately return to Virtue' These are the Words of *Gaspar d'Auvergne*, who has been quoted before in the Notes of Chap XV I thought proper to put them down here, in order to shew that *Machiavel's* Doctrine is founded in Reason, and therefore ought not to be condemned upon a slight Inquiry

Prince ought to be strictly upon his Guard, not to let a Word drop from him which does not favour of the five Qualities above-mentioned; and to judge of him by his Looks and Discourse, he should seem to be all Goodness, Sincerity, Humanity and Religion. There is nothing of which it is more necessary to have the Appearance than of this last Quality; because Men in general judge by Sight, and not by Feeling; every one having the Faculty of seeing, few that of Perception.

and impious Man of his Time, was always successful in Deceit, because he perfectly knew the Weakness of Mankind, with regard to Credulity. Now I will venture to affirm, that the Success of Pope *Alexander* was owing not so much to the Credulity of Man, as to certain Events and Circumstances of that Time, and especially to the Rivalship between *France* and *Spain*, to the Divisions and Animosities that prevailed among the chief Families of *Italy*, and to the Passions and Weakness of *Lewis* XII.

Don *Lewis de Haro*, an able Politician, looked upon Deceit as an Error in Politicks. He used to say of Cardinal *Mazarin*, that his Eminence had one great Fault in his political Character, which was, that he always cheated. The same *Mazarin* wanting to employ the Marshal *de Faber* in making a slippery Treaty; Permit me, my Lord, says *Faber*, to refuse cheating the Duke of *Savoy*, especially in a trifling

ption. All fee what you appear to be, few know what you really are, and these few dare not contradict the Opinion of the Multitude, which is backed by the Majesty of Government. In the Actions of all Men, and particularly in those of Princes, (against whom there ies no Appeal) People fix their Eyes on the Event. For this Reason let a Prince only take care to maintain his Power, and every one will praise the Means as honourable,

trifling Affair The World knows that I am an honest Man, be pleased therefore to reserve my Integrity for some other Occasion, when it may do Good to my Country.

To fay nothing either of Honour or Virtue: but only to confider the Interest of Princes; I fay it is bad Policy in them to impose upon and dupe the World, for they are never fure of fucceeding but once, and by one Act of Deceit they lose the Confidence of all their Neighbours.

A certain Power very lately published a Manifesto, fetting forth the Reasons of her Conduct; and prefently after acted in a manner quite oppofite to all her Pretences It must be owned that fuch glaring Deceitfulness must needs make one forfeit the Confidence of others, for the fooner the Contradiction follows the Proteftation, 'tis the more palpable. The Church of *Rome,* to avoid the like Inconfiftency. has very wifely prefcribed a Noviciat of a hundred Years to those whom it

places

nourabled, becaufe the Vulgar always judge by Appearances and the Event of Things. Almoft the wholeWorld comes under thisDenomination, and the Opinion of the Few only takes Place where the Multitude have nothing

to

places in the Number of its Saints; in which Time the Memory of their Faults and Extravagancies is entirely loft, thofe who knew them perfonally when living, and could fwear againft them, are dead and gone, and nothing obftructs the Notion of Saintfhip, which the Church would impofe upon the Publick.

The Reader, I hope, will pardon this little Digreffion. To return to *Machiavel*; I own there are fome unhappy Cafes, when a Prince cannot help breaking his Treaties and Alliances. But he ought to do it with as much Honour as he can, by giving timelyNotice of it to hisAllies, and fhewing that he is forced to it by the greateft Neceffity, and for the Prefervation of his People, which are the only Cafes wherein it is allowable.

I fhall conclude this Chapter with making one more Remark. Obferve how fertilely one Vice propagates

d *Nhil glouofum, nfi tutum, et omnia retinenda dominationis honefta* Saluft "Nothing is glorious but " what is fafe, and there are " no Means of maintaining " Dominion but are ho- " nourable" "In a Prince " or Commonwealth, fays

' *To exhbde* nothing is un- " juft that is beneficial' *Tacitus* relate, that *Agrippina*, *Nero's Mother*, thought no Price too great for a Crown *Decus, pudorem, corpus, cuncto regno viliora habere* Ann 2

to judge by. A certain Prince now living, whom it is not proper to name, talks of nothing but Peace and Fidelity; but had he practised either, he must frequently have lost both his Dominions and Reputation[e].

propagates another in the Hands of *Machiavel.* 'Tis not enough for his Prince to be cruel, deceitful, perfidious and irreligious: he must crown all his Vices with that of Hypocrisy. *Machiavel* thinks the People will be more gained by his Devotion, than offended with his Oppressions. There are others of the same Opinion. For my own part, the World, methinks, is very indulgent as to Errors in Speculation, when they are such as do not necessarily corrupt and vitiate the Heart: A People will always be better affected to an unbelieving Prince, if he is an honest Man, and a good Master, than to one who is orthodox, but a Villain or a Tyrant. 'Tis not upon a Prince's Opinions, but upon his Actions only, that the Happiness of his People depends.

[e] Meaning *Ferdinand* King of *Castile* and *Arragon*, who by his Innocency and Perfidy conquered *Italy* and *Navarre.* An *Italian* Prince, his Cotemporary, used to say, that he would never trust to *Ferdinand's* Oaths, till he swore by some God in whom he believed

CHAP.

CHAP. XIX.

Princes ought to beware of growing odious or contemptible.

HAving now confidered the moft important of the Qualities above-mentioned, I fhall briefly treat of the
reft under this geneial Head; That a Prince
fhould endeavour (as I hinted before) to avoid
fuch things as may rendei him odious or
contemptible; and that while he fucceeds in
this, he acts his Pait well, and will find
himfelf in no Dangei from the Imputation
of any othei Vices

Nothing makes a Piince more odious, as
I faid above, than ufuiping the Piopeities,
and debauching the Wives, of his Subjects,
which are two things he ought carefully to
avoid;

OBSERVATIONS.

Fondnefs foi Syftein is not a Folly peculiar to
Philofophers, but grown common to them and
Politicians. Our Author is as much infected with
it as any Writei whatevei: He would prove, that a
Prince ought to be wicked and knavifh; thefe in-
deed are the faciamental Words of his Religion.
Machiavel

avoid, for as long as a whole People are un-
molested in their Possessions, and unpreju-
diced in their Honour, they live contented;
and their Prince has nothing to struggle with
but the Ambition of a few particular Persons, which may be curbed many Ways, and
with great Ease

A Prince is contemptible, who is counted
inconstant, light, effeminate, pusillanimous
or irresolute, and these are Faults which
he ought to avoid as so many Rocks; en
deavouring in all his Actions to shew a Greatness of Mind, Courage, Gravity and Forti-
tude, to make all his Determinations in the
private Affairs of his Subjects irrevocable,
and to keep up such a Reputation among
them, that they may never think of deluding
him or averting him from his Purpose.

There

Machiavel has all the Wickedness of those Monsters whom *Hercules* overthrew, but has not
their Strength; so there is no need of the Club of
Hercules to demolish him. What can be more
simple, more natural, and more suitable to Princes,
than

Vitellium factis officiis,
aut intempestiva blandi-
tis, mutabilem et time-
nebat me-
tuebant ⁝ Tacit. Hist. 2.
" The despised Vitellius,
" and created him, as a

" Man who was apt to be
" suddenly changed by every
' Gust of Passion, or by
' any wild Strain of Flat-
" tery

There is no Prince who has this Reputation but is in great Esteem; and in this Case, it will not be an easy Matter for any of his Subjects to conspire against him, nor for any of his Neighbours to invade him, as having a Character of great Worth, and of being respected by his People For a Prince should always have two Objects of his Fear; the one at Home, with regard to his own Subjects, and the other Abroad, with regard to his powerful Neighbours. Against the latter he defends himself by good Arms, and good Allies As he will always have good Allies when he is well armed, so when he is in no Danger from Abroad, he will always be safe at Home, unless Affairs have been already perplexed by some former Conspiracy When he is threatened with any Invasion, if he is provided in the Manner I men-

than Justice and Goodness? If this Position is true, *Machiavel*'s Politicks must necessarily be false; and it is so evident, that we need not go about to prove it For if he maintains, that a Prince established in the Throne ought to be cruel, knavish, perfidious, and so forth, he endeavours to make him wicked merely to undo him. And if he recommends all those Vices to a Prince who obtains

mentioned before, and is not wanting to himself, he will never fail to baffle the Attacks of his Enemies; as I have already shewn was the Case of *Nabis* Tyrant of *Sparta*.

When Things are quiet Abroad, what the Prince has to fear, is some secret Conspiracy at Home; and he sufficiently provides against this, by not rendering himself odious or contemptible, and by making his Subjects always satisfied with his Government; the Necessity of all which I have shewn before at large. One of the best Remedies a Prince can use against Conspiracies, is not to be hated or despised by the Body of the People, for no Man plots, but when he thinks to gratify the People by the Death of the Sovereign; whereas

obtains his Crown by Usurpation, he gives him such Advice as would set all Princes and States against him For how is it possible, that a private Man should usurp a Sovereignty, but either by dethroning the lawful Prince, or by assuming the supreme Authority of a Republick? Certainly this is not a Practice which the Princes of *Europe* will encourage or approve. Had *Machiavel* published a Collection of Rules and Examples for the Instruction of Highwaymen, he would not have written a worse Book than this.

whereas his believing that it would offend them, deters him from any such Enterprize: And in all Conspiracies there are infinite Difficulties. We find by Experience, that many have been set on foot, but that very few have succeeded, for no Man can conspire alone, nor can he chuse a Confederate but out of those whom he thinks discontented And you no sooner discover your Thoughts to a Malecontent, but you give him an Opportunity of coming into Favour, and the Prospect of any Gratification by revealing your Secret [b] So that, as the Profit is

I must however take Notice of some of the false Reasonings in the Chapter before us Machiavel pretends, that a Prince renders himself odious, when he unjustly seizes the Properties of his Subjects, and makes Attempts upon the Modesty of their Wives. Certainly a selfish, unjust, violent, and cruel Prince, cannot fail to be hated by his Subjects : but it is not so with respect to Gallantry.

Julius

[b] There is a remarkable Instance of this in *Tacitus* *Volusius Proculus* had been employed by *Nero* in assassinating his Mother *Agrippina*, but not meeting with that Preferment afterwards, which he thought so great a Service had merited, he discovered his Discontentment and made grievous Complaints to *Epicharis*, a Woman who was then in a Conspiracy against the Emperor's Life, and to her he declared his settled Resolution of

P taking

is certain on one side, and extremely hazardous and precarious on the other, he muſt either be a rare Friend to you, or an implacable Enemy to the Prince, if he does not betray you [c]. In ſhort, on the ſide of the Conſpirators there is nothing but Fear, Jealouſy, and the Dread of Puniſhment, which intirely diſ-

---

Julius Cæſar, whom they ſtyled at *Rome* the Huſband of all their Wives, and the Wife of all their Husbands, *Lewis* XIV. who was a great Lover of Women, the late *Auguſtus*, King of *Poland*, who enjoyed them in common with all his Subjects, none of theſe Princes were hated on account of their Amours And if *Cæſar* was aſſaſſinated; if

---

taking Vengeance the firſt Opportunity. It encouraged *Epicharis* to let him into her Secret, which he had no ſooner learned, but he went and betrayed it to *Nero* Erat Chilia ſhus in ea claſſ *Volusius Proculus*, occisa de matri N-10, s inter miniſtros, non ex magnitudine ſceleris provectus, ut rebatur Is mulier ——avum merita erga Neronem ſua, & quam in irritum ceciaſſent, aperit, adjectoque queſtus, & deſtinatioem viod Iæ, ſi facultas oriretur, ſpem dedit poſſe impelli Ergo Epicharis omnia ſcelera principis or-

d t , —accingeret modò, ravaret operam, & militum acerrimos duceret in partes, ac digna pret a expectaret—— *Proculis* ea quæ audierat ad *Neronem* detalit Ann 15 The Man to whom you truſt your Secret, becomes Maſter of your Liberty, ſays *M de Roub faucault*, in his Memoirs

[c] The Affection which your Accomplice bears you muſt needs be very great, if the Danger to which he expoſes himſelf by the Conſpiracy, does not appear much greater, ſays *Machiavel*, Chap VI of his Diſcourſes.

dishearten them [d] But on the side of the Prince, there is the Majesty of Government, the Laws, the Assistance of his Allies and State;

of *Rome*, for its Liberty, plunged so many Daggars in his Breast, it was because *Cæsar* was an Usurper, not because he was a Man of Gallantry.

It may be objected, perhaps, in favour of our Author, that the Kings of *Rome* were expelled for the Attempt upon the Modesty of *Lucretia*. I answer, that it was not the Love which young *Tarquin* made to *Lucretia*, but the violent Manner in which he made it, that raised the Insurrection at *Rome*: and as this Outrage revived in the Memory

[d] *Tacitus*, in the 15th Book of his Annals, points out all the Causes that may render a Conspiracy abortive 1 The Hopes of Impunity, which is always an Enemy to great Attempts *Impunitatis cupido, magnis semper conat.bus adversa, and promissa impunitas* 2 Hope and Fear *Spes atque metus* 3 Dilatoriness *Accendere conjuratos, lentitudinis eorum pertæsa* 4 The Fear of being betrayed *Metus proditionis* 5 Jealousy, for he observes, that *Piso* refused to kill *Nero* in his Country-house, whither *Nero* often resorted, for fear that *Silanus* should succeed him, or that the Consul *Vestinus* should re-establish Liberty and the Commonwealth, or else make an Emperor of his own 6 *Proditio* Treachery itself, which often happens the very Day before the Conspiracy should be executed, *pudor insidiarum* 7 *Præmia perfidæ, immensa pecunia & potentia* The Hopes of Recompence, as also the Fear of being prevented by some other of the Conspirators *Multos adstitisse, qui eadem ad sint, nihil profuturum unius silentium, at præmia penes unum fore, qui judicio prævenisset* There is, besides, another sort of Treachery,

State [e]; which defend him fo effectually, that if the Affection of the People is added, it is impoffible any Man fhould be rafh enough to confpire againft him. For if, in moft Cafes, the Confpirator has Reafon to be afraid only before the Execution of his Defign,

mory of the People, the other Violences committed by the *Tarquins*, they took that Opportunity of avenging themfelves, and vindicating their Liberty After all, the Adventure of *Lucretia* is perhaps a mere Romance

I am far from faying this by way of Excufe for the Gallantry of Princes, which may be morally

Treachery, that of the Mien and Countenance, which often betray the inmoft Thoughts of the Confpirator *Ipfe mæftus & vagâ cogitationis manifeftus erat* 8 Imprudence, for Example, the making Preparations for the Confpiracy, in the Prefence of Servants, as ordering them to whet a Poniard, or the like *Pugionem afperari faxo & in mucronem ardefcere juffit*, which gives them fome Sufpicion of your Defigns, *arreptis fufpicionibus de confequentibus* 9 The Sight or Tortures *Tormentorum afpectus ac metus* 10 The Fear

that fome of the Confpirators have already betrayed all, and that it is in vain to be longer filent *Cuncta jam patefacta ei deferis, nec illum filentii emolumentum, edidit cæteros* To all this we may add Chance, which often prevails in thofe Cafes Thus the Earl of *Leicefter* failed in his Enterprize upon *Leyden*, for one of the Confpirators being feized for Debt, moft of the reft ran away, believing that fome of their Number had betrayed them

[e] *Illum quidem*, fays *Germanicus* to the Legions that mutinied againft *Tiberius, fua majeftas, imperium Romanum,*

fign, in this Cafe, he ought to be as much afraid after it, as having offended the whole People, and therefore left himfelf no Refuge.

Many Examples of this might be produced; but I fhall content myfelf with one, which happened in the Memory of our Fathers. *Hannibal Bentivoglio*, Grandfather of the prefent *Hannibal*, was Prince of *Bologna*, and affaffinated by the *Canneschi*[1], who had confpired againft him, nor was there any of of the Family left, except his Son *John*, who was

rally bad · I only touch upon it to fhew that Gallantry does not make a Prince odious The Amours of a good King are always deemed a pardonable Weaknefs, if they are not attended with Injuftice and Violence. Make Love like *Lewis* XIV. or *Charles* II. King of *England*, or *Auguftus*, King of *Poland*, and you will be refpected and careffed · But beware of imitating the Amours of a *Nero* or a *David*.

P 3 The

num, cætera exercitus defidebit "*Tiberius* will be defended by the Majefty of "hisCharacter, by theRoman "Empire, and by the other "Armies" He had told them a little before, that *Italy* and *Gaul* were faithful to *Tiberius*, and that all the reft of

the Empire was in a State of Tranquillity *Italiæ confenfum, Galliarum fidem extollit nil ufquam turbidum aut difcors* Ann 1

[f] A Family that rivalled the *Bentivoglio's* in the Year 1445

was then an Infant g. No sooner was the Murder committed, but the People rose up in Arms, and slew all the *Canneschi.* Now this proceeded only from the Affection which the People of *Bologna* had at that time for the House of *Bentivoglio* And it was so great, that after *Hannibal*'s Death, being informed there was a natural Son of the Family at *Florence* h, who till that time had passed for the Son of a Smith, they sent for him, conducting him ho-

The following, methinks, is a downright Contradiction *Machiavel* would have his Prince gain the Affection of his Subjects, in order to prevent Conspiracies and in the XVIIth Chapter he says, that a Prince ought especially to endeavour to make himself feared, because he can more rely upon Fear, which is in his own Power, than upon Affection, which is in the Option of others Which of the two is our Author's real Opinion? He speaks the Language of an Oracle, and may be interpreted both

g In Book VI of his History of *Florence* he says, That *John* was then 1 Years of Age

h He was the natural Son of *Hercules Bentivoglio*, *Hannibal*'s first Cousin, and was called *Santi*, he passed at *Florence* for the Son of one *Angelo da Cascese* *Mach at* ibid Where he adds, that *Santi*'s Conduct was so prudent, that whereas his Predecessors had all been killed by their Enemies, *Santi* lived in great Peace and Reputation, and died lamented

honourably to the City, and invested him with the Government, which he continued to possess till *Hannibal's* Son came of Age.

From whence I conclude, that a Prince has but little Occasion to be afraid of Conspiracies, if the People are his Friends; but there is no Man nor Thing which he ought not to fear, when the People are his Enemies. Indeed it has been the constant Business of all wise Princes, and of all well-modelled States, to content the People, and not to drive the Nobles to Despair; and this is one of the most essential Duties of a Prince. Among the best-modelled States in our Times, the Kingdom of *France* is one [i],

which

both ways; but this, by-the-bye, is the Language of Knaves.

I must observe in general, upon this Occasion, that Conspiracies and Assassinations are now grown rare, and that Princes are safe in this respect. Those Crimes are worn away, and no longer in Fashion, and the Reasons which *Machiavel* alledges are good. There is nothing, at most, but the Enthusiasm of Priests, which can occasion such horrible Villainies. Among the judicious Observations which *Machiavel* makes

P 4

upon

---

[i] That Kingdom, says *Machiavel*, Chap I Book III of his Discourses, is more subject to the Laws, than any other we know of.

which has a great many excellent Inftitutions, both with regard to the Liberty of the People, and the Security of the Sovereign : The moft confiderable of thefe is the Parliament k, and the Authority with which it is invefted.   For he who modelled that State, was fenfible, on the one hand, of the Ambition and Arrogance of the Nobles, and therefore judged it neceffary to bridle them   On the other hand, he knew how much they were feared, and for that Reafon hated, by the Commons, and was therefore defirous to

pro-

upon Confpiracies, there is one, remarkably good in itfelf, but grows bad by coming from his Pen. A Confpirator, fays he, is difturbed by the Apprehenfion of Punifhment, whereas the King is fupported by the Majefty of Government, and by the Authority of the Laws   Methinks it ill becomes our political Author to talk of Laws, he who breathes nothing but Intereft, Cruelty, Tyranny, and Ufurpation. *Machiavel* acts like the Proteftants, who make ufe of the Arguments of Unbelievers, to refute the Tranfubftantiation of the Church of *Rome*, and of the Arguments which the Catholicks produce for Tranfubftantiation, to refute Unbelievers.

Ma-

---

* He fpeaks only of the Parliament of *Paris*, which gives Motion to all the reft, and which, he obferves, is the inviolable Executor of the Laws   *Ibid.*

protect them: But as he intended, that neither of these should be the Affair of the King alone, left the King should at any time be obliged to offend either the Nobles, by favouring the Commons, or the Commons, by encouraging the Nobles; he instituted a third Judge, who, without casting any Odium upon the King, might both curb the Nobility and protect the People. Nor could any Institution be more prudent or more beneficial, or attended with more Security, both to the Sovereign and the State. Here we may make another Remark, that Princes ought to delegate invidious Affairs to their Ministers, and reserve to themselves the Distribution of all

Machiavel very justly advises a Prince to make himself loved, both by the Grandees and People, to throw upon others what might procure him the Hatred of either of these States, and for this purpose to appoint Magistrates, who may judge of such Differences as arise between them. He alledges the Government of *France* as an Example. Is it not strange that so keen an Advocate for despotick Power and Usurpation, should approve of the Authority which was formerly vested in the Parliaments of *France?* For my own part, if there was any Constitution, which for its Wisdom should be proposed as a Model, methinks it is that of *England,* where the Parliament is the

Ar-

all Favours!   To conclude, a Prince ought
fo to regard and value his Nobility, as not to
render himſelf odious to his People.

To many, perhaps, who conſider the Mif-
fortunes that befel feveral of the *Roman* Emperors, it may appear that their Lives diſprove
the Opinion I have advanced. For even of
ſuch Emperors who poſſeſſed great Qualities,
and always acted with great Wiſdom, ſome
were depoſed, and ſome murdered by Con-
ſpiracies   In order to anſwer this Objection,
I ſhall examine the Characters and Conduct
of ſome of thoſe Emperors, ſhew the Rea-
                                        ſons

Arbiter between the King and the People, and
the King has every Power to do Good, without
any to do Ill.

Machiavel enters next into a large Diſcuſſion
upon the Lives of the *Roman* Emperors, from
Marcus Aurelius, down to the two *Gordians*   He
aſcribes the many Revolutions that happened in
it, to the Venality of the Empire ; but this is not
the only Cauſe of them. *Caligula, Claudius, Nero,
Galba, Otho, Vitellius*, were all murdered, though
they did not buy *Rome*, like *Didius Julianus*.
Venality was indeed an additional Motive for
                                        aſſaſ-

---

[1] This is agreeable to what
Xenophon ſays, that a Prince
ought to delegate to others
the Care of inflicting Pu- niſhments, and to beſtow all
the Rewards and Favours
himſelf

sons of their Miscarriage and Ruin, which will not appear different from the Reasons I have before alledged, and make some Remarks, by the way, upon the History of those Times. I shall confine myself, in this Inquiry, to the Emperors between *Marcus* the Philosopher, and *Maximinus*; and these are *Marcus*, his Son *Commodus*, *Pertinax*, *Julian*, *Severus*, *Antoninus*, his Son *Caracalla*, *Macrinus*, *Heliogabalus*, *Alexander*, and *Maximinus*.

It is first to be observed, that whereas other Princes had nothing to struggle with but the Ambition of the Grandees, and the Insolence of the People, the *Roman* Emperors had a third Difficulty to surmount, which was the Cruelty and Avarice of the Soldiers And this occasioned the Ruin of many

assassinating those Emperors; but the true Cause of so many Revolutions, was the Form of the Government. The *Pretorian* Guards were in those Days what the *Mamelucks* have been since in *Egypt*, the *Janisaries* in *Turkey*, and the *Strelits* in *Russia*. *Constantine*, with great Ability, cashiered the *Pretorian* Bands, but at length new Misfortunes which befel that Empire, exposed the Emperors to be assassinated or poisoned. I shall only observe, that the bad Emperors were generally cut off by violent

many of thofe Princes; for the Task is extremely difficult to content both the Soldiery and the People; becaufe the People prefer Peace, and therefore a Prince of a mild and peaceable Difpofition; whereas the Soldiers love one of a martial Turn, one who is infolent, cruel, and rapacious [m] And thefe were the Qualities which the *Roman* Army had a mind the Prince fhould exert againft

violent Deaths; but *Theodofius* died a natural Death, and *Juftinian* reigned in Profperity four and twenty Years. Now this is what I infift upon, there is fcarce any wicked Prince who is long fuccefsful, nor did *Auguftus* reign in Peace till he became virtuous The Tyrant *Commodvs*, the Succeffor of the divine *Marcus Avrelius*, was put to Death,

---

[m] *Erant quos memoria Neronis, ac defiderium prioris licentiæ accendebat* Hift 1 "Some were tranfpored with a Fondnefs for the Memory of *Nero*, and with a Paffion for recalling the Licentioufnefs which under him they had enjoyed" *Neque exercitus, aut legatos ac duces, magnâ ex parte luxûs, egeftatis, fcelerum fibi confcios, nifi pollutum obftrictumque meritis fuis principem paf-* *furos* Hift 2 "I cannot imagine that the Armies, or the Lieutenant-Generals and Leaders, Men, for the moft part, wallowing in Prodigality, preffed by Indigence, and under the Guilt and Horrors of Enormities black and manifold, would have fuffered any Prince to reign over them, except one polluted with Crimes, and under Obligations to them for their wicked Services

againſt the People, that their Pay might be the more increaſed, and their Avarice and Cruelty glutted. Whence it happened, that thoſe Emperors who had not Credit or Art enough to keep both theſe Parties in Order, always miſcarried: Moſt of them, and eſpecially ſuch as had riſen from a private Fortune,

Death, notwithſtanding the great Veneration which was had for his Father's Memory. *Caracalla* was not able to maintain his Authority becauſe of his Cruelty. *Alexander Severus* was killed by the Treaſon of that *Maximinus* the *Thracian*, who paſſed for a Giant; and the ſame *Maximinus*, having

" Services done him " One of the Cauſes why *Galba* loſt both the Empire and his Life, was a Saying of his, *That he had choſen his Soldiers, and not bought them* Legi à ſe militem, non emi Hiſt 1 Another was, that he had uſed too much Severity towards thoſe who were diſuſed to the antient Diſcipline, and accuſtomed by *Nero* to Licentiouſneſs *Nocuit antiquus rigor, & nimia ſeveritas, cui jam pares non ſumus* And elſewhere, *Laudata olim & militari famâ celebrata ſeveritas ejus, angebat coaſperſantes veterem diſciplinam, atque ita XIV*

annis a Nerone aſſuefactos, ut haud minus vitia Principum amarent, quàm olim virtutes venerabantur Hiſt. 1 " That Severity of *Galba*, a Quality ſo admired " of old, and by the antient " Armies ever diſtinguiſhed " with Applauſe, was very " grievous to a ſlothful Sol- " diery, who ſcorned the " primitive Diſcipline, and " for fourteen Years were " ſo much habituated to the " baſe Reign of *Nero*, that " at this Time they no leſs " admired the Vileneſs and " Vices of their Princes, " than of old they had adored " their Virtues "

tune, perceiving the Difficulty of managing these two different Tempers, applied themselves only to content the 'Army, and made but little account of the Injuries they did to the People   Such a Conduct, indeed, was very necessary, for if a Prince cannot help being odious to some particular Persons, he should make it his chief Endeavour, in the first place, to avoid the Hatred of the whole Body of his Subjects: and when that is impracticable, to avoid the Hatred of the stronger Party.

Accordingly those Emperors who had need of extraordinary Support, as being new Princes, courted rather the Soldiers than the People . nevertheless this Conduct proved beneficial or hurtful, just as they knew how to keep up their Reputation with the Army For these Reasons it happened, that *Marcus Aurelius, Pertinax,* and *Alexander,* who were

having exasperated the whole Empire by his Barbarities, was assassinated in his turn. *Machiavel* pretends, that this Emperor was destroyed because of the Contempt in which he was held for his obscure Birth. But this is a Mistake : A Man, who by his Courage and Ability raises himself to an Empire, has no longer any Parents . His Subjects

were all mild and good Princes, Lovers of Juſtice, Enemies of Cruelty, humane and beneficent, came all to an untimely Death; except *Marcus*, who lived and died extreme-ly honoured: And the Reaſon was, that *Marcus* ſuccceded in the Empire by Inherit-ance, without having any Obligation for it either to the Army or the People · Beſides, as he poſſeſſed many Virtues that gained him Eſteem and Veneration, he was able, during his whole Reign, to keep both theſe Parties within their proper Bounds, without being either hated or deſpiſed. *Pertinax*, on the contrary, was created Emperor againſt the Will of the Soldiers; and theſe being accuſtomed to a licentious and diſſolute Life under *Commodus*, could never endure that Regularity and Virtue, to which *Perti-nax* endeavoured to bring them back : And therefore this Prince having incurred their Hatred, and fallen beſides into Contempt, on

jects conſider his Power and Dignity, rather than his Extraction. *Pupian* was the Son of a Coun-try Farmer, *Probus* of a Gardener, *Dioclefian* of a Slave, *Valentinian* of a Rope-maker, and yet they were all reſpected. *Sforza*, who con-quered *Milan*, was the Son of a Peaſant , *Crom-well,*

on account of his great Age ⁿ, was cut off in the very Beginning of his Reign *.

Here

ⁿ Old Age renders Princes contemptible *Ipsa ætas Galbæ & irrisui & fastidio erat assuetis juventæ Neronis* Hist 1 " To those " who were accustomed to ' behold the Youth and gay " Person of *Nero*, even the " Age of *Galba* was matter " of Derision and Hate " Either because old Men are less enterprising, *reputante Tiberio extremam ætatem* Ann 6 Or because their Enemies think they are not able to defend themselves *Artabanus senectutem Tiberii ut inermem despiciens* Ann 6 Or because it is thought they begin to dote, *fluxam sero mentem objectando* Ibid Besides, old Age is often the Cause of their suffering themselves to be governed by others *Invalidum senem, T Vinius & Cornelius Laco, odio flagitiorum oneratum contemptu inertiæ destruebant* Hist 1 " *Titus Vinius* and *Cornelius* " *Laco*, *Galba's* worthless " and wicked Ministers, de- " rived upon him the " Weight and Infamy of all " their own numberless " Crimes, brought Scorn " upon the Impotency of " the Administration, and " involved their Prince, al- " ready enfeebled with Age, " in utter Ruin " Add, that those who enter upon the Ministry towards the End of the Prince's Reign, make haste to enrich themselves by plundering all manner of ways ——*Offerebant venalia cuncta præpotentes liberti servorum manus subitis avidæ, & tanquam apud senem festinantes* " *Galba's* Freed- " men, indulged in immo- " derate Power, exposed to " common Sale all the Ho- " nours and Emoluments of " the State His Bondmen " too were greedy to make " Advantage of their pre- " sent Sunshine, and eager " to convert into hasty " Gains the short Reign of " an antient Master " And so much the rather, because a declining Sovereign is but little feared *Cum apud infirmum & credulum minore metu, & majore præmio peccaretur* Hist 1 " Under " a Prince so feeble and cre- " dulous, the Iniquities of " his Ministers were attend- " ed with the smaller Peril, " and with the greater " Gains '

* In the third Month.

Here it muſt be obſerved, that Hatred is procured as well by good Actions as bad °; and therefore, as I ſaid before, a Prince who would maintain his Dominions, is often forced not to be good. For when that Party, whoſe Support you find neceſſary, whether it is the People, or the Army, or the Grandees, is grown corrupt and vicious, you are not at Liberty to be good; you muſt needs gratify their Humour; and in this Caſe good Actions would be prejudicial and pernicious.

But let us come to *Alexander*, of whom, among other Encomiums which have been given him, it is related, that during the fourteen

well, who ſubjected *England*, and made all *Europe* tremble, was the Son of a Country Gentleman. The great *Mahomet*, Founder of the moſt flouriſhing Religion in the Univerſe, was bred up a Merchant; *Samon*, the firſt King of *Sclavonia*, was a *French* Merchant; the famous *Piaſt*, whoſe Name is ſtill revered in *Poland*, was elected King,

Q   while

° His Eaſineſs of Acceſs, his flowing Courteſy, (ſays *Tacitus* of *Venones*) were Virtues unknown to the *Parthians*, and by them reputed ſo many Vices, every Part of his Manners, good or bad, was equally ſubject to Hatred, becauſe foreign from their own *Et quia moribus ipſorum aliena, perinde odium pravis & honeſtis* Ann 2.

teen Years of his Reign, he governed with
fo much Equity and Goodnefs, that no Man
was ever put to Death without a fair Trial.
Neverthelefs, as he paffed for effeminate, and
for being under the Management of his Mother, he quickly fell into Contempt, and the
Army confpired againft him, and murdered
him *. On the other hand, *Commodus,
Severus, Antoninus, Caracalla,* and *Maximinus,* were extremely cruel and rapacious;
and, to fatisfy the Soldiers, committed all
manner of Injuftices and Outrages againft the
People. Thefe Emperors however came all
to an untimely Death, except *Severus,* whofe
Reign was profperous and happy: For *Severus* was a Prince of fo great Courage and
Magnanimity, that notwithftanding he grie-
voufly oppreffed the People, yet both the
People and the Army fo admired him for his

great

while he ftill wore wooden Shoes; and he lived
many Years in great Refpect. How many Generals, how many Minifters of State and Chan-
cellors, have we feen of the loweft Extraction?
Europe is full of fuch Inftances, and is the hap-
pier for it; thefe being the Rewards of Merit,

and

---

* With his Mother at *Mayenne.*

great Qualities, that the former were, in some measure, stunned and amazed, and the latter always obedient and submissive. As the Actions of this Emperor, considered as a new Prince, were very remarkable, I shall briefly shew how well he knew to put on both the Fox and the Lion; two Animals whose Natures, as I said before, it is necessary for every Prince to imitate.

Severus, knowing the Slothfulness and Effeminacy of the Emperor *Julian*, persuaded the Army under his Command in *Sclavonia*, to go to *Rome*, and revenge the Death of *Pertinax*, who had been murdered

and Incitements to it. I say not this with a View to shew any Disrespect for the Blood of the *Vitikins*, the *Charlemaigns*, or the *Ottomans*: I ought on the contrary, for more Reasons than one, to love the Blood of Heroes; but I love Merit still more.

It must not here be omitted, that *Machiavel* is greatly mistaken in believing, that in the Time of *Severus*, an Emperor needed only to preserve the Good-will of the Soldiery in order to maintain his Power: This is what the History of the Emperors contradicts. The more those indisciplinable Pretorian Bands were courted, the more they felt their own Strength and Importance, and it was equally dangerous to flatter and to check them. The

Sol-

dered by the *Pretorian* Guards [p]. Under this Colour, without shewing any Ambition for the Empire, he marched his Army directly to *Rome*, and was in · *Italy* before his Departure was known. Being arrived at *Rome*, the Senate, through Fear, elected him Emperor, and *Julian* was put to Death. After this prosperous Beginning, he had but two Difficulties to remove, in order to make himself Master of the whole Empire; one was in *Asia*, where *Pescennius Niger*, General of the *Asiatick* Army, had taken the

Soldiery at present are but little to be feared, as they are all divided into small Bodies, which keep a Watch upon each other; as the Sovereign has the Disposal of all Preferments; and as the Execution of the Laws is better secured. The Reason why the *Turkish* Emperors are so liable to be strangled, is, because they have not made use of this Political Institution: For the *Turks* are the Slaves

---

[p] *Scelus cujus ultor est, & qui successit* Hist. i. The Murder of a Prince " is a Crime which his Suc- " cessor, whoever he be, is " sure to revenge. *Omnes conquiri & interfici jussit non honore Galbæ, sed tradito Principibus more, munimen-* tum ad præsens, in posterum ultionem Ibid. " *Vitellius* " commanded Search to be " made for the Murderers " of *Galba* and *Piso*, and all " of them to be put to the " Sword, not from any " Tenderness or Regard for " *Galba*, but out of a Po- " licy

the Title of Emperor; the other in the West*, where *Claudius Albinus* likewise set up for Emperor. Thinking it dangerous to declare against both these Competitors at once, he resolved to attack *Niger*, and to couzen *Albinus*: He wrote therefore to *Albinus*, that being chosen Emperor by the Senate, he was willing to share that Dignity with him; accordingly he gave him the Title of Emperor, and with the Consent of the Senate admitted him his Collegue. All this

Slaves of the Sultan, and the Sultan of his Janisfaries. In *Christendom* a Prince must treat equally well all the different Orders of Men over whom he reigns, and avoid making any Distinctions, which would never fail to raise Jealousies fatal to his Interest.

Q 3

The

" licy common and traditional among Princes, and which is a sort of Security against such Traitors, during their own Reigns, and a Precedent of Vengeance left by them to their Successors." *Claudius* put to Death *Chereas* and *Lupus*, who had killed *Caligula*, though that Murder was the Occasion of his being made Emperor As *Vitellius* ordered all those who had been concerned in the Murder of *Galba* and *Piso* to be slain, so *Domitian* put to Death *Epaphroditus* for helping *Nero* to kill himself, though *Nero* had been condemned by a Decree of the Senate *Ferdinand*, Great Duke of *Tuscany*, put to Death *Branca Capella*, his Sister-in-law, who had poisoned the Grand Duke *Francis*, her Husband

* In *France*

this was accepted by *Albinus*, and taken in good Earneſt But after *Severus* had overcome and ſlain *Niger*, and ſettled the Affairs of the Eaſt, being returned to *Rome*, he complained in the Senate of *Albinus*, as of a Perſon upon whom he had laid great Obligations, and who notwithſtanding had endeavoured treacherouſly to murder him; and told them, that he was obliged to go and puniſh his Ingratitude Whereupon *Severus* marched into *France*, deprived *Albinus* of his Authority, and put him to Death.

If therefore we ſtrictly examine the Conduct of *Severus*, we ſhall find that he had in him the Ferocity of the Lion, and the Craftineſs of the Fox; and that he was feared and reſpected by his People, without being odious to his Army Nor will it be thought ſurpriſing, that this Prince, who from a private Fortune raiſed himſelf to ſo vaſt an Empire, was able to preſerve it; for his great Re-

The Model of *Severus*, which *Machiavel* propoſes to ſuch as raiſe themſelves to an Empire, is therefore as pernicious, as that of *Marcus Aurelius* would be beneficial. But how is it poſſible

Reputation protected him against the Hatred which the People might have conceived against him on account of his Rapine. His Son *Antoninus* was likewise a Man of extraordinary Parts, which gained him the Admiration of the People and the Affection of the Soldiers; for he was martial by Nature, patient of Labour and Hardships, and a great Despiser of all Sensuality and Softness; and this highly recommended him to the whole Army Nevertheless his Fury and Cruelty were so enormous, as having upon many private Occasions destroyed great Numbers of the People at *Rome*, and all the Inhabitants of *Alexandria*, that he became extremely odious to the whole World, and began to be dreaded even by those who were about his Person; so that he was murdered by a Centurion in the very Middle of his Camp.

Here it is to be observed, that Assassinations of this kind, which proceed from the ob-

___

sible to propose in the same Breath, *Severus*, *Cæsar Borgia*, and *Marcus Aurelius*, as Models? This is uniting Wisdom, and the purest Virtue, with the most horrible Villainy. I cannot conclude without ob-

serving

obſtinate Courage of a ſingle Man, cannot be avoided by any Prince; for every one who deſpiſes his own Life, has the Prince's in his Power[e]: But theſe Aſſaſſinations are the leſs to be feared, as they happen but ſeldom. The Prince muſt only beware of doing any grievous Injury to thoſe who are near his Perſon, either in the Service of his Houſhold, or in that of the State. This was the Error of *Antoninus*, who had put a Brother

ſerving once more, that the inhuman *Cæſar Borgia*, with all his Abilities, died very miſerable, and that *Marcus Aurelius*, that Imperial Philoſopher, always good and always virtuous, met not with the leaſt Reverſe of Fortune during his whole Reign.

[e] *Quiſquis vitam ſuam contempſit, tuæ dominus eſt* " Whoever deſpiſes his own " Life, is Maſter of yours ' *Periculum ex ſingulis*, ſaid *Veſpaſian* to thoſe who exhorted him to ſeize the Empire, *quid enim profuturas cohortes alaſque, ſi unus alterque, præſenti facinore, paratum ex diverſo præmium petat?--facilius univerſos impelli, quam ſingulos virar.* Hiſt 2 " There is not an " individual Soldier, from " whom Danger is not to ' be apprehended For indeed what Security can " Squadrons of Horſe and " Battalions of Foot afford, if one particular " Man, or two, are reſolved " by a bold Murder to earn " a ready Reward from the " oppoſite Party? 'Tis a " much eaſier Task to excite them in a Body to any " Deſign, than to eſcape the " wicked Deſigns of any " particular Man "

ther of that Centurion to an ignominious Death, and was daily threatning the Centurion himself †, and yet continued him in his Guards: Now this was a rash and pernicious Action, and sufficient to ruin him, as it actually did.

As for *Commodus*, he might have easily kept the Empire, because he had come to it by Inheritance, as the Son of *Marcus*; and might have contented both the Army and the People, had he only followed his Father's Footsteps. But being of a cruel and brutal Disposition, and wanting to plunder and oppress the People, he indulged the Army in all manner of Licentiousness. Besides, as he prostituted his Dignity, by descending often upon the Theatre to fight with Gladiators, and by many other vile Actions, much beneath the Majesty of an Emperor, he quickly grew contemptible to the Army. Thus as he was hated by one Part, and despised by the other, they conspired against him, and murdered him. It only now remains that we speak of *Maximinus*.

The

---

† To threaten any Man, is to furnish him with Arms against you.

The Army, having flain *Alexander*, whom for his Effeminacy they defpifed, as I mentioned before, chofe *Maximinus* in his room: This was a very warlike Prince, but did not long enjoy the Empire‡, for two Reafons: One was the Meannefs of his Birth, which rendered him contemptible in the Eyes of all his People; for it was univerfally known, that he had been a common Shepherd in *Thrace* The other was his neglecting to repair immediately to *Rome*, upon his coming to the Throne, and to take Poffeffion of his Imperial Seat; for the Barbarities committed in the mean time by his Lieutenants over the whole Empire, and particularly at *Rome*, gave him the Reputation of being extremely cruel, and this rendered him highly odious: Infomuch that being univerfally fcorned for the Meannefs of his Birth, and univerfally hated and dreaded for his Fury and Cruelty; firft *Africk*, then the Senate, with the whole People both of *Rome* and *Italy*, confpired againft him; and were joined afterwards by his own Army, who were then laying Siege to *Aquileia*. Whereupon his Soldiers, harraffed with the Length of that Siege, ab-

‡ Scarce above two Years.

abhorring *Maximinus* for his Cruelty, and fearing him less, as they saw he was universally hated, fell upon him and slew him [f].

I shall pass over *Heliogabalus, Macrinus,* and *Julian,* because they were all Men of contemptible Parts, and were therefore quickly destroyed.

To conclude this Discourse, I say, that modern Princes have much less Occasion to content the Soldiery by extraordinary Means; for though some Consideration must always be had for them, yet as no Prince in our Time has Armies inveterated in the Government of any Part of his Dominions, as was the Case of the *Roman* Armies, he has less Occasion to court them, than the *Roman* Emperors had. For if in those Times it was necessary to content the Soldiers rather than the People, because the Soldiers were the stronger Party [g], it is at present necessary for every Prince to content the

[f] They killed his Son also, though still a Child, saying, That of so wicked a Race not one ought to be left alive.

[g] Witness the *German* Legions, who boasted that they had the *Roman* Empire in their own Hands. *Suâ in manu sitam rem Romanam,* *suis victoriis augeri Remp. in suum cognomentum adscisci imperatores Ann. 1.* "In "their Hands lay the Power "and Fate of *Rome,* by "their Victories the Empire "was inlarged, and from "them the *Cæsars* took, by "way of Compliment, the "Sur-

the People rather than the Soldiers, becaufe the People are more powerful. I except the *Turk* and the Sultan of *Egypt*: For as the former is always attended with a Guard of Twelve thoufand Foot and Fifteen thoufand Horfe, upon whom the Security and Strength of his Empire depend, he is obliged to preferve their Friendfhip and Attachment, without any Confideration for the People. The Empire of the Sultan is like that of the *Turk*, as being entirely in the Power of the Soldiers; fo that the Sultan is likewife obliged to wave all Regard for the People, and keep the others his Friends at any Rate.

Here it may be obferved, that the Government of the Sultan is very different from all other Principalities, and refembles that of the Pope in *Chriftendom*, which cannot be called either hereditary or new; not hereditary, becaufe the Sons of the deceafed Prince are not his Heirs and Succeffors in the Empire; for it goes to him who is chofen by thofe who

---

" Surname of *Germanicus* " Evulgato imper : arcano, poffe princpern alibi quamRomæ fieri: Hift 1 "The Secret " of Government was then " firft difclofed, that an Emperor might be created

" elfewhere than at *Rome* " Ana poffe ab exercitu principem fieri. Hift 2 "They " difcovered that an Empe- " ror might be created by " the Army "

who have the Power of Election: And as this Custom of electing is antient, the Principality cannot be said to be new, because it is not accompanied with any of the Difficulties that are met with in new Principalities; for though the Power and Title of the Prince are new, yet the Laws and Ordinances of the State are old and settled, and by virtue of them he is received as if he were an hereditary Prince.

But to return to my Subject. Whoever considers what I have said, will find that the Ruin of those Emperors proceeded only from Hatred or Contempt; and will be able to judge how it happened that some of them following one Course, some another, in their Administration, Part succeeded, and Part miscarried, on both Sides. *Pertinax* and *Alexander* were new Princes, and therefore it was not only a vain, but a fatal Attempt in them to imitate *Marcus*, who had succeeded by Right of Inheritance. Nor was it less fatal Conduct in *Caracalla*, *Commodus* and *Maximinus*, to take *Severus* for their Pattern, since they had not Ability enough to follow his Footsteps. Upon the Whole, a new Prince, as he cannot imitate the

the Actions of *Marcus*, and has no need of imitating those of *Severus*, ought to copy the latter in what is necessary for founding and establishing his Principality, and the former in what conduces to preserve it with Reputation and Glory, after it is settled and firm

CHAP. XX.

Whether Citadels, and many other Things which Princes often make use of, are useful or prejudicial.

SOME Princes, for the greater Security of their Dominions, have disarmed their Subjects, others have kept up Parties and Divisions in their Towns; some have created Enemies on purpose,

others

OBSERVATIONS.

The Heathens represented *Janus* with a double Face, to denote his thorough Knowledge of Things past and future. Taken in an allegorical Sense, the Image of that God is very applicable to Princes. They ought like *Janus* to see backward into the History of all former Ages, which furnishes them with useful Instructions for their Conduct and Behaviour,

others have endeavoured to gain such as they suspected in the Beginning of their Reign; some have built Cities, and others have demolished them. Though in all these Cases no certain and fixed Rule can be prescribed, without particularly considering the State where it is to be used; nevertheless I shall speak of them all in as general a manner as the Subject will permit.

New Princes were never known to disarm their Subjects; on the contrary, when they found them disarmed, they have always put Arms into their Hands: For these Arms with which you trust them, are employed in your

haviour; like *Janus* they ought to look forward, with that Force of Discernment and Penetration which draws Inferences from the Likeness of Circumstances, and in the present Conjunctures reads those that must naturally follow.

Machiavel proposes five Questions to Princes, as well to those who have made new Conquests, as to others whose Politicks wholly turn upon securing their old Possessions. Let us see what Prudence will advise in comparing the past with the future, and in forming such Conclusions as are always consonant to Reason and Justice.

His first Question is, Whether a Prince ought to disarm the People whom he conquers? We must constantly remember, how much the Method of making

your Service; those whom you suspected become faithful, those who were faithful are confirmed, and all your Subjects side with you. As it is impossible to arm them all, so if you are favourable to those whom you have armed, you can act more safely with respect to the rest; for by distinguishing the former, you lay them under Obligations[a]; and the others will readily excuse you, thinking it must needs be that those have most Merit, who are most exposed to Danger: Whereas, if you disarm them, you give them Offence, and shew them that you are distrustful either of their Courage or their Fidelity;

making War is altered since *Machiavel*'s Time. Countries are now defended always by disciplined Armies, more or less strong; and a Body of armed Peasants would be greatly despised. If in Sieges sometimes the Burghers take Arms, the Enemy does not allow of it, and in order to prevent it, threatens

[a] Thus the fourteenth Legion continued always faithful to *Nero*, and had always great Regard for his Memory, in Return for the Honour he had done them, in chusing them, as the most valiant Legion of his Army, for the reducing of *England*, which at that time had revolted *Addiderat* (*Quartadecumanis*) *gloriam Nero, eligendo ut potissimos, unde longa illis erga Neronem fides, et erecta in Othonem studia* (Their great Attachment to *Otho*'s Person and Cause, proceeded from the Resemblance between his Temper and *Nero*'s) Hist 2

delity; and your fufpecting either of the two
tends to make them hate you: As you cannot
fubfift without Soldiers, you will be forced in
this Cafe to entertain mercenary Troops, the
Nature of which I have formerly defcribed; and
even if it were fafe to employ them, they can
never be numerous enough to defend you both
againft powerful Enemies, and fufpected Subjects. Wherefore, as I faid before, a new Prince,
in a new Principality, has always armed his
Subjects; as appears from numberlefs Examples in Hiftory. But when a Prince conquers a new State, and annexes it, as a Member, to his old Dominions, it is then necef-

fary

threatens them with Bombs and red-hot Bullets. In
general, Prudence feems to require, that the Inhabitants of a conquered Town fhould be difarmed at
firft, efpecially if there is any Caufe to fear a Revolt. The *Romans*, having fubdued *Great Britain*,
and finding it impoffible to keep that Country
quiet, on account of the turbulent and warlike
Difpofition of the Inhabitants, made it their Bufinefs to effeminate them, in order to quell their
fierce and martial Inftinct, which in the End fucceeded to their Wifh. The *Corficans* are a Handful of Men not lefs brave and refolute than thofe
old *Brittons*, and in my Opinion nothing but Prudence and Moderation will fubdue them at laft. To
maintain the Sovereignty of that Ifland, I think

R

is

fary his new Subjects fhould be difarmed, all
but fuch as appeared for him in the Conqueft, whom neverthelefs he ought to take
all Opportunities of rendering foft and effeminate, that in Time the whole Strength
of his Dominions may be transferred to his
natural Troops, which he is accuftomed to
keep up in his hereditary State.

Our Anceftors, and thofe efpecially who
were accounted wife Men, ufed to fay, that
it was neceffary to keep *Piftoia* by Factions,
and *Pifa* by Fortreffes· Accordingly in feveral Towns under their Subjection, they fomented Parties and Divifions, in order to
preferve them with more Eafe This indeed
was a prudent Conduct at that Time, when
Italy was unfettled, and in a State of Suf-
pense;

it abfolutely receffary to difarm the Inhabitants,
and to foften their Manners. One may obferve
by the way, from the Example of the *Corficans,*
how much the Love of Liberty infpires Men with
Courage and Bravery, and that in fuch a Cafe
Oppreffion is as dangerous as it is unjuft.

The fecond Queftion turns upon the Confidence
which a Prince, after having juft fubdued a Country, ought to repofe either in fuch of his new Subjects as affifted him in the Conqueft, or in fuch as
preferved their Fidelity to their lawful Prince.
When

pense; but I am far from thinking that it
should be made a Precept for us to follow:
Nor indeed can I believe that Factions and
Divisions do any Good at all; for a Town
that is divided, must needs fall into the Hands
of the Enemy as soon as ever he approaches,
because the weaker Party will be sure to
join with him, and the other will not be
able to hold out. The *Venetians* fomented
the Factions of the *Guelfs* and *Ghibelins*
in the Towns that were under their Jurisdiction; and though they never suffered
them to come to Blows, yet they encouraged their Animosities, for no other
Reason, I believe, but that the Townsmen
taken up with their Feuds, might have no
Leisure

When a Town is taken by Intelligence, and by
the Treachery of some of the Inhabitants, it
would be highly imprudent to trust the Traitors, as
they may probably betray you, and it is to be presumed that those who were loyal to their old Masters, will likewise prove so to their new Sovereigns For it is commonly wise Men, and such as
are happily settled in a Country, who love Order,
and to whom every Change is prejudicial. Nevertheless it is a prudent Maxim to trust none rashly.
   Let us suppose, that a People roused by Oppression, and forced to shake off the Yoke of Tyran

R 2   ny,

Leifure to think of revolting. Neverthelefs this Policy did not anfwer the Expectation of the *Venetians:* For after they
were defeated at *Vayla**, one of the Factions took Arms againft them, and ftripped
them of all their Dominions.

Such a Conduct as this argues the Weaknefs of a Government: For one that is
found and vigorous, will never fuffer fuch
Divifions †; becaufe they are ufeful only in Times of Peace, when perhaps they
may contribute to the more eafy Management of the People, but when War comes
on,

ny, fhould call in another Prince to govern them:
I am of Opinion, that the Prince ought in all re-
fpects to anfwer the Confidence that has been placed
in him, and that if on this Occafion he fhould not
keep his Word to thofe who have trufted him with
every thing they value moft, it would be the bafeft
Return of Ingratitude, and would fix a perpetual
Reproach on his Memory. *William* Prince of
Orange preferved to the End of his Life his Confidence and Friendfhip for thofe who put the Crown
of

---

* A Village in the Country
of *Ghiarra d Adda*
† Witnefs the King of
France, (fays *Machiavel*,
who fuffers nobody to call
himfelf of the King's Party),
becaufe that would imply
there was a Party againft
him, whereas the King will
fuffer no Parties at all Chap
2 Book III of his Dif-
courfes

on, the Fallacy of those Councils quickly appears. It is not to be doubted but that Princes aggrandise themselves when they surmount the Difficulties and Obstacles that oppose them; and therefore Fortune, when she would exalt a new Prince, who has more Need of Reputation than one who is hereditary, raises up Enemies, and encourages Enterprizes against him, that he may have an Opportunity of conquering them, and ascending to a greater Height of Power by such Steps as his Enemies have supplied him with [b]. For this Reason

of *England* upon his Head; such as opposed him, left their Country, and followed King *James*. In elective Monarchies, where the greatest Part of Elections are procured by Intriguing, and where the Crown is venal, I believe, whatever others

R 3 may

[b] Thus Fortune used *Tiberius*, whose Life, before he came to the Empire, was full of Dangers and Crosses *Casus primâ ab infantiâ ancipites——Ubi domum Augusti privignus introiit, multis æmulis conflictatus est, dum Marcellus & Agrippa, mox Caius Luciusque Cæsares viguere——Sed maxime in lubrico egit, acceptâ in matrimonium Juliâ, impudicitiam uxoris tole-* *rans aut declinans. Tacit.* Ann 6 " From his first " Infancy his Life was chec- " quer'd with various Turns " and Dangers ——When ta- " ken in the Quality of Son- " in-law into the Family of " *Augustus,* he long struggled " there with many potent " Rivals, during the Lives " of *Marcellus* and *Agrippa,* " and next of the young " Cæsars, *Caius* and *Lucius.* "——But

Reaſon many have thought that a wiſe Prince, when Opportunity offers, ſhould artfully encourage and foment ſome Enmity againſt himſelf, that by deſtroying it afterwards he may increaſe his own Reputation and Power c.

Princes, and particularly ſuch as are new, have met with more Fidelity and Aſſiſtance from thoſe whom in the Beginning of their Reign they ſuſpected, than from others in whom at that Time they truſted moſt. *Pandolphus*

may think. that the new Sovereign will find it an eaſy Matter to buy off thoſe who had oppoſed him, in the ſame manner as he procured the Favour of thoſe who choſe him to that Dignity.

Poland furniſhes us with Examples of this. The Crown there is ſo groſsly ſet to Sale, that it ſeems

to

" —But nothing threatened " or diſtreſſed him ſo much " as his Marriage with *Ju-* " *lia*, whether he bore the " Proſtitutions of his Wife, " or relinquiſhed the Daugh- " ter of *Auguſtus*" Thus Fortune uſed *Caractacus, qu m multa ambigua, multa proſpera extulerant, ut ceteros Britannorum Imperatores præmineret* Ann 12 ' *Ca- ractacus, who ſurpaſſed in* " Credit all the other *Britiſh*

" Commanders, was a Man " renowned for many Vic- " tories and many Diſaſters " And thus ſhe uſed that *Roman* General, whoſe Diſtreſ- ſes as well as Proſperities had rendered him intrepid *Cæcina ſecundarum ambiguarumque rerum ferens, eoque interritus* Ann 1

e In this Senſe *Diogenes* ſaid, That it was neceſſary to have rude Enemies.

dolphus Petrucci Prince of *Siena* employed
in the Government of his State rather thofe
whom he had fufpected, than others But
as this Matter cannot be treated of in a general manner, becaufe it varies according to
particular Circumftances, I fhall only fay,
That if thofe who oppofed the Prince in
the Beginning of his Government, are fuch
as want the Support of others, he will
hardly find any Difficulty to gain them;
and they will be the more obliged to ferve
him with Fidelity, as they know it is only
their good Carriage that can remove the unfavourable Opinion he had of them. Thus
will

to be done at a public Market. The Liberality
of a King of *Poland* removes all Oppofition: He
has it in his Power to gain over the great Families
by Palatinates, Governments, and other Employments, which he confers upon them, but as in point
of Favours the *Poles* have a very fhort Memory,
he will often be obliged to return to the Charge:
In a Word, the Republick of *Poland* may be compared to the Sieve of the *Daraids*, the moft generous King will fhower his Favours upon them to
no Purpofe; they will never be full Neverthelefs,
as a King of *Poland* has a great many Favours to
beftow, he may keep many Refources in Store, by
being liberal only to thofe Families whofe Affiftance he has need of.

R 4 *Machiavel's*

will the Prince always receive more Benefit by them, than by others, who serving him with more Security, commonly neglect his Affairs [d]. This Subject will not suffer me to omit reminding the Prince, who has newly acquired a Country by means of the Inhabitants, to consider well upon what Motive they acted in assisting him; whether they were guided by any natural Affection to his Person, or only by Pique and Animosity against the former Government.

Machiavel's third Question properly regards the Security of a Prince in a hereditary Kingdom; Whether it is better for such a one to promote Unity or Division among his Subjects? Possibly there might have been room for this Question at *Florence* in the Time of *Machiavel*'s Ancestors; but at present I do not think any Politician would adopt it, blunt and indigested as it is, without some Mitigation. It would be sufficient to quote here the beautiful and well-known Fable of *Menenius Agrippa*, by which he restored Unity among the *Roman* People. Commonwealths indeed ought to encourage a sort of

---

[c] Thus *Marius Celsus*, who was *Galba*'s faithful Friend to the last, proved afterwards as faithful to *Otho Marum Celsum Conf. Galbæ usque in extremas res amicum fide* *que Hist :* *Otho* n tra intimos habuit ——*Mansitque Celso velut fataliter etiam pro Othone fides integre.* Ibid

ment. In this laſt Caſe it will coſt him infinite Trouble and Difficulty to keep them
his Friends, becauſe it will be impoſſible
for him to content them: If we look either
into modern or antient Examples, we ſhall
find the Reaſon of this to be, that it is
much eaſier for a Prince to gain the Friendſhip of thoſe who lived quietly under the
former Government, and conſequently were
his Enemies, than of ſuch as were diſcon-
tent, and therefore became his Friends, and
helped to make him Maſter of that State.

It has been a Cuſtom among Princes, for
the greater Security of their Dominions, to
build

of Jealouſy between their Members, becauſe if
one Party does not watch over another, their
Form of Government will be changed into a Monarchy.

There are Princes who look upon a Miſunder-
ſtanding between their Miniſters as neceſſary for
their Intereſt: They fancy they are leſs in Danger
of being impoſed upon by Men whom a mutual
Hatred

e *Multi odio præſentium, et*
cupidine mutationis. Ann. 3
" Many are guided in their
" Actions by their Hatred
" of the preſent Adminiſtra-
" tor, and a Deſire of
" Change" *Privatas ſpes* | *agitantes, ſine publicâ curâ.*
Hiſt. 1 " Several are in-
" fluenced by their private
" Views and Hopes, with-
" out any Concern about
" the Publick"

build Fortreſſes, in order to bridle and overawe the Mutinous, and to have a ſure Place
of Refuge in Times of Rebellion. I approve
of this Method, as it is of old Standing. Nevertheleſs in our own Times *Nicolas Vitelli* thought fit to demoliſh two Fortreſſes
in the City of *Caſtello*, in order to preſerve
that Place *Guidubaldo* Duke of *Urbin*, having recovered his Dutchy, of which he had
been diſpoſſeſſed by *Caeſar Borgia*, demoliſhed
all the Fortreſſes of that Province f, thinking
it would be more difficult to diſpoſſeſs him
a ſecond time, if his State was not guarded
with

Hatred obliges to watch over one another's Actions. But if this Hatred produces ſuch an Effect,
it likewiſe produces one of a very dangerous Kind ;
for whereas theſe Miniſters ought to concur in ſerving their Prince, it happens that, while they ſtudy
to hurt, they continually thwart one another, and
confound the Intereſt of their Sovereign, as well
as the Good of the People, in their particular
Quarrels Nothing contributes more to the Strength
of a Monarchy, than a cloſe and inſeparable Union
between

---

f He ſays Chap 24 Book
III of his Diſcourſes, that
the Duke of *Urbin* demo-
liſhed them, becauſe being
beloved by his Subjects, he
was afraid of loſing their Affect on by ſhewing any Diſ-
truſt of them, and beſides,
he was not able to defend
theſe Fortreſſes againſt his
Enemies, without having an
Army in the Field.

with Citadels: And the *Bentivoglio's* did the like after their Return to *Bologna*[8].

Fortresses therefore are ufeful or not, according to the State of Affairs; and if in some Cafes they do Good, they do as much Mifchief in others. A Prince, for Example, who is more afraid of his Subjects, than of his Neighbours, fhould build Fortresses. But he

between all its Members; and to fettle this ought to be the Purpofe of every wife Prince.

My Anfwer to *Machiavel's* third Queftion may in fome meafure ferve as a Solution to his fourth Problem. Let us however examine in a few Words, Whether a Prince ought to foment Factions againft himfelf, or whether he ought to gain the Affection and Friendfhip of his Subjects? A Man who makes Enemies in order to overcome them, what elfe does he but raife up Monfters for himfelf to contend with? It is more agreeable to Nature, Reafon and Humanity, to make Friends: Happy are the Princes who know the Charms of Friendfhip! more happy ftill are thofe, who deferve the Love and Affection of their People.

I come now to *Machiavel's* laft Queftion, *viz.* Whether a Prince ought to have Fortresses and Citadels,

[8] The *Bentivoglio's* grew wife at the Expence of Pope *Julius* II who having built a Citadel at *Bologna*, and appointed a Governor who caufed many of the Citizens to be affaffinated, loft both that and the Town, as foon as the Townfmen took Arms. Ibid

he who fears his Neighbours more than his Subjects, ought to dispense with them. The Castle which *Francis Sforza* built at *Milan*, has done and will do more Mischief to the Family of *Sforza*, than any Disorder whatever in that State [b]. There is no better Fortress, than not to be hated by the

tadels, or whether he ought to demolish them? As to what concerns petty Princes, I think I have given my Opinion on this Head in the tenth Chapter. Let us now consider it with regard to Kings. In *Machiavel*'s Time the World was in a general Ferment, the Spirit of Revolt and Sedition prevailed every-where; there was nothing to be seen but Factions and Tyrants. Frequent Revolutions obliged Princes to build Citadels upon the Emi-

[b] Because the *Sforza*'s became more bold, and consequently more violent. If you build Fortresses, says *Machiavel*, in the same Chapter, you will find them serviceable in Time of Peace, because they make you more bold in oppressing your Subjects. But in Time of War they will be of no Advantage, for they will be attacked both by your Enemies and your Subjects, and cannot possibly hold out against both —If you would recover a State that is lost, it will never be done by Fortresses, unless you have an Army strong enough to fight your Enemy who has dispossessed you. Now, if you have such an Army, you will be able to recover your State without any Fortresses at all. As for the Castle of *Milan Machiavel* adds, that in Time of Distress it was of no Service either to the *Sforza*'s or the *French*, but on the contrary did them hurt, as it made both neglect to treat the People better.

the People. Nor will any Fortress be sufficient to protect you, if the People are your Enemies, because they will no sooner take Arms but Foreigners will come in to their Assistance. In our Times we have not seen any Instance of the Advantage of these Fortresses, except

Eminences of Towns, in order to bridle the restless Disposition of the Inhabitants.

Since that barbarous Age, whether it be that Men are grown weary of destroying one another, or rather that Sovereigns have a more absolute Power over their Subjects, we do not hear so much of Revolts and Seditions; and that turbulent Spirit, after having sufficiently fatigued itself, may be said to be reduced at present to a State of Tranquillity; so that there is no further Occasion fo Citadels to secure the Fidelity of Towns and Provinces. It is not so with regard to such Fortifications as are designed against foreign Enemies, and as a further Security to the State.

Armies and Fortresses are of equal Service to Princes, for their Armies, in case they are worsted, may retire under the Cannon of their Fortresses; and if the Enemy attempts the Siege of them, the Prince has Time to recover himself, and to levy new Troops, with which and the rest, he may raise the Siege.

In the late Wars in *Flanders* between the Emperor and *France*, hardly any Progress was made, by reason of the Multitude of strong Places in that Country: Victories won by an Army of a

Hun-

except one The Countess of *Furli** after the Murder of Count *Jerom*† her Husband, was able, by means of her Citadel, to withstand the Fury of the Populace, till Succours arrived from *Milan*, and re-established her in the Government. And such was the State of Affairs at that Time, that Foreigners were

not

Hundred thousand Men over another equally numerous, were only followed by the Surrender of a Town or two. By the next Campaign the Enemy, having had Time to repair their Losses, appeared again in the very Field where they had been defeated, and disputed a Victory which had been decided the Year before In a Country that abounds with fortified Places, Armies numerous enough to cover two Miles of Ground may make War for thirty Years together, and if they are prosperous, may gain after twenty Battles a Country ten Miles in Compass In an open Country it is quite otherwise, a Battle, or a Campaign or two, terminates the War, and makes the Conqueror Master of whole Kingdoms. *Alexander*, *Cæsar*, *Gengiskan*, *Charles* XII owed their Glory to their meeting with few fortified Places in the Countries they subdued The Conqueror of the *Indies* made but two Sieges in all his glorious Campaigns, the

Arbiter

---

*Catherine Sforza, Daughter of Francis, and Sister of Lewis the Moor, both Dukes of Milan.

†Jerom Rear, Nephew of Pope Sixtus IV

not in a Condition to affist the People. But afterwards, when she was attacked by *Cæsar Borgia*, who was joined by her own Subjects, she found it had been more prudent Conduct, both at that Time and before, to have gained the Good-will of the People, than to have depended upon Fortresses. Upon the Whole, I approve of those who build Fortresses, and of those who do not; but I must needs blame those who trust so much to them, as to make but little Account of being hated by their Subjects.

Arbiter of *Poland* never made more. *Eugene, Villars, Marlborough, Luxemburg*, were great Generals; but the Brightness of their Successes and Glory was damped, as it were, by the Number of Fortresses they met with. The *French* are very sensible of the Usefulness of Fortresses, for from *Brabant* to *Dauphiny* there runs, as it were, a double Ridge of strong Places. The Frontier of *France* towards *Germany* resembles the open Jaws of a Lion, guarded with two Rows of dreadful Teeth, that seem prepared to devour every thing. This may suffice to shew the great Usefulness of fortified Towns.

C H A P.

CHAP. XXI.

How a Prince ought to act in order to gain Reputation.

Nothing makes a Prince so highly esteemed, as great Enterprizes, and giving signal Proofs of his Abilities. We have in our Days an Example of this in *Ferdinand* King of *Arragon*, the present King of *Spain*, who may not improperly be called a new Prince, as having from a small and weak King become, for Reputation and

Glory,

OBSERVATIONS.

This Chapter of *Machiavel* contains some Lessons that are good, and some that are bad. I shall first point out his Errors, and confirm what is just and commendable in him, and afterwards venture to give my own Sentiments upon some Things that have a natural Connection with this Subject.

Our Author proposes the Conduct of *Ferdinand* of *Arragon,* and of *Bernard* of *Milan,* as a Pattern to those who would distinguish themselves by great Enterprizes, and by Actions that are singular and extraordinary.

Mc

Glory, the first Monarch in *Christendom*. If
we consider his Exploits, we shall find them
all great and remarkable, and some of them
extraordinary. In the Beginning of his Reign,
he invaded the Kingdom of *Granada*, and
that Enterprize was the Foundation of his
Grandeur. He began it leisurely, and without any Suspicion of meeting with Obstacles;
he kept the Barons of *Castile* employed in
that Service, and so intent upon the War,
that they had no Leisure to think of Innovations; whilst in the mean time he got Reputation,

Machiavel hunts after the Marvellous, both with
regard to the Boldness of the Enterprizes, and to
the Rapidity of their Execution. That may be
great, I own; but can only be commendable so far
as the Enterprize of the Conqueror is just. " You
" who boast of exterminating Robbers, said the
" *Scythian* Embassadors to *Alexander*, are your-
" self the greatest of all Robbers, for you have
" conquered no Nation which you have not plun-
" dered: If you are a God, you should be bene-
" ficent to Mortals, and not strip them of what
" they lawfully enjoy, if a Man, remember what
" you are."
Ferdinand of *Arragon* was not always content with
making War; but often employed Religion as a
Veil to cover his Designs; and made no Scruple
to profane the Sanctity of Oaths; Justice was in all
S   his

putation, and ere they were aware, increased his Authority over them. He found out a way to maintain his Army, at the Expence of the Church and the People, and by the Length of that War to establish such Order and Discipline among his Troops, that afterwards they gained him many glorious Victories. Besides, to prepare himself for greater Enterprizes, *Ferdinand*, always making Religion his Pretence, had Recourse to a sort of pious Cruelty, and plundered and banished all the *Jews*, nor could there be a more deplorable, or more signal Instance of his Conduct

his Professions, but Injustice and Violence in all his Actions. In his Conduct *Machiavel* commends every thing that others blame in it

Our Author produces in the next Place the Example of *Bernard* of *Milan*, to insinuate that Princes ought to reward and punish in some conspicuous manner, in order that all their Actions may bear a Stamp of Grandeur and Excellence. Generous Princes will never fail to get Reputation, especially if their Generosity proceeds from a Greatness of Mind, and not from Self-love, the Goodness of their Hearts may alone make them greater than all other Qualities *There is nothing greater in your Fortune,* said *Cicero* to *Cæsar, than the Power of saving so many Citizens: nor is there any thing more worthy of your Goodness, than the Will to do it.* The

Punish-

Conduct than this. Under the same Cloak of Religion, he invaded *Africa*, made his Expedition into *Italy*, and has now at length attacked *France*. Thus *Ferdinand* has been continually employed in some Attempt, which always kept the Minds of his Subjects in Suspense and Admiration, and busied in attending to the Event· And these Enterprizes have so grown out of one another, that the People have never had Time to rest, or to plot against him.

It is likewise of great Advantage to a Prince, to give Proofs of his Abilities in his Administration at home (such as are related of
Bernard

Punishments therefore which a Prince inflicts, should be less than the Offence, and the Rewards which he bestows greater than the Service he receives.

But here follows a downright Contradiction. In this Chapter our Political Doctor would have Princes observe their Alliances, and in the eighteenth Chapter he expresly discharges them from their Engagements. He acts like those Fortune-tellers, who say White to some, and Black to others.

If thus far *Machiavel* reasons ill, his Observations are just concerning the Prudence with which Princes ought to avoid engaging, upon slight Occasions, with others who are more powerful, and who instead of succouring would oppress them. This Maxim was well known to a great

Prince

Bernard Lord of *Milan*), when he wants
a Man to perform something in the Government that is either signally good, or signally
wicked, and to find some Means of reward-
ing or punishing him, that may be much
talked of in the World. But especially the
Prince should endeavour in all his Actions
to aim at a Reputation of Greatness and Excellence[b] A Prince is likewise much esteemed
when he shews himself a true Friend, or a
true Enemy. By a true Enemy I mean one
who without Hesitation openly declares in
favour of one Party against another, which is
always

Prince in *Germany*, equally esteemed by his Friends
and Enemies Whilst this Prince with all his Troops
assisted the Emperor upon the *Rhine*, in the War
against *France*, the *Swedes* invaded his Dominions.
His Ministers, upon the News of this sudden Ir-
ruption, advised him to call in the Czar to his Assistance: But having more Penetration than his Ministers,

[a] And these under *Philip
de Comines* relates of *Lewis*
XI his Master He dealt in
Purshments, says that Au-
thor, *to make himself feared,
and that he might not lose
the Obedience of his People
He would displace Statesmen,
superior Officers, retrench Pen-*

*sions, and make and unmake
whom he pleased, and was
more talked of in* France
than any King whatever
Mem Book III Chap 8

[b] *Præcipua rerum ad famam dirigenda,* says *Tacitus,*
Ann 4 "One of the main
"Designs of a Prince in all
"his

always better Policy than standing neuter. For when two of your powerful Neighbours are at War, they are either so strong, that you have Reason to be afraid of the Victor, or they are not. Now in both Cases it is most prudent to declare yourself, and to make a fair War. For if you stand neuter, you will always fall a Prey to the Victor, and it will be a great Pleasure to the Vanquished, to see you his Fellow-sufferer. Nor will you meet with Pity or Protection, for the Victor will have no suspected Friends, and such as will not assist him in his Misfortunes; and

---

nisters, he answered, That the *Russians* were a sort of Boars whose Chains it was dangerous to take off, lest it should be impossible to put them on again; and therefore he generously resolved to be his own Avenger, and had no Cause to repent his Resolution. If I was to live in the next Age, I should certainly mention this Article of History, with suitable Reflections; but it is not for me to judge of the Conduct of modern Princes: and in Affairs of this World a Man should know where to speak and where to be silent.

S 3

The

" his Conduct should be to " gain himself Reputation " Like *Mucianus*, he should give a sort of Grace and Ornament to every thing he says or does *Omnium quæ diceret, aut ageret, arte quâdem ostentator. Hist 2,*

and the Vanquiſhed will not receive you, becauſe you would not take Arms, and with
him expoſe yourſelf to the Chance of War.

Antiochus upon the Invitation of the
Etolians, paſſed into *Greece*, in order to
expel the *Romans*, and ſent Embaſſadors to
perſuade the *Achaians*, who were then in
Alliance with the *Romans*, to obſerve a
Neutrality: On the other hand, the *Romans* ſent to perſuade them to take Arms
on their Side. The Affair was debated in
the Council of *Achaia*, where the Embaſſador ſent by *Antiochus* preſſing them to
ſtand neuter, the *Roman* Embaſſador replied *As for what he endeavours to perſuade you, that it is moſt uſeful, and moſt
conſiſtent with the Intereſt of your State,*

not

The Subject of Neutrality is as well handled
by *Machiavel*, as that of Alliances. Long Experience has ſhewn, that a Prince who ſtands neuter,
expoſes his Country to the Depredations of both
the contending Parties, that his Dominions become the Theatre of War, and that he is ſure to
loſe on the one hand by a Neutrality, without
ever being able to make any ſolid Acquiſition on
the other. There are two ways by which a King
may aggrandize himſelf, one by Conqueſt, when
a warlike Prince by the Force of Arms extends

the

not to engage in the War between us, no-
thing can be more prejudicial to you, for if
you declare on neither Side, you will be
sure to fall a Prey to that which conquers,
without any Merit with them, or Reputa-
tion to yourselves [c]. And it will always
happen, that he who is not your Friend,
will intreat you to stand neuter, and that he
who is, will prefs you to declare yourself, and
to take Arms for him. Imprudent Princes,
to avoid some present Danger, commonly
take

the Limits of his Empire, the other by good
Government, when an industrious Prince encourages all the Arts and Sciences, and by making
them flourish, renders his Dominions more powerful, and better regulated. As this whole Book
treats only of the first way of aggrandizing a
Prince, I shall say something here of the second,
which is much more innocent and just than the
other, and not lefs useful.

S 4 The

[c] *Quippe sine disputate*
pretium victoris eritis Li-
vius, Book 35 " You will
" be the Booty of the Vic
" tor, without any Reputa-
" tion to yourselves' No
Prince should stand neuter
between two Neighbours
at War, but when he is
more powerful than either
of them, for in this Cafe
he can make himself Ar-
biter of their Differences
whenever he pleases Neu-
tralities are always prejudicial to petty Princes So
that you must either be
strongest yourself, or side
with the strongest.

take the neutral Way, and are commonly undone by it. But when you boldly declare for one Party, though the Prince to whom you adhere is more powerful than yourfelf, and therefore has you at his Difcretion, if he overcomes, yet he is connected with you both by Obligation and Friendfhip: And Men are never fo difhoneft, as to opprefs, with the moft fhameful Ingratitude, thofe who have obliged them. Befides, Victories are never fo clear and complete, as to difengage the Victor from all Confiderations, and efpecially from thofe of Juftice But if your Confederate is worfted, he will be fure to receive, and to affift you, when he can, and you become the Companion of his Fortune, which may poffibly be retrieved.

In

The Arts that are moft neceffary in Life, are Agriculture, Commerce, and Manufactures: Thofe that do moft Honour to the Mind of Man are Geometry, Philofophy, Aftronomy, Eloquence, Poetry, Painting, Mufick, Sculpture, Architecture, Engraving, and the other polite Arts.

As the Nature of Countries is very different, fo there are fome whofe Riches and Strength depend upon Agriculture, others upon Vineyards, fome upon Manufactures, and others upon Commerce; and in fome few Countries we fee all thefe Arts flourifh

In the second Cafe, when the contending
Parties are not of fuch Strength, that you
have Reafon to fear the Conqueror, you
ought in Prudence to declare yourfelf the
fooner; becaufe by affifting one, you contribute to the Ruin of the other, whom your
Confederate, had he been wife, ought rather
to have preferved; and as, with your Affiftance, he muft needs overcome, he muft, of
Courfe, lie at your Mercy. Here it is to be
obferved, that a Prince fhould always beware
of affociating with one who is ftronger than
himfelf, in an offenfive War, unlefs he is
compelled to it by Neceffity, as I faid before *. For if your Affociate overcomes, you
are

flourifh together. Princes therefore who chufe
this mild and amiable way of increafing their
Power, will be obliged to ftudy the particular
Nature of their Country, in order to know which
of thofe Arts is moft likely to thrive in it, and
confequently which of them they ought moft to
encourage. The *French* and *Spaniards* have at
length perceived their want of Trade, and therefore have contrived to ruin the Trade of the
Englifh If they fucceed, *France* will increafe its
Power more confiderably by this means, than by
the Conqueft of twenty Towns, and a thoufand
Vil-

* Chap XIII.

are wholly at his Difcretion; and there is nothing which Princes ought moie carefully to avoid, than expofing themfelves to the Difcretion of others. The *Venetians*, without any real Neceffity, affociated with *France* againft the Duke of *Milan*, and this Affociation was the Caufe of their Ruin. Eut when fuch a Step cannot be avoided, as happened to the *Florentines*, when the Pope and the King of *Spain* fent their Aimies to invade *Lombardy*, the Prince, in this Cafe, ought to affociate, foi the Reafcns abovementioned. Nor let any Piince or State imagine, that in fuch Cafes they can take a fure and infallible Courfe. For there is not

any

Villages; and *Englana* and *Holland*, the two fineft and richeft Countries in the World, will dwindle away bv Degrees, like a Man who is continually dying of a Confumption

In Countries whofe Riches confift in Corn and Vineyards, two things are to be confidered: In the firft place, it is neceffary to grub up all the untilled Land, that there may hardly be a fingle Spot of Ground which does not yield fomething: In the next place, Care muft be taken to increafe the Sale of that natural Produce, to make the Tranfportation of fuch Merchandizes cheap and eafy, and to be able to fell them at low Prices.

As

any Courfe whatever, but is doubtful and hazardous; and fuch is the Condition of all Affairs, that there is no Poffibility to avoid one Inconvenience without running into another: It is the Part of a wife Man to know the Nature of Inconveniencies and Dangers, and always to make Choice of the leaft [d].

A Prince ought befides to fhew himfelf a Lover of all the valuable Arts, and to honour thofe who excel in them. Nor muft he neglect to encourage his Subjects in their feveral Employments, and efpecially in Merchandize and Agriculture, that finding themfelves

As for Manufactures of all kinds, thefe, perhaps, of all other things, are the moft ufeful and profitable. as they provide not only for the Neceffities, but for the Luxury of your Inhabitants, impofe upon your Neighbours a fort of Tribute to your Induftry, and, while they hinder the exporting of your own, promote the importing of foreign Coin.

I

[d] He who waits for all Conveniencies, (fays Machiavel, Book II of his Hiftory) either undertakes nothing, or mifcarries in all his Undertakings I have obferved in all Affairs of this World, fays another Italian Politician, that nothing more precipitates a Man into Dangers, than too much Care to avoid them, and that too much Prudence commonly degenerates into Imprudence Father Paul

felves fecure and unmolefted, they may neither forbear to improve their Eftates, through
the Apprehenfion of lofing them, nor to inlarge their Trade, for fear of Impofitions *:
Nay, he ought to propofe Rewaids to be be-
ftowed on thofe who fet any Improvements on
foot, for enriching his Dominions. Befides in,
the proper Seafon of the Year, the People ought
to be entertained with Feftivals and publick
Shews e; and as every City is divided either
into

I have always believed, that the want of Ma-
nufactures partly occafioned thofe prodigious Tranf-
migrations of People from the North, of thofe
Gotbs and *Vandals*, who fo often over-run the
Southern Countries. In thofe early Times, no
Art was known in *Sweden*, *Denmark*, or the
greateft Part of *Germany*, except Agriculture and
Hunt-

---

* Sir *William Temple* juftly obferves, that Trade never flourfhes in a defpotick
Government, becaufe no
Man is fure of long enjoying
his Property, whereas the
Lofs of it is not to be apprehended in a free State
Whereupon he concludes,
that a Republick feems to be
much more proper than a
Monarcical Government,
for cultivating and preferving
Trade, witnefs *Tyre*, *Car-*
thage, *Athens*, *Syracufe*,
Agrigentum, and *Rhodes*,
where it began to decline, as
foon as thofe Cities fell into
the Hands of an abfolute
Prince See Chap 6 of his
Obfervations upon the *Ne-*
therlands
e Thus the *Romans*, as
Tacitus obferves, fubdued
Nations rather by Voluptuoufnefs than by Arms *Vo-*
luptatibus, quibus Romani
pl is adverfis fubjectos, quàm
armis

into Companies or Wards, the Prince fhould have a Value for thefe feveral Societies, be fometimes prefent at their Entertainments f, and give Inftances of his Goodnefs and Magnificence,

Hunting: Arable Lands were divided among a certain Number of Proprietors, who tilled them, and whom they were fufficient to fubfift. But as the Race of Men has always been very fertile in thofe cold Climates, it foon happened, that they had twice as many Inhabitants as could fubfift by Agriculture: Whereupon the younger Sons of good Families herded together, and were forced by Neceffity to become illuftrious Robbers, to invade and plunder other Countries, and difpoffefs their Proprietors. Accordingly we find, that both in the Eaftern and Weftern Empire, thofe Barbarians

---

arms valent Hift 4. And particularly *Agricola*, who, by introducing Luxury and Voluptuoufnefs among the *Britons*, diffolved the fierce Courage of that Nation to fuch a Degree, that they gave the Names of Politenefs and Humanity to what was really Part of their Servitude *Ut homines difperfi ac rudes, eoque bello feroces, quieti & otio per voluptates affuefcerent ——Idque apud imperitos humanitas vocabatur, cùm pars fervitutis effet* Tacit in *Agricola*

f As *Auguftus* did *Indulferat et ludicro Auguftus—neque ipfe abhorrebat talibus ftudiis, & civile rebatur mifceri voluptatibus vulgi* Ann I " *Auguftus* had countenanced the Players in the " *Roman* Games, and their " Art, nor indeed had he " any Averfion to thofe fa- " vouriteAmufements of the " Populace, he rather judged " it an acceptable Courtefy " to mingle with the Multi- " tude in their Pleafures" For the People, who are fond of their Pleafures, are de-

nificence, but always keeping up the Majesty of his Rank s; for that muſt never be laid aſide upon any Occaſion.

barians commonly demanded nothing but Lands to cultivate for their Subſiſtence. The Northern Countries are not leſs populous at preſent, than they were in thoſe Days : But Luxury, as it has wiſely multiplied our Wants, ſo it has produced Manufactures, and all thoſe Arts, that ſupport and maintain whole Nations, who would otherwiſe be forced to ſeek their Subſiſtence elſewhere

These ways of rendering a State proſperous and flouriſhing, are, as it were, Talents that are truſted with the Wiſdom of Sovereigns, and which they muſt always put to Uſe, and improve. The ſureſt Proof we can have, that a Country is under a wiſe and happy Government, is when the polite Arts ſpring up and flouriſh in it. Theſe are Flowers

that

delighted to find the Prince their Companion in them *Ut eſt vulgus cupiens voluptatum, &, ſi eodem Princeps trahat, lætum* Ann 14 And thus did *Vitellus* Co— *a Conſulum cum candidatis civiliter celebrans, omnem infimæ plebis rumorem in theatro ut ſpectator, in circo, ut fautor, affectavit* Hiſt 2 " *Vitellus,* in holding the Aſſemblies for " creating Conſuls, aſſiſted " with great Moderation, " and behaved towards the " Candidates as their Equal.

" Nay, he ſtudied to gain " the good Graces and Applauſe of the Rabble, " whom he courted by frequenting the Theatre as a " Spectator among them, " and the Circus as a Partizan '

Ita ut nec illi, aut facilitas auctoritatem, aut ſeveritas amorem diminuat In *Agricola* " His Compliance muſt neither weaken " his Authority, nor his Severity make him leſs amiable "

that never fail to bloom in a rich Soil, and a happy Climate, but that wither and die off, when the Soil is barren, or the Air tempestuous.

Nothing makes a Reign more illustrious, than when Arts flourish under its Protection. The Age of *Pericles* is as famous for the Men of Genius who then lived at *Athens*, as for the Battles which were then fought by the *Athenians*. That of *Augustus* is more remarkable for producing *Cicero*, *Ovid*, *Horace* and *Virgil*, than for the Proscriptions of that cruel Emperor, who, after all, owes great Part of his Reputation to the Writings of *Horace*, and the Esteem that is had for them. That of *Lewis* XIV. is more illustrious for the *Corneilles*, *Racines*, *Molieres*, *Boileaus*, *Descartes*, *Le Bruns*, and *Girardons*, whom it produced, than for the marvellous Passage of the *Rhine*, which has been so much exaggerated, than for those Sieges where *Lewis* himself was present, and for the Battle of *Turin*, which Marshal *Marsin*, by Order of the Cabinet Council, made the Duke of *Orleans* lose.

When Princes distinguish and reward Men of uncommon Merit, when they encourage those superior Genius's who devote themselves to the perfecting of our Knowledge, and the Discovery and Improvement of Truth, they do Honour to human Nature. Happy are those Sovereigns who themselves cultivate the Sciences, and who think with *Cicero*, that *Roman* Consul, who was the Saviour of his Country, and the Father of Eloquence, " These are Studies that form and " improve us in our younger Years, and soften " and chear us in our old Age; they adorn us " in Prosperity, and comfort and relieve us in

" Ad-

" Adverfity; whether we are at home or abroad,
" in the World or in Solitude, at all Times and
" in all Places, thefe are the Delights and Em-
" bellifhments of our Life."

Laurence of *Medicis*, the greateft Man of his
Nation, was the Peace-maker of *Italy*, and the
Reftorer of the Sciences. His Probity procured
him the general Confidence of all the Princes of
his Age. *Marcus Aurelius*, one of the greateft
Emperors of *Rome*, was not a lefs fortunate War-
rior than wife Philofopher; and joined the Practice
of the fevereft Morality, with the Profeffion he
made of it. Let us conclude with thefe Words:
When a King in all his Actions is guided by
Juftice, the Univerfe is his Temple, and every
virtuous Man his Prieft.

C H A P. XXII.

Of the Secretaries of Princes.

THE chufing of Minifters is not an
Affair of little Importance; and the
Choice is either well or ill made,
according to the Wifdom of the Prince: The
firft Judgment that is paffed of his Capacity,
is from thofe who are about his Perfon [a]:
When

---

[a] *Tacitus* obferves, that
the Choice wh en *Nero* made
of *Corbulo* for his General,
was looked upon as a happy

Omen of his future Reign;
as it fhewed, that a Door was
now open for Merit, and
that *Nero* employed good
Coua?

When they are Men of Parts and Fidelity, you may always infer that he is a wife Prince, becaufe he has been able to know their Worth [b], and to keep them faithful. But when

OBSERVATIONS.

There are two forts of Princes in the World; thofe who fee with their own Eyes, and govern their Dominions themfelves; and thofe who truft to the Integrity of their Minifters, and fuffer themfelves to be governed by fuch as have got an

T

Afcen-

Counfellors *Datarum plané documentum, honeftis, an fecùs, amicis uteretur, fi ducem egregium, quàm fi pecuniofum, & gratiâ fubnixum deligeret* And a few Lines after, *Læti---quod Dominum Corbulonem præpofuerat, videbaturque locus virtutibus patefactus* Ann 13 "The "Senate fincerely rejoiced, "that for the Re-conqueft "of *Armenia*, *Nero* had "preferred *Domitius Corbulo*, whence a Door "feemed to be opened for "the Reward of Virtue "and Merit" And, methinks, (fays *Philip de Comines*, Chap 3 Book II of his Memoirs) one of the greateft Proofs a Prince can give of his good Senfe, is to employ about his Perfon

Men of Virtue and Honefty, for the World will believe, that he is of the fame Difpofition and Nature with thofe who are near him It was for this Reafon the Prince of *Orange* faid, That one might judge of the Cruelty of *Philip* II King of *Spain*, by the many Cruelties which the Duke of *Alva* committed with Impunity in the *Netherlands*

[b] For as one can never judge well of a Statuary, Painter, or Sculptor, without being Mafter of his Art, fo none but a wife Man can difcover the Wifdom of another *Ut enim de pictore, fculptore, fictore, ni artifex judicare, ita nifi fapiens non poteft perfpicere fapientem.* Plin Ep 10 Lib I

when they are not, you may always conceive
an unfavourable Opinion of him, for in the
very first thing he did, which was chusing his
Ministers, he committed an Error. There
was no Man who knew *Anthony da Venefio*
to be the Minister of *Pandolphus Petrucci*,
Prince of *Siena*, but judged that *Pandolphus*
was a very wise Prince, because he had such
a Minister. Now the Capacities of Men may
be divided into three Classes. Some under- [c]
stand things of themselves; others understand
as much as is explained to them, and others
neither understand of themselves [c], nor by
any Explanation. The first sort of Capacity
is excellent, the second commendable, and
the

Ascendant over them. Sovereigns of the first
sort, are the Life and Soul of their Dominions;
the Weight of their Government rests upon themselves, like the World upon the Shoulders of
Atlas, they regulate Affairs both foreign and
domestick: and fill at once the Posts of first Magistrate of Justice, of General of the Armies, and of
High Treasurer. In Imitation of the Supreme
Being,

[c] An antient Poet says,
*Laudatissimus est, qui per se
cuncta videbit. Sed laudan-
dus & is, qui paret recta
monenti.* He who sees things
himself, is highly to be com-
mended. And he deserves
Commendation likewise,
who follows the good Ad-
vice of others

the third quite ufelefs. One muft therefore
neceffarily agree, that if *Pandolphus* was not
of the firft Clafs, he was of the fecond. For
when a Prince has Judgment enough to
know the Good or the Bad in the Words or
Actions of others, though he has no Inven-
tion himfelf, yet he knows the good and bad
Actions of his Minifter; he rewards the one,
and punifhes the other; and the Minifter, as
he cannot hope to impofe upon him, will
continue to act honeftly [d].

To

Being, who employs Intelligences fuperior to Men,
in the Execution of his Will, they have Men of
Penetration and Induftry, to execute their Defigns,
and to accomplifh every particular Part of what
they have projected in general, and their Minifters are properly no more than the Tools and
Utenfils of a fkilful Artificer

Sovereigns of the other kind, for want of Genius, or from a natural Indolence, are plunged in
a fort of lethargick Indifference If the State,
ready to fink, becaufe of the Imbecillity of the
Sovereign, muft be fupported by the Wifdom and
Application of the Minifter, the Sovereign is

T 2   nothing

[d] For this Reafon *Sejanus*,
who well knew the Ability
and Penetration of *Tiberius*,
at firft endeavoured to gain
the Reputation of a wife and

faithful Counfellor *Sejanus*,
.. iprente adhuc potentiá, bo-
nis confiliis notefcere volebat
Ann 4

To distinguish between a good and a bad Minister, there is one Rule that never fails. When you see that your Minister thinks more of himself than of you, and that all his Actions have a private Tendency to his own Advantage; you may always conclude, that he is a bad Minister, and that you can never repose any Confidence in him [e] For he who has the Do-

nothing but a Shadow, though a necessary one, because he represents the State; we can only wish that he may make a happy Choice.

It is not so easy a Matter as is imagined, for a Sovereign to sound the Disposition and pry into the Characters of those whom he would employ; and as, on the one hand, a Prince can hardly conceal his most secret Thoughts from the Eyes of the Publick, so, on the other, a private Man may easily disguise himself before the Prince, and elude his Penetration. If *Sixtus Quintus* could impose upon seventy

---

[e] After *Sejanus* had exposed his Life to save *Tiberius*, in a Cave at a Villa, thence called *Spelunca*, *Tacitus* says, that *Tiberius* put an intire Confidence in him, as a Man who had been more careful of the Prince's Life than of his own. *Major ex eo, &c, ut non sibi anxius, cum fide audiebatur.* Ann. 4. And *Tigellinus*, to undo his Rivals, alledged to *Nero*, that he was not in the same Case with *Burrhus*, who had several Pretensions and Hopes, whereas all his Ambition was to watch over the Safety of the Prince. *Non se, ut Burrhum, diversas spes, sed solam incolumitatem Neronis spectare* Ann 14. All Ministers make the same Professions, but their Hearts and their Actions often give their Mouths the Lye

Dominions of a Prince in his Management, ought never to mind his own, or any Interest, but that of the Prince; nor to entertain him with any Discourse that is foreign to it [f]. The Prince, on the other hand, to keep his Minister faithful, ought to have as much

seventy Cardinals, who ought to have perfectly known his Character, how much easier must it be for a private Man to impose upon his Prince, who has not so many Opportunities of observing him? The Prince, indeed, if he is a Man of Parts, may easily judge of the Parts of those whom he would employ; but as for their Integrity and Fidelity, it is scarce possible to discover them beforehand. How many Men have appeared virtuous, only for want of an Opportunity

T 3   to

[f] For this Reason *Tiberius* turned a Senator into Ridicule, who pretended to discourse in the Senate of the private Affairs of his own Family. *Nec ideò à majoribus concessum est, egredi aliquandò relationem, & quod in commune conducat loco sententiæ proferre, ut privata negotia, res familiares nostras hic augeamus ——Efflagitatio intempestiva & improvisa, cùm aliis de rebus convenerint patres, consurgere* Ann 2. "Our Ancestors, when "they permitted any Man "to depart from the Que-"stion, permitted it in or-"der to hear some Affair of "greater Importance to the "State, and not that we "might in the Senate talk "of our domestic Affairs, "and seek to augment our "private Rents But this, "indeed, is not a Petition "of *Hortalus*, it is a De-"mand made against Order, "and made by Surprize, "whilst you are assembled "upon other Affairs, he "stands up, and interrupts "your Proceeding".

much Regard for his Interest g, to honour
him, enrich him, attach him to himself, and
confer such Dignities and Employments upon him, that he may have no Occasion to
desire more Wealth, or more Honour; and
that, perceiving it would be scarce possible for
him to keep, under another Master, what he
enjoys

to shew their Wickedness? How many have
renounced all Honesty, as soon as their Virtue
was put to the Trial? *Tiberius, Nero, Caligula,*
had no bad Reputation at *Rome,* before they
ascended the Throne But Opportunity ripened
and displayed the Wickedness of their Nature,
which perhaps would have otherwise produced no
Effect.

There

g This was *Tiberius* s Sense
of the Matter, when he said to
*Sejanus, Ipse, quid ut a ani-
mum volutaverit, quibus adhuc necessitudinibus remiscere
te mihi parem, oratam ad
præsens referre Id tantum
aperiam, nihil esse tam excel-
sum, quod non virtutes istæ,
tuusque in me animus, mere-
antur, datoque tempore, vel
in senatu, vel in concione non
retcelo Ann* + "The
secret and constant Pur-
poses of my Heart towards
you, and with what fur-
ther Ties of Affinity I am
contriving to bind you

"still faster to me, I shall at
"present forbear to men-
"tion Thus much only I
"will declare, that there is
"nothing so high, but those
"Abilities, and your singular
"Zeal and Fidelity towards
"me, may justly claim, as,
"when Opportunity pre-
"sents, either in the Senate,
"or in a popular Assembly,
"I shall not fail to testify"
Philip II King of *Spain,* used
to say to *Ruy Gomez,* his first
Minister, *Do you mind my
Affairs, and I will mind
yours.*

enjoys by the Favour of the prefent, he may
be afraid of fuffering by any Change.
When the Prince and his Minifter act in this
manner, they may always rely upon one
another; but when they act otherwife, either
the Minifter or the Prince muft needs be undone at laft.

There are fome Men who have great Wit,
great Cunning, and many Talents, but are withal
in their Nature full of Perfidy and Ingratitude;
and there are others who poffefs all the Qualities
of the Heart, without excelling fo much in thofe
of the Head. Wife Princes have commonly preferred the latter in domeftick Employments, and
the former in foreign Negotiations. For as at
home it is only neceffary to maintain Order and
Juftice, in this Cafe Honefty is fufficient; whereas,
when there is occafion for perfuading foreign
Princes, and difcovering the Intrigues of a neighbouring Court, Probity is not fo much wanted, as
Addrefs and Penetration.

A Prince, methinks, can never fufficiently
reward the Fidelity and Zeal of his Minifters:
There is in our Nature fome Sentiment of Juftice,
which, as it were, forces us to be grateful. Befides, the Intereft of the Great abfolutely requires
that they reward with Generofity, as well as punifh
with Clemency. But certainly Minifters, when
they perceive that Virtue will be the means of raifing
their Fortune, will never have recourfe to Vice;
and muft naturally prefer the Bounty of their
Mafter, to the Bribes of others. Prudence there-

T 4 fore

fore and Juſtice agree perfectly in this Point ·
And without queſtion, it is not more ungenerous
than imprudent in a Prince, to put the Fidelity of
his Miniſter to a dangerous Trial, by neglecting
to reward it.

There are ſome Princes who give into another
Error, not leſs dangerous than the former; they
change their Miniſters upon the ſlighteſt Occaſions, and puniſh the leaſt Irregularity in their
Conduct with exceſſive Rigour. Miniſters who
are employed under the immediate Inſpection of
the Prince, when they have been ſome time in
Place, cannot wholly conceal their Faults from
him; and the more he is penetrating, the ſooner
will he diſcover them. Sovereigns who are not
Philoſophers, quickly loſe their Patience, take
Offence at the Weakneſſes of thoſe who ſerve
them, and diſgrace and ruin them.

Princes who reaſon more profoundly, know
Men better, and remember that they all bear ſome
diſtinguiſhing Mark of Humanity . that there is
nothing perfect in this World , that great Qualities are allayed, and, as it were, balanced, by as
great Defects ; and that Men of Genius partake of
both. For theſe Reaſons, except in Caſes of Pre-
varication, they continue their Miniſters, with all
their Faults, and prefer thoſe whom they have
tried and ſounded, to others who are new to them ;
much in the ſame manner, as ſkilful Muſicians
chuſe rather to play upon Inſtruments whoſe Ex-
cellencies and Defects they know, than upon others
with whoſe Properties they are not acquainted.

CHAP. XXIII.

How Flatterers are to be avoided.

I Will not pass by one Error of very great Consequence, which it is hard for Princes to guard against, unless they have great Prudence and Discernment: It is that of suffering themselves to be flattered, of which we have numberless Instances in all Histories [a]. For Men have commonly so much Self-love, and so easily impose upon themselves in their own Affairs, that it is

cx-

OBSERVATIONS.

There is not a single Book, moral or historical, where the Weakness of Princes, with regard to Flattery, is not severely censured. The World justly desires, that every Prince should love Truth, and be accustomed to hear it: But, as indeed it often happens, they expect things that are contradictory. They expect that Princes should have so much Self-love, as to be fond of Glory, and perform great Actions; and at the same time so much Self-denial, as willingly to renounce the Reward of their Atchievements. They would have them

en-

[a] Adulation is an Evil as old as Government *Vetus* *id in republicâ malum,* says *Tacitus,* Ann 2

extremely difficult for them to escape this
Contagion; and in endeavouring to escape
it, they expose themselves to another Danger, which is that of falling into Contempt:
For as there is no other way of guarding
against Flattery, but letting Men know that
they do not offend you by telling you the
Truth, so, if every one has leave to tell it,
you quickly lose Respect b. Wherefore a
prudent Prince ought to take a third way,
which is that of chusing out of his Subjects
a few wise Men, and permitting them only
to declare the Truth to him, and only in
such Things as he inquires of them, never
suf-

endeavour to purchase Fame, and to despise it.
This is expecting too much from human Nature:
It is doing Princes great Honour, to suppose that
they should have more Power over themselves,
than over others.

Contemptus Virtutis ex contemptu fama There
have been no Princes indifferent as to Fame, who
were not voluptuous Men, abandoned to Sloth
and Effeminacy, mere Lumps of some contemptible Substance, animated with no Virtue. Some
cruel

b For this Reason *Tibe-
rius*, though he hated Flattery, could not suffer Freedom
of Speech, so that it was
scarce possible to know how
to speak to him *An usta
& lubrica oratio sub Principe, qui libertatem metuebat,
adulationem oderat* Ann
2

suffering them to talk to him of any thing
else · But then he ought to be inquisitive about
all Affairs, to listen to their Opinions, and
afterwards take such a Resolution as is agreeable to his own Sentiments; always be-
having to each of them in such a manner,
that they may find, the more freely they
speak, the more they are acceptable to
him *. As he ought to give Ear to none
but them, so he should be slow to take his
Resolution, but afterwards firm and inflexible
in the Pursuit of it. The Prince who acts
otherwise, must either be distressed by his
Flatterers, or often change his Mind, according

cruel Tyrants, indeed, have loved Praise; but in
them it was an odious Vanity, and even a Vice,
as they desired Esteem, whilst they deserved Infamy

With vicious Princes, Flattery is a deadly
Poison, which multiplies the Seeds of Vice. With
those who have Merit, it is a sort of Rust, that sticks
to their Glory, and diminishes the Lustre of it.
A Man of Sense is immediately shocked at gross
Adulation, and repels the unskilful Flatterer.
There is another sort of Flattery, which aims at
ex-

* After the Example of
John II King of *Portugal*,
who being asked by one of
his Courtiers to bestow a
vacant Post upon him, an-
swered, *I keep it for a Man
that never flattered me*

ing to the Diverſity of Opinions c; and thus fall into Diſeſteem.

I ſhall here give one Example in our own Times: Father *Lucas*, ſpeaking of his Maſter *Maximilian*, the preſent Emperor, ſaid, *That his Majeſty never conſulted any body, and yet never did any thing his own way.* This proceeded from his acting contrary to what we have mentioned: For the Emperor is very reſerved, communicates his Secrets to none, and takes nobody's Advice: But when his Deſigns are to be executed, and

come

extenuating the Faults of Princes by its ſophiſtical Rhetorick, ſupplies them with Reaſons for indulging their Paſſions, gives Juſtice the Character of Auſterity, and draws ſo perfect a Reſemblance between Generoſity and Profuſion, that it is hard to diſtinguiſh one from the other: This ſort of Flattery would diſguiſe Debauches under the Veil of Amuſements and Pleaſures, and is particularly intent upon amplifying the Vices of others, in order to erect a Trophy to its Hero. Moſt Men

give

c As weak Princes do, *Ipſe modò huc illuc, ut quemque ſuadentem audierat, promptus:* " *Claudius*, ſays " *Tacitus*, was now inclined " to one Wife, then to " another, and was always " led by his laſt Adviſer "

Ann 12 *Hùc illùc circumagis, quæ juſſerat, vetare, quæ vetuerat, jubere* Hiſt 3. " *Vitellius* was toſſed about " from one Deſign to an- " other, would forbid what " he had juſt ordered, and or- " der what he had juſt forbid

come to be known, thofe who are about him begin to oppofe them; and *Maximilian*, being of an eafy Temper, prefently gives them over: Thus what he does one Day, he undoes the next; no Man can ever know what he defires or defigns, nor depend upon any of his Refolutions [d].

A Prince therefore ought always to confult others; but to do it at his own Pleafure, and not at theirs. Nay, he fhould deter them from offering him their Advice in any Affair, when he does not demand it: But he ought not to be fparing in his Demands, and fhould patiently hear what they anfwer; and if he finds that any one conceals the Truth upon any Confideration whatever, he ought to fhew his Difpleafure and Refentment.

Thofe

give into the kind of Flattery, which juftifies their Tafte, and is not wholly falfe: They can have no Averfion to thefe who fpeak well of them for what they are convinced merits Commendation. Of all Flatteries, that which refts upon a folid Bafis, is the moft fubtle; and great Difcernment is neceffary, in order to difcover the Shadowings

---

[d] A Failing which it is faid the Emperor *Leopold* inherited from *Maximilian* I

Thofe who think that a Prince who has the Reputation of Wifdom, may owe it not to his own natural Parts, but to the good Counfellors he has about him, are certainly miftaken[e]. For it is a general and never-failing Rule, that a Prince who is not prudent himfelf, can never be prudently advifed, unlefs by chance he puts himfelf wholly under the Management of a fingle Perfon, who has great Sagacity. In this Cafe he may indeed be well governed, but cannot reign long; for that Governor will in a fhort time fet up for himfelf, and turn him out. If fuch a

Prince

dowings which it gives to Truth. It will never fend Poets to attend the Prince at a Siege, in order to write his Hiftory, it will never compofe Opera-Prologues, ftuffed with Hyperboles, or infipid Prefaces, or fervile Epiftles; it will never ftun the Hero with high-fwollen Accounts of his Victories; but will put on the Air of Sentiment, ufher itfelf in with great Delicacy, and appear

frank

[e] The Worth of the Minifter, fays a wife *Spaniard*, has never leffened the Glory of his Mafter, on the contrary, all the Honour of the Succefs falls to the Mafter, as well as the Blame of a Mifcarriage Fame always applies itfelf to the principal Authors, and never fays, *This Man had good or bad Minifters,* but *This Man has been a good or bad Prince* A Prince muft therefore endeavour to chufe his Minifters well, fince upon them depend his Fame and Immortality *Gratian,* in his Manual Oracle

Prince employs more Counfellors than one, their Counfels will be divided, and the Prince has not Parts enough to unite them[f]; each of thefe Counfellors will be byaffed by his own private Interefl s, and the Prince will not be able to correct or even to difcover this Error: Nor is it poffible for to him find others that are lefs interefted; for Men will always be wicked, unlefs you lay them under a Neceffity to be virtuous. I conclude therefore, that good Counfels, whomfoever they come from, muft needs be owing to the Wifdom of the Prince, and not the Wifdom of the Prince to them.

frank and natural   How can any Man, and much more a Prince, or a Hero, be difpleafed to hear a Truth, which the Vivacity of a Friend feems to let flip from him? How could *Lewis* XIV who perceived that his Air could alone command Refpect, and who took Delight in that Superiority over Men, be offended at an old Officer, who trembled and faltered when he fpoke to him, and ftopping fhort in his Difcourfe, told him,

[f] *Neque alienis confiliis reg., neque fua expedire* Hift 3   "*Vitellius* would "neither follow the Coun-"fels of others, nor execute "his own"

[g] *Sibi quifque tendentes* Hift 1   *Quia apud infirmum in minore metu, & in majore praemio peccatum* Ibid

him, *Sir, I do not tremble thus before your Ene-*
mies ?

Princes who have been Men before they were
Kings, will remember what they were, and not
so easily accustom themselves to the Food of Flattery. Those who have reigned all their Lives,
have always had Incense offered to them, as to the
Gods ; and would be starved, if they were not
flattered.

It would therefore be more just, methinks, to
lament the Condition of Kings, than to condemn
them. It is Flatterers, and still more Calum-
niators, who deserve the Censure and Hatred of
the Publick, as well as all those who are Enemies enough to the Prince to conceal the Truth
from him. But let us distinguish Flattery from
Praise. *Trajan* was animated to Virtue by *Pliny's*
Panegyrick, and *Tiberius* was confirmed in Vice
by the Adulation of the *Roman* Senators.

CHAP. XXIV.

How the Princes of Italy came to lose their Dominions.

WHEN those things which I have
mentioned, are prudently followed, the new Prince appears a
Sovereign by Inheritance, and quickly becomes more secure and better settled in his
Principality, than if it had been transmitted

to him by a long Succession of his Forefathers: For as the Actions of a new Prince are more narrowly examined, than of one who succeeds by Inheritance, so when they are known to be prudent and judicious, they gain upon and oblige the People much more than the Antiquity of Descent: And the Reason is, that Men are more affected with things which are present, than with those that are past; and when they find themselves happy in their present Condition, they sit down to enjoy it, without looking out for any thing else [a]; nay, when in other things the Prince is not wanting to himself, the People will in this Case employ all their Strength in his Defence.

Thus

OBSERVATIONS.

The Fable of *Cadmus*, who sowed in the Earth the Teeth of the Serpent, which he had overcome, from whence sprung up a People of Warriers who destroyed one another, is an Emblem of the *Italian* Princes in *Machiavel*'s Time: The Perfidies and Treacheries which they committed against each other, were the true Cause of their Ruin. Whoever reads the History of *Italy* towards the latter End of the fourteenth Century as far as the

U

Be-

---

[a] *Tuta & præsentia, quàm vetera & periculosa malunt.* Ann 1 *Arteponunt præsentia dubiis* Hist 1

Thus he gains double Honour, as having laid the Foundation of a new Principality, embellished it, fortified it by good Laws, good Forces, good Allies, and good Examples, whereas he who is born a Prince incurrs a double Infamy, by losing his Principality through his own Imprudence.

If we consider the Conduct of the Sovereign Princes of *Italy*, who in our Times have lost their Dominions, as the King of *Naples*, the Duke of *Milan*, and others; first we shall find one Error common to them all, which is that of employing Mercenary or Auxiliary Troops, as I have shewn before at large: In the next Place it will appear, that some of them either were hated by the People; or if beloved by them, knew

not

Beginning of the fifteenth, will meet with nothing but Cruelties, Seditions, Violences, Confederacies among them to extirpate one another, Usurpations, Assassinations, and, in short, a most enormous Multitude of Crimes, the very Idea of which will inspire him with Horror.

The Prince who, according to *Machiavel's* Precepts, endeavours to destroy Justice and Humanity, aims at nothing less than destroying Mankind, for a Deluge of Crimes would quickly dispeople the whole Globe. As the Iniquities and

Bar-

not how to secure themfelves againft the
Grandees: For without thefe Errors, no
Principality can be loft, that has Men and
Money enough to keep an Army in the
Field.

Philip of *Macedon*†, not the Father of
Alexander the Great, but he who was con-
quered by *Titus Quintus*, had but a fmall
Territory, when compared with that of the
Romans and *Grecians*, who both attacked
him; neverthelefs, as he was a martial Prince,
and knew how to keep the Good-will of the
People, and to fecure himfelf againft the
Grandees, he fuftained a War for feveral
Years againft both thefe Nations; and if at
length

Barbarities of thofe *Italian* Princes coft them their
Dominions, fo the falfe Politicks of *Machiavel*
muft inevitably ruin thofe who have the Folly to
be guided by them.

Not but I muft own, that the Sloth and Cowardice of fome of thofe Princes may have concurred with their Wickednefs to bring on their
Ruin. The Weaknefs of the Kings of *Naples*
unqueftionably diftreffed their Affairs But in
fpite of all the political Arguments and Subtleties
you can ufe, of all the Examples you can produce, and of any Syftem you can form, you will
find

† The Father of *Perfeus*, the laft King of *Macedon*.

length he loſt a few Towns, yet he was able to preſerve his Kingdom. For theſe Reaſons our *Italian* Princes, who for many Years had been ſettled in their Dominions, muſt not impute the Loſs of them to Fortune, but to their own Sloth For as it is a common Failing among Men, not to think of a Storm when the Weather is calm; ſo theſe Princes, in Times of Peace, had no Apprehenſion of a Change, and therefore, when they were invaded, they thought of making their Eſcape, not their Defence, in Hopes that the People, loathing the Inſolence of the Con-

find yourſelf at length obliged to have recourſe to Juſtice.

I would ask *Maurice*, what he means by ſaying, That a new Prince, (that is, *an Uſurper*) who is prudent and judicious. will gain the Attachment of the People more than one who owes his Greatneſs to his Birth, becauſe Men are more affected by the preſent, than the paſt; and, when they find their preſent Situation happy, ſit down to enjoy it, without looking out for any thing elſe? Does he ſuppoſe, that of two Men, equally brave, and equally wiſe, a whole Nation will prefer him who is the Uſurper, to the other who is their lawful Prince? Or does he mean a Prince void of all Merit, and an Uſurper who is a Man of Courage and Capacity? The firſt can hardly be ſuppoſed

Conquerors, would foon recal them. Such
a Refolution is good, when no other can be
taken. But to neglect all other Securities,
and truft to that alone, is certainly much to
be blamed. No Man will fuffer himfelf
to fall, in Hopes that fomebody will come
by and take him up For either that does
not happen, or if it does, you are not fafe,
becaufe the Means of your Relief are contemptible, and do not proceed from yourfelf. And there is no good, certain and lafting Defence, which does not proceed from
the Prince's own Courage and Ability.

to be our Author's Meaning, becaufe it is contrary to common Senfe. Nor will any Nation
ever prefer an Ufurper to a lawful Prince who is
every way equal to him in Merit.

Machiavel muft therefore mean an Ufurper
who is fuperior in Parts to the lawful Prince: And
even in this Cafe his Pofition is almoft as abfurd
as in the other. For let that Ufurper have ever
fo great Qualities, it will be granted that the
Action by which he attains his Authority is a
flagrant Injuftice. Now what can the People
expect from a Soveregn who begins his Reign
with an Act of Violence and Wickednefs, but a
violent and tyrannical Government? It is the
fame Cafe with that of a Husband, who fhould
find his Wife guilty upon the Wedding-Day;

me-

methinks he would not much depend upon her being chaster afterwards.

In this Chapter *Machiavel* passes Sentence of
Condemnation against himself. He expresly
affirms, that without the Affections of the People,
and of the Grandees, and without an Army, it is
impossible a Prince should maintain himself in the
Throne. Truth itself seems to have wrung this
Confession from him, and to have forced him to
pay this Homage to it; much in the same manner
as Divines tell us, that the Angels of Darkness
own the Deity, while they blaspheme him   For
how is it possible for a Prince to gain the Affections
of the People and the Grandees, without having not
only a Capacity for Affairs, but a Fund of Virtue,
Humanity and Beneficence ?

It is with the Office of a Prince, as with all
others ; no Man, whatever his Employment may
be, can gain the Confidence of others, without
Justice and Integrity, as well as Prudence : The
most vicious Men always chuse to deal with the
most virtuous ; in the same manner as those
Princes who have the least Capacity for Governing, trust to him who passes with them for having
the most. And why should Vice be more necef-
sary to the Office of Sovereignty, than to that of
the meanest Magistrate ? Upon the whole, a
Prince who would preserve his Dominions, as he
must gain the Hearts of the People, so for that
purpose he is obliged to be just, virtuous, and
beneficent, and not, as *Machiavel* through the
whole of this Work endeavours to form him, unjust, cruel, ambitious, and solely intent upon aggrandizing himself, by any means whatever.

Thus

Thus have I endeavoured to unmask this Politician, who paffed in his own Age for an extraordinary Man, whom feveral Minifters of State have thought a dangerous Writer, and yet have followed his abominable Maxims, and recommended the Study of them to their Mafters, an Author who yet was never exprefly anfwered, and whom feveral Statefmen follow, without thinking it any Reproach to them. Happy would be the Man who were able to banifh fuch Doctrines out of the World! I have here endeavoured to fhew the Inconfiftency of them; and it is incumbent on thofe who rule over others, to fhew it by their Example, and to fet the Publick right, with regard to the falfe Notion they entertain of Politicks, which fhould only be a Syftem of Wifdom, but commonly paffes for a Breviary of Fraud and Impofture: It is incumbent on them to banifh Subtleties and Infincerity, which are fo common in Treaties; to revive Honefty and Candour, which, in Truth, are very rare among Sovereigns, and to fhew themfelves as indifferent about conquering the Provinces of their Neighbours, as jealous of preferving their own. The Prince who would poffefs every thing, is not lefs abfurd than the Man who would devour every thing, and expects he could digeft as much as he devours. Whereas he who is content to govern wifely what he juftly poffeffes, is like the Man who loads his Stomach with nothing more than it is able to digeft.

U 4   CHAP.

CHAP. XXV.

How great Influence Fortune has in Human Affairs, and in what Manner she may be withstood.

I KNOW it has been, and is still the Opinion of many, that the Affairs of this World are so governed by Fortune and Providence, that human Wisdom cannot amend or alter them, or even apply any Remedy at all From whence they would infer, that we need give ourselves but little Trouble about any thing, and should leave all to the

Govern-

OBSERVATIONS.

The Question concerning the Liberty of the Will is one of those Problems that have put Philosophers to the greatest Nonplus; and has often forced Anathema's from the Divines. The Partizans of Liberty alledge, that if Men are not free, it must be God that acts in them, and that in Cases of Murther, Robberies, or any other Crimes, they are no more than the Tools of the Divine Power; a Doctrine which is manifestly opposite to the Nature of the Deity. In the next Place they alledge, that if the Supreme Being is the Author of Vices, those that commit them, as they cannot be charged

with

Government of Chance a.   This Opinion has the more prevailed in our Times, by reason of the many strange Revolutions that have lately been seen, and daily happen, beyond all human Conjecture.

When

with any Guilt, so they ought to suffer no Punishment, and there will be neither Vice nor Virtue in the World.   Now, as it is impossible to think of this hideous Doctrine, without perceiving all the Contradictions it implies, we can do no better, say they, than declare for the Liberty of the Will.

The

a *Tacitus*, who was an *Epicurean*, says something like this, in the sixth Book of his Annals *Mihi---in incerto judicium est, fato ne res mortalium, & necessitudine immutabili, an forte volvatur.* " For my own part, whilst " I listen to these and the " like Relations, my Judg- " ment wavers,   whether " Things human are in their " Course and Rotation de- " termined by Fate, and im- " mutable Necessity, or left " to roll at random " He adds a little after, *Fatum quidem congruere rebus putant, sed non è vagis stellis, verùm apud principia & nexus natu- talium caussarum , ac tamen electionem vitæ nobis relin- quit quam ubi elegeris, cer- tum in nae itium ordinem* " Others believe a Fate to " preside over Events, a " Fate however not result- " ing from wandering Stars, " but coeval with the first " Principle of Things, and " operating by the conti- " nued Connexion of natu- " ral Causes Yet their Phi- " losophy leaves the Course " of our Life in our own " freeOption, but that, after " the Choice is made, the " Chain of Consequences " is inevitable " As for what *Machiavel* says, that human Prudence has no Influence in Affairs of the World, or at least

When I fometimes reflect on this, I am a little inclined to their Opinion: Neverthelefs, that our Free-will may not be quite exploded, I think it may be faid, that Fortune is the Miftrefs of one half of our Actions, but leaves the other half, or little lefs, to be governed

The Partizans of abfolute Neceffity alledge, on the other hand, that God would be worfe than a blind Workman, or one at leaft who works in the Dark, if, after having created this World, he had been ignorant what fhould happen in it: A Watchmaker, fay they, knows the Action of the fmalleft Wheel in the Watch, fince he knows the Movement which he has given it, and the End for which it is defigned, and fhall God, a Being infinitely wife and powerful, be thought the curious and

---

leaft very little, *Tacitus* gives a beautiful Example of it, fpeaking of *Claudius*, vhom Fortune defigned for the Empire, when any other Succeffor was expected *Mihi quanto plus a recentium, feu veterum revolvo, tanto magis ludibria rerum mortalium cunctis in negotiis obfervatur. quippe famâ, fpe, veneratione, potius omnes deftinabantur imper o, quàm quem futurum Principem fortuna in occulto tenebat* Ann 3 " To me, the more I revolve

" the Events of late, or of
" old, the more of Mockery
" and Slipperinefs appears in
' all human Wifdom, and
" the Tranfactions of Men,
" for in popular Fame, in
" the Hopes, Wifhes, and
" Veneration of thePublick,
" all Men were rather de-
" ftined to the Empire, than
" he for whom Fortune had
" referved the Sovereignty
" in the Dark " Fortune, fays *Gratian*, which is fo famous, and yet fo little known, is nothing but that great

governed by ourselves [b]. Fortune I compare to a rapid and impetuous River, which, when it swells and rages, overwhelms the Plains, destroys the Trees and the Houses, forces away the Earth from one Place, and carries it to another; every one flies before it, and dreads its Fury, without being able to resist it. Yet this does not hinder, but that when it is quiet and calm, there may be Ditches, Banks,

and impotent Spectator of human Actions! How should that Being, all whose Works bear so many Marks of Harmony and Order, and are all subject to certain and invariable Laws, suffer Man alone to enjoy Independence and Liberty? The World, in this Case, would be no longer governed by Providence, but by the Caprice of Men. Since therefore we must make our Option between the Creator and the Creature, which of the two is the mere Machine? Is it not more reasonable to believe that it is the Being who is weak and dependent,

great Parent of Accidents, and that Offspring of the sovereign Providence, which concurs with all secondary Causes, either by moving them, or permitting them to act. Fortune is a Queen absolute, impenetrable, inexorable, smiles upon some, and frowns upon others, sometimes a Mother, at other times a Stepmother, not through an Effect of Passion, but by an incomprehensible Secret of the divine Appointments. Chap 10 of his Hero.

[b] Success, says *Seneca*, Ep 14 is not in the Power of the Wise, we begin Things, but it is Fortune that finishes them

Banks, and other Preparations made to confine it, so that when it swells again, it may either be carried off by some Canal, or at least be less impetuous and destructive. So it is with Fortune, who shews her Power where there is no Preparation made to withstand it, and turns all her Force and Impetuosity where she knows there are no Banks, or other Fences, to restrain her. If you consider

dent. than the Being in whom resides all Power? Accordingly Reason and the Passions are, as it were, the invisible Chain by which the Hand of Providence guides Mankind, and makes all their Actions terminate in those Events which Divine Wisdom had ordained to happen in the World, that each Individual might fulfil his Destiny.

Thus, to avoid *Charybis*, they run upon *Scylla*; and Philosophers force each other into an Abyss of Absurdities, while Divines grope in the Dark, and devoutly damn one another out of Charity. These two Parties carry on their War much in the same manner as the *Carthaginians* and the *Romans* did of old. When it was feared that the *Roman* Army would invade *Africa*, the Scene of War was presently shifted to *Italy*, and when the *Romans* wanted to rid themselves of *Hannibal*, they sent *Scipio* at the Head of their Legions to besiege *Carthage*. Philosophers, Divines, and most of the Heroes in Argument, have the Genius of the *French* Nation; they make a vigorous Attack, but are undone if you

sides *Italy*, which is the Theatre of all these Revolutions, and even has set them in Motion, you will find it an open Field, without any Trench or Bank to secure it; and that if it had been sufficiently fenced, like *Germany*, *Spain* and *France*, such an Inundation of Foreigners would never have happened, or at least would not have made so great Progress.

I shall say no more with respect to opposing Fortune in general; and shall now confine myself to Particulars. It is not rare to see a Prince happy and flourishing one Day, and ruined the next, without observing the least Change in his Disposition or Conduct. This, I be-

you reduce them to the Defensive For this Reason it was said by a Man of Wit, that God was the Father of all religious Sects, since he had equally supplied them all with good Arms, and given them a strong Side and a weak one.

This Question concerning Liberty and Predestination is transplanted by *Machiavel* from Metaphysicks to Politicks: But this nevertheless is a Soil which is entirely improper for it, and can never nourish it, for in Politicks, instead of reasoning whether we are or are not free, whether Fortune or Chance has any or no Influence upon our Actions; we must only consider how far our Penetration and Prudence may be perfected.

Fortune

I believe, proceeds from the Causes which I have mentioned before at large; for the Prince who relies wholly upon Fortune, is undone whenever she changes. I likewise believe, that he whose Manner of Proceeding agrees with the Times, is happy; and that he is unhappy, who cannot accommodate his Conduct to them. For we see that Men, to arrive at the End which they all propose, namely the acquiring of Glory and Riches, take very different Courses; one acts with Moderation, another with Impetuosity, one with Violence, another with Art, one with Patience, another with Fury, and yet they may all arrive at the same End. We see

Fortune and Hazard are Words without any Meaning. and in all Probability owe their Rise to the profound Ignorance in which the World groped when they gave loose and indefinite Names to Effects whose Causes they knew not. What is commonly called the good Fortune of *Cæsar* signifies properly all those Conjunctures which favoured the Designs of that ambitious Man. What is meant by the bad Fortune of *Cato*, are those unforeseen Accidents which happened to him, those Crosses and Disappointments where the Effects so suddenly followed their Cause, that his Prudence could neither forefee nor prevent them.

What

see likewise that of two Persons equally moderate, one succeeds, the other miscarries; and that two Persons of different Turns, one moderate, the other impetuous, are equally successful: This proceeds from nothing but the Nature of the Times, which either suits or disagrees with their Manner of proceeding. Thus it happens, as I said before, that two different Persons, who take different Courses, attain the same End; and of two others, who take the same Course, one succeeds,

What is meant by Hazard cannot be better explained than by a Game at Dice. It is owing to Hazard, say you, that my Dice come up twelve rather than seven To unravel this Phænomenon in a physical manner, one must have Eyes quick enough to see the Way in which the Dice are put into the Box, the Motions of the Hand more or less strong, more or less repeated, which make them turn, and communicate to them a Motion more or less swift: And these Causes taken all together are what goes by the Name of Hazard.

Whilst we are but Men, that is, Beings very much circumscribed, we shall never be superior to what we call the Blows of Fortune. We ought to make all Advantages of Hazard, as soon as it happens. But our Life is too short, and our Understanding too limited, to perceive all its Combinations.

I shall

ceeds, the other miscarries. Upon this also depend the Vicissitudes of Good; for when a Man acts always with Moderation and Patience, if the Times and Affairs turn so favourably as to suit his Conduct, he prospers; but if the Face of Affairs and the Times change, he is undone, because he does not change likewise[c]. Nor is there any Man so wise as to know how to suit himself always to the Times, either because he cannot resist his

I shall mention two Events which will clearly shew the Insufficiency of Human Wisdom. The first is the Surprize of *Cremona* by Prince *Eugene,* an Enterprize concerted with all imaginable Prudence, and executed with infinite Valour. It miscarried after this manner· The Prince was admitted into the Town in the Morning through one of the common Sewers, which was opened to him by

[c] *Peter Soderini,* says Machiavel, proceeded with great Gentleness and Humanity, in all Affairs, and whilst his Conduct was suitable to the Times, he and his Country (Florence) prospered But when the Times changed, and it was necessary to lay aside Moderation and Humility, Peter was at a Loss, could not depart from his former Measures, and therefore he and his Country were both ruined Chap 9 Book III of his Discourses And Chap 3 he observes that if *Peter* had exerted all that Authority which belonged to him as Gonfalonier for Life, he might have ruined all the Family of *Medicis,* and by that means preserved the Liberty of his Country, which he had restored

his natural Inclination, or becaufe he can hardly be perfuaded to take a different Courfe from that which has always carried him to his End: Accordingly a moderate Man cannot act with Impetuofity, when the Times require it, and therefore is ruined, whereas, could he turn with the Times, Fortune would never forfake him [d].

Pope *Julius* II. in all his Enterprizes acted with Paffion and Vehemence; and the Times and Circumftances of Affairs were fo fuitable to his Manner of proceeding, that he always came off with Succefs   Confider

his

by a Curate with whom he held Intelligence; and he would infallibly have made himfelf Mafter of the Place, if two unforefeen Accidents had not happened.   Firft, a Regiment of *Swifs*, who were to perform their Exercife that Morning, were in Arms

X   fooner

[d] What makes Fortune abandon a Man (fays *Machiavel* in the fame Chap 9) is that fhe changes the Times, and he does not change his Meafures   A King of *Sparta*, being accufed of Inconftancy, anfwered, *It is not I that change, but Affairs*   To fhew that we muft fall in with the Times, *morem accommodari, prout conducat*   Ann 12   *Remiffum aliquid & mitigatum quia expedierit*   Ann 3   It has always been efteemed the Part of a wife Man, fays *Cicero*, to yield to the Times, and to comply with the Neceffity of Affairs   *Tempori cedere, id eft, neceffitati parere; femper fapientis eft habitum*   Ep 9 Book I

his first Enterprize against *Bologna*, when *John Bentivaglio* was still living: The *Venetians* took Umbrage at it, the Kings of *Spain* and *France* complained of it; the Pope nevertheless marched to *Bologna*, himself, and by his Ferocity and Impetuousness kept both the *Spaniards* and the *Venetians* in Suspense and Inaction; the *Venetians* were afraid to stir, and the *Spaniards* ambitious to recover the whole Kingdom of *Naples*;

sooner than ordinary, and made Resistance till the rest of the Garison were brought together. In the next Place, the Guide who led the Prince of *Vaudemont* to one of the Gates of the Town, of which that Prince was to make himself Master, missed his Way, and therefore that Detachment arrived too late

The second Event is the separate Peace which *England* made with *France* towards the End of the War concerning the Succession in *Spain*. Neither the Emperor *Joseph*'s Ministers, nor the greatest Philosophers, nor the ablest Politicians, could ever have suspected, that a Pair of Gloves would have changed the Destiny of *Europe*; and yet this is literally true. The Dutchess of *Marlborough* was Groom of the Stole to Queen *Anne* at *London*, whilst her Husband was gathering Laurels and Riches in his Campaigns in the *Netherlands*. The Dutchess by her Favour at Court supported the Interest of the Hero, and the Hero by his Victories abroad

sup-

Naples; whilst the King of *France*, seeing the Pope already in Motion, and being desirous to make him his Friend in order to humble the *Venetians*, thought he could not deny him his Assistance without doing him an open Injury.

Thus

supported the Credit of his Wife. The Tories who opposed them, and wished for Peace, were able to do nothing, whilst that Dutchess was all-powerful with the Queen. She lost her Favour by a very slight Accident. The Queen and the Dutchess had both given Orders at the same time for a Pair of Gloves. The Dutchess was so impatient for hers, that she pressed the Glover to serve her before the Queen. In the mean time *Anne* was likewise in Haste for her Gloves: A Lady whose Name was *Masham*, and who was an Enemy to the Dutchess, informed the Queen of all that had passed, and aggravated every thing with so many malicious Particulars, that the Queen from that Moment considered the Dutchess as a Favourite whose Insolence was no longer to be supported. The Glover soured the Queen still more by the Account she gave of the Affair, which she told her with all imaginable Malignity. This Leaven, though but slight, was sufficient to put all the Humours into Fermentation, and to season every thing that accompanies a Disgrace. The *Tories*, and Marshal *Tallard* at their Head, made a proper Use of this Accident, which gave a decisive Blow to their Antagonists The Dutchess

X 2

of

Thus Pope *Julius*, by his violent and impetuous Meafures, fucceeded in an Enterprize, which no other Pope, with all the Wifdom of Man, could ever have effected; for had he put off his Departure from *Rome* till every thing was fettled and prepared, as

any

of *Marlborough* was foon difgraced; and with her fell the *Whig* Party, and that of the Emperor's Allies   Such are the Frolicks of Fortune in the moft important Things of this World.   Providence laughs at human Wifdom, and human Greatnefs.   Caufes frivolous, nay fometimes ridiculous, often determine the Fate of entire Monarchies.   Upon that Occafion a forry Quarrel among Women delivered *Lewis* XIV. from a calamitous War, out of which all his Wifdom, Forces and Power would perhaps have proved infufficient to extricate him, and reduced the Allies to a Neceffity of making Peace   Such Events, I own, happen but feldom. fo that their Authority alone is not fufficient to difcredit human Prudence and Penetration   It is with them as with fome Difeafes, which, though they may impair our Health for fome time, do not hinder us from enjoying for the reft of our Lives the Advantage of a vigorous Conftitution.

It is therefore neceffary that thofe who are appointed to govern others, fhould endeavour to perfect their Penetration and Prudence: But this is not all; for in order to captivate Fortune, they muft learn to make their Tempers pliable to the different Conjunctures of Affairs; which indeed is no eafy

Task.

any other Pope would have done, *France* would have made a thousand Excuses, and the other Powers would have given him a thousand Apprehensions, and thus his Attempt must needs have miscarried. I shall pass by the rest of his Enterprizes, which were

Task. I only speak in general of two Sorts of Tempers, one bold and enterprising, and the other wary and slow, and as these moral Causes proceed from one that is physical, it is almost impossible a Prince should be so much Master of himself as to assume all Colours like the Chameleon. There are some Ages which favour the Glory of Conquerors, and of those bold and enterprising Men who seem to be born for mighty Wars, and mighty Revolutions. But they are especially favourable to those giddy, daring and fiery Spirits, who embroil Sovereigns, and furnish the common Enemy with an Opportunity of profiting by their Quarrels. And to such Men almost all Conquerors owe their Success; even *Ferdinand Cortez* was favoured in the Conquest of *Mexico* by the civil Broils of the *Americans*.

There are other Times when it would seem that the World, being less ruffled and disturbed, requires to be governed only by Gentleness and Moderation; and when nothing is necessary but Circumspection and Prudence. This is a sort of happy Calm in Politicks, which commonly follows a Storm; then it is that Negotiations are more effectual than Battles, and that you may gain by the Pen what could not be acquired by the Sword.

were all of the fame Kind, and all equally
fuccefsful. The Shortnefs of his Reign faved
him from any Reverfe of Fortune; for had
he lived to fee fuch Times as made it neceffary to proceed with Caution and Moderation,

A Prince who would make Advantage of both
thefe different Conjunctures, muft learn to accommodate himfelf to each of them, and always to
fteer, like a skilful Pilot, according to the Times.
If a General was bold and wary upon the proper
Occafions, he would be almoft invincible. *Fabius*
fupplanted *Hannibal* by his Delays; he was not
ignorant that the *Carthaginian* Army wanted both
Recruits and Money, and therefore would quickly
dwindle to nothing, if a Battle was avoided. *Hannibal*'s Policy on the other hand was to come to
an Engagement. His Power was only temporary
and tranfient, he was willing therefore to lofe no
Time in making all the Advantages of it that
were poffible, in order to render it more lafting
and folid, by that Terror which bright and fhine-
ing Actions never fail to fpread, and by thofe
Refources which are met with in a conquered
Country.

In

---

e *Nard.* obferves that Pope
Julius owed his conftant
Succefs rather to his Fortune than his Prudence,
and that he could not have
choſen a Time more fortu-
nate or more glorious for his
Popecom. Book 6 of his
Hiftory. To this Pope we
may juftly apply that Saying
of *Paterculus, Vir, inquies,
et ultra fortem temerarius*
Though a Man of great Bravery, yet he was ftill more
rafh than brave.

sion, he would have certainly been ruined;
because he could never have departed from
his natural Impetuosity.

I conclude therefore, that as Fortune is
changeable, the Prince who always persists
in the same Measures, succeeds as long as
the Times fall in with them, but is sure to
miscarry.

In the Year 1704. if the Elector of *Bavaria*
and Marshal *Tallard* had not left *Bavaria*, and advanced as far as *Blenheim* and *Hockstedt*, they
would have continued Masters of all *Swabia*; for
the Army of the Allies, not being able to subsist in
Bavaria for want of Provisions, would have been
obliged to retire towards *Mentz*, and even to separate. It was for want of Circumspection therefore
at a Time when Circumspection was seasonable, that
the Elector put to the Hazard of a Battle, for ever
memorable and glorious for the *Germans*, what was
in his own Power to preserve. This Imprudence was
punished by the total Defeat of the *French* and
Bavarians, by the Loss of *Bavaria*, and of all that
Country which lies between the Upper Palatinate
and the *Rhine*.

Those who have been undone by their Temerity,
are commonly forgot; and the few are only remembered whose Rashness was favoured by Fortune. It is
with them as with Dreams and Prophecies; we
preserve the Memory only of the few that have
been accomplished; the rest are sunk in Oblivion.
The World ought to judge of Events by their
Causes, and not of Causes by the Event.

X 2   I con-

miscarry when the Times alter I believe indeed, that of the two it is better to be impetuous, than cautious; because Fortune is a Woman with whom it is impossible to succeed without Blows and Violence; and it appears by Experience, that she more easily submits

I conclude therefore, that a People venture much when their Prince is bold and enterprising, and are threatened with continual Danger; whereas a wary Sovereign, if he is not fit for atchieving great Exploits, seems to be more fit to govern than the other; one ventures, but the other preserves.

If either of them would be great Men, they must come into the World at a seasonable Time; otherwise their Talents will be more pernicious than profitable. Every reasonable Man, and especially those whom Heaven hath appointed to govern others, ought to lay down some Plan of their Conduct, and to make it as well connected and as conclusive as a geometrical Demonstration. By closely adhering to such a System, they will be sure to act consistently, without ever departing from their main Design. By this means every Conjuncture and Event might be made to promote, and every thing to concur in, the Execution of these Projects which they have concerted.

But who are those Princes from whom we expect so many rare Talents? They will always be Men, and it may be truly said, that human Nature is not sufficient for so many Duties. The Phenix of the Poets, the Unity of the Metaphysicians, will sooner be

submits to those who are fierce and boiste-
rous, than to such as are cool and deliberate,
and that, like Woman, she favours young
Men, because they are more rash, audacious and violent.

be met with than such a Man as *Plato* describes.
Justice requires that the People should be content
with those Efforts which Sovereigns make to arrive at Perfection; among whom the best accomplished will always be those whose Characters are
most remote from that of *Machiavel*'s Prince. It
is but an Act of Justice to bear with their Failings,
while these are counterpoised by the Qualities of
the Heart, and by good Intentions; we must never
forget, that Error and Weakness are the Lot of
every Man, and that there is nothing perfect in
this World. There is no Country so happy as
that where a mutual Indulgence prevails between
the Sovereign and his Subjects, and gives Society
those

' Witness what *Tacitus*
says of *Cerialis*, one of *Vefpafian*'s Relations and Generals *Cerialis parùm tempo-ris
ad exfequenda imperia da-
bat, fubitus confiliis, fed even-
tu clarus adeat fortuna,
etiam ubi artes defuiffent*
" *Cerialis* indeed allowed his
" Men but little Time for
" executing his Orders, he
" was sudden in forming his
" Refolutions, yet he gained
" fignal Renown from the
" Event of them. Fortune
" aided him even where his
" Conduct failed." *Han-
nibal* therefore had good
Reason to call Fortune the
Step-mother of Prudence.
The Marquis of *Marignan*
said to the Emperor *Charles*
V that she was not only in-
conftant like Woman, but
capricious and wanton like
Youth. *Gratian*, Chap 21
of his Hero.

those Charms without which, Life itself would be a
Burden, and this World a Valley of Bitterness instead of a Scene of Pleasures.

CHAP. XXVI.

An Exhortation to deliver Italy from the Barbarians.

WHEN I reflect upon all that has
been said in the preceding Chapters, and confider with myself whether the present Juncture of Affairs in *Italy*
would be favourable to a new Prince, and
furnish him with an Opportunity of introducing such a Form of Government as might
do

OBSERVATIONS.

Of the different Sorts of Negotiations, and of the Reasons which may be called just for making War.

We have seen in the Course of this Work, the
Fallacy of those Arguments with which *Machiavel* pretended to impose upon us, by disguising
Villains under the Mask of great Men. I have
endeavoured to pull off that Veil of Virtue with
which he would cloak Vice, and to undeceive the
World in an Error held by many, with regard to the Politicks of Princes. I have told
Kings, That their true Policy was to excel their Subjects

do Honour to himself, and prove beneficial to the whole Country; methinks so many Things concur to promote such an Enterprize, that I know not whether there was ever a Time more proper for it than the present. If, to discover the Worth of *Moses*, it was necessary, as I said before, that the *Israelites* should be Captives in *Egypt*; to shew the Magnanimity and Courage of *Cyrus*, that the *Persians* should be oppressed by the *Medes*; and to display the excellent Qualities of *Theseus*, that the *Athenians* should be banished and dispersed*; so, to evince the Courage and Capacity of an *Italian* Spirit,

it

jects in Virtue, that they might not find themselves obliged to condemn in others what their own Practice authorized. I have observed, that bright and glorious Actions were not alone sufficient to establish their Reputation, and that true and lasting Fame was only to be purchased by such Actions as tend to the Benefit of Mankind. I shall here add a few Remarks upon the Subject of Negotiations, and upon the Reasons, which may truly be called just, for undertaking a War.

The Ministers of foreign Courts are Spies by Privilege, who are to watch the Conduct of those

Princes

---

* See Chap VI where he treats of the three Lawgivers.

it was neceſſary that *Italy* ſhould be reduced to its preſent Condition, that it ſhould be in greater Servitude than the *Jews*, in greater Subjection than the *Perſians*, more diſperſed than the *Athenians*, without Head, without Order or Laws, harraſſed, plundered, mangled and over-run, and ſhould have been involved in every ſort of Calamity.

Though from time to time ſome Man of ſuperior Courage has ſtarted up, whom it was hoped that God had ſent for the Deliverance of *Italy*, yet ſo it has always happened, that in the very Height of his Career, Fortune has caſt him off, inſomuch that *Italy*, now ready to expire, ſtill looks for ſome Deliverer, who may put an End to the Devaſtations in *Lombardy*, to the oppreſſive and galling

Princes with whom they reſide, to pry into their Deſigns and Proceedings, and to foreſee their Actions, in order to give their Maſters early Intelligence. The principal Deſign of their Embaſſy is to ſtrengthen the Tyes of Friendſhip between Princes; but inſtead of being the Artificers of Peace, they are often the Inſtruments of War. By Flattery, Cunning, and Seduction, they endeavour to delude Miniſters into a Diſcovery of the Secrets of State; they gain the Weak by their Addreſs, the Proud by their Fawning, and the Intereſted by their

galling Taxations in the Kingdom of *Na-ples* [a], and in *Tuscany* [b], and heal up all those Wounds, and festered Sores, which Length of Time has rendered almost incureable. 'Tis evident that she prays God to send her some Person who may deliver her from the Cruelty and Insolence of the Barbarians: 'Tis evident how much she is prepared and disposed to follow the Standard which any one sets up. And now at length she can have

their Bounty: In short, they do all the Mischief they can; their Profession allows them to transgress; they sin out of Duty, and are sure of Impunity

'Tis against the Wiles of those Spies that Princes ought to be chiefly upon their Guard. When the Subject of the Negotiation grows important, they ought to examine the Conduct of their Ministers with the greatest Rigour, in order to discover whether any Shower of *Danaë* may not have melted away the Austerity of their Virtue.

In

[a] *Machiavel* speaks here to his Patron *Laurence* of *Medicis*, agreeably to the Predictions of the Astrologers which were made in the Beginning of the Popedom of *Leo X viz.* That *Julian* his Brother should be King of *Naples*, and *Laurence* his Nephew Duke of *Milan* Nardi's History of *Florence*, Book VI

[b] The same Historian relates in two Passages of the same Book, that *Laurence* had a mind to make himself Sovereign of *Florence*

have no Hopes but in your illustrious Family, whose Valour and Fortune, favoured both by God and the Church, of which it now holds the Principality, may induce it to become the Champion of her Deliverance; nor will the Task be difficult, if you place before you the Lives and Actions of the Princes above-mentioned.

Though

In more critical Junctures, when they treat of Alliances, their Vigilance must be still greater; they must diffect the very Nature of those Articles which they are willing to yield, that they may be able to fulfil their Engagements. A Treaty considered only in the Lump, is very different from one that is examined in all its Views, and with all its Consequences. What appears at first Sight a real Advantage, will often be found, upon strict Examination, a wretched Palliative, which tends to the Ruin of the State. To these Precautions must be added great Care in defining and clearing up the Terms of the Treaty; and the punctilious Grammarian should always take place of the skilful Politician, that no room may be left for any fraudulent Distinction between the Letter and the Spirit of the Treaty.

In Politicks, one should make a Collection of all the Errors which Princes have committed through Precipitation, for the Use of those who would make Treaties or Alliances: The Time which they employed in reading it, would give
them

Though these were Men of rare and wonderful Abilities, nevertheless they were but Men, and none of them had so fair an Opportunity as the present. Their Enterprizes were not more just or more easy, nor was God more their Friend, than yours. Justice is on your Side, for every War is just that is necessary; and it is an Act of Piety towards our Country, to take Arms for it, when Arms are its only Resource. The People are universally disposed; and where the Disposition is so great, the Difficulty cannot be considerable, if you do but follow the Example of such as I have proposed

them Leisure to make Reflections that could not fail to be useful.

Negotiations are not all carried on by Persons of Figure; Ministers are often sent without any Character to neutral Places, where they make Proposals with the more Freedom, as they no-wise endanger the Honour of their Master. The Preliminaries of the late Peace between the Emperor and *France* were concluded in this manner, without the Knowledge of the Empire, and of the maritime Powers: This Accommodation was made in the House of a Count*, whose Estate lies upon the *Rhine*.

Victor Amadeus, the most able, and withal the most artful Prince of his Time, perfectly knew the Art

* The Count of *Newwied*

poſed for your Imitation. Beſides, we here ſee Things extraordinary and unparalleled effected by the divine Power: The Sea has been opened, a Cloud has pointed out the Way, a Rock has yielded Waters, the Heavens have rained down Manna, every thing has concurred in promoting your Greatneſs; the reſt is left for you to effect. God will not do every thing himſelf, that he may not deprive us of our Free-will, and of that Share of Glory which belongs to us. Nor is it ſurpriſing that none of the fore-mentioned *Italians* were able to do what may be hoped from

Art of concealing his Deſigns. *Europe* was impoſed upon more than once by his Fineſſe; eſpecially when Marſhal *Catinat*, in a Monk's Habit, and under Pretence of taking care of the Salvation of that Prince, withdrew him from the Emperor's Intereſt, and made him a Proſelyte to *France*. That Negotiation between the King and the General, was concluded with ſo much Dexterity, that the Alliance between *France* and *Savoy*, which immediately followed, was to *Europe* a moſt unexpected and extraordinary Phænomenon in Politicks.

I am far from propoſing the Conduct of *Victor Amadeus* in this Caſe, to the Imitation of Sovereigns. I only commend his Ability and Diſcretion; Qualities which, when they are made uſe of to promote

from your illustrious Family: If, in so many Revolutions, and so long Continuance of War in *Italy*, it has always appeared that our military Valour was extinct, the Reason is, because our old Discipline was not good, and nobody was able to invent a better.

Nothing does so much Honour to a new Prince, as inventing new Laws, and new Discipline, which, if they are well founded, and give an Idea of Grandeur, make him venerable

promote a good End, are absolutely necessary to every Prince.

It is a general Rule, That in difficult Negotiations, you must employ Men of the most exquisite Parts; that you must not only chuse those who are cunning, intriguing, supple, and insinuating, but those who have so quick and piercing an Eye, as to read in the Faces of others, the Secrets of their Hearts, in order that nothing may escape their Penetration, and the Force of their Reasoning.

Cunning must not be too often employ'd: It is with this, as with Spices, the too frequent Use of which blunts the Taste, and takes off that Tartness, which a Palate that is but seldom used to them, always feels. Probity, on the contrary, is for all Times, and resembles that simple and natural Food which agrees with every Constitution, and renders the Body robust, without over heating it.

Y   A Prince

nerable and awful; and *Italy* is fufcept-
ible enough of any new Form. It is not her
Soldiers that are wanting in Courage, but
their Commanders. Witnefs Duels and
Combats, in which the *Italians* have the Advantage by their Strength, their Dexterity,
and Stratagem; whereas, in Battles, they are
generally worfted, which is owing to the
Inability of their Generals For thofe who
pretend to have Skill, will never obey; and
every

A Prince whofe Candour is known, will never
fail to gain the Confidence of *Europe*; he will be
fuccefsful and happy without having recourfe to
Fraud, and powerful by means of Virtue alone. The
Peace and Profperity of the State are, as it were, a
Center, where all the Paths of Politicks ought to
unite; and to which all Negotiations ought ulti-
mately to tend.

The Tranquillity of *Europe* is principally founded upon the Support of that wife Equilibrium, by
which the fuperior Force of a fingle Monarchy is
counterbalanced by the united Powers of feveral
Princes. If this Equilibrium fhould fail, it might
be feared left an univerfal Revolution fhould happen, and a new Monarchy be eftablifhed upon the
Ruins of Princes weakened by their Difunion.

The Politicks of the Princes of *Europe* feem
therefore to require them never to neglect Alliances and Treaties, by which they may match the
Power

every one thinks himself skilful: Nor has any Man to this Day, been raised by his Valour and Fortune, to such a Height of Reputation, as to prevail with others to obey him. From hence it happened, that in the many Wars, during the last twenty Years, no Army that consisted only of *Italians*, has been successful; as appeared first at *Tarus*, afterwards at *Alexandria, Capua, Genoa, Vayla, Bologna*, and *Mestri*. If therefore your illustrious

Power of an ambitious Prince: They ought always to be distrustful of those who would sow Dissention among them: Let them remember that Consul, who, to shew the Necessity of Union, made several vain Attempts to pull away the Tail of a Horse all at once, but when he had separated the Hairs, and plucked one after another, he easily succeeded. This Lesson is as proper for certain Sovereigns in our Time, as for the *Roman* Legionaries: Nothing out their reuniting will be able to make them formidable, and to maintain the Peace and Tranquillity of *Europe*.

The World would be very happy if there was no other way but that of Negotiation to maintain Justice, and to re-establish Peace and Concord among Nations. Arguments would then be employ'd instead of Arms, and People would dispute with, instead of butchering one another. An unhappy Necessity obliges Princes to have recourse to Means that are much more cruel, there are Occa-

sions

illustrious Family would tread in the Steps of those excellent Persons, who delivered their Country from a foreign Yoke; it is necessary, as the true Foundation of all great Enterprizes, to provide yourselves with an Army of your own Subjects, who will always be more faithful, and better Soldiers than any others And though each of them is brave, yet, if they are united, they will be more so, when they find themselves commanded, preferred and rewarded by their own Prince

It

sions where the Liberty of the People, whom the Enemy would oppress by Injustice, must be defended by Arms; where you must obtain by Violence what is unjustly refused, and where Sovereigns must commit the Cause of their People to the Fate of Battles It is in such Cases the Paradox is true, that a good War procures and confirms a good Peace

What makes a War just or unjust is the Cause of it The Passion or Ambition of Princes often casts a Mist before their Eyes, and represents the most criminal Actions in the most advantageous Colours. War is a Resource in Extremity; so it ought only to be employ'd with Precaution, and in desperate Cases; and a Prince should well examine, whether he is induced to it by the Illusion of Pride, or by solid and indispensable Reasons.

Some

It is neceſſary therefore to be furniſhed with theſe Forces, befoie you can be able with *Italian* Valour to vindicate your Country from the Oppreſſion of Foreigners. Though the *Swiſs* and the *Spaniſh* Infantry aie counted terrible, yet both have their Defects; inſomuch that a third Soit of Infantry might be com-

---

Some Wars are defenſive, and theſe unqueſtionably are the moſt juſt. Some Wars are made for Inteieſt, when Kings are obliged to undertake them in order to maintain their conteſted Rights; they plead their Cauſe with Sword in Hand, and Battles decide the Validity of their Reaſons.

There are ſome Wars made for the Sake of Precaution, and which Princes do well to undertake: They are offenſive indeed, but juſt. When the exceſſive Grandeur of a Prince threatens to overwhelm and ſwallow up the Univerſe, Prudence requires that Ditches and Banks ſhould be made to oppoſe him, and to ſtop the impetuous Courſe of the Torrent, while that is practicable. We ſee Clouds that gather, a Storm that is approaching, and Lightning that foretels it; and the Sovereign who is threatened with ſuch a Danger, without being able to eſcape the Tempeſt, will unite himſelf, if he is wiſe, with all thoſe who may be involved in the ſame Diſtieſs, and conſequently have the ſame Intereſt with him. If the Kings of *Egypt*, of *Syria*, and *Macedon*, had joined together againſt the *Roman* Power, it would never be able to have overturned thoſe Empires: An Alliance wiſely concerted, and

a War

composed, that would be able not only to
withstand, but to defeat them: For the *Spaniards* cannot sustain the Charge of the
Horse; and the *Swiss* have Reason to be afraid
of the Foot, when they meet with such as
are as obstinate as themselves. Accordingly
we have seen, and may yet see, by Experience,
that the *Spaniards* cannot sustain the Fury of
the

a War vigorously pushed, would have rendered
those ambitious Designs abortive, the Accomplish-
ment of which fettered the Universe. As it is
Prudence to prefer lesser Evils to greater, as well
as Certainty to Chance, a Prince ought rather to
engage in an offensive War, when he has it in his
Power to make his Option between the Olive and
the Laurel, than to wait till desperate Times come
on, when a Declaration of War can only put off
his Slavery and Ruin for a few Moments. It is a
certain Maxim, That a Prince should rather prevent, than be prevented. Great Men have always
been successful, when they made use of their Forces
before their Enemies had taken such Measures as
tied their Hands, and suppressed their Power.

Many Princes have been engaged by Treaties,
in the Wars of their Allies, and obliged by Stipu-
lation, to furnish them with a certain Number of
auxiliary Troops. As Sovereigns cannot be without
Alliances, since there is no Prince in *Europe* who can
support himself against the rest by his own Power
alone, they engage mutually to assist one another

in

the *French* Cavalry; and that the *Swifs* have been overthrown by the Infantry of *Spain*. Of this laſt indeed we have had no perfect Experiment: Neverthelefs, we had ſome Inſtance of it at the Battle of *Ravenna*; where the *Spaniſh* Foot being engaged with the *German* Battalions, (which obſerve the ſame Order and

in cafe of Need; and this contributes to their Security and Preſervation. The Event determines which of the Allies reaps moſt Advantage by the Alliance, At one time, a lucky Opportunity favours one of the contracting Parties; at another time, ſome unexpected Incident promotes the Intereſt of another; It is therefore, not only an honeſt, but a wiſe Conduct in Princes, religiouſly to keep their Faith and Promiſe, and to be punctual in fulfilling their Engagements; the rather becauſe their Alliances make the Protection which they give to their Subjects more effectual and laſting.

All Wars therefore, whoſe ſole Deſign is to guard againſt Uſurpations, to maintain unqueſtionable Rights, to guarantee the publick Liberty, and to ward off the Oppreſſion and Violence of the Ambitious, are agreeable to Juſtice. When Sovereigns engage in Wars of this Kind, they have no room to reproach themſelves with Bloodſhed, as they are forced to it by Neceſſity; and in ſuch Circumſtances War is a leſs Evil than Peace.

This Subject naturally leads me to ſpeak of Princes, who deal in the Blood of their People; a Sort of Merchandize unknown in ancient Times:

Their

and Discipline with the *Swiss*) the *Spaniards*
by the Agility of their Bodies, and the Protection of their Bucklers, broke in upon their
Pikes, and killed them securely, while the
Germans could make no Defence, and would
have been all cut off, had not their Enemies
been charged by the Horse.   Wherefore, as

the

Their Court is, as it were, a publick Market, where
their Troops are sold to those who bid the greatest
Subsidies. Soldiers were originally designed for the
Defence of their own Country: To hire them out
to others, like Dogs and Bulls, to bait and be
baited, is, methinks, perverting at once the De-
sign both of Trade and War.   It is said,
That sacred Things are not allowed to be sold:
What can be more sacred than the Lives of
Men?

As for Civil Wars about Religion, they are, for
the most part, the Effect of the Princes Imprudence: He must needs have unseasonably favoured
one Sect, at the Expence of another. He must
either have too much promoted, or too much
discouraged, the publick Exercise of certain Forms
of Worship. He must have added Weight to
Party Quarrels, which are only transient Sparks
of Fire when the Sovereign does not interfere, but
become Conflagrations when he foments them.

To maintain the Civil Government with Vigour,
to grant every Man a Liberty of Conscience, to
act always like a King, and never to put on the
Priest, is the sure Means of preserving a State from
those

the Defects of thefe two Sorts of Infantry are known, it is poffible to invent a third Sort that may be able to withftand the Horfe, and may yet have no need of fearing the Foot. And this will be effected, not by changing their Arms, but their Difcipline. 'Tis this Sort of Inventions and Improvements, that gives Reputation and

Autho-

thofe Storms and Hurricanes, which the dogmatical Spirit of Divines is continually labouring to conjure up.

Foreign Wars about Religion are the very Height of Injuftice and Abfurdity. To leave *Aix la Chapelle*, and go Sword in Hand to convert the *Saxons*, as was done by *Charles* the Great, to equip a Fleet for *Egypt*, in order to propofe the Chriftian Religion to the Sultan, are very ftrange and unaccountable Enterprizes. The Fury of Crufades is now over: Heaven grant it may never return!

War in general is fo full of Calamities, the Event of it is fo uncertain, and its Confequences are fo ruinous to a Country, that Princes cannot be too cautious of engaging in it. The Violences which your Armies commit in your Enemies Country, are inconfiderable Advantages, when compared with the Misfortunes which immediately fall upon your own Dominions. To undertake a War is fo ferious and important a Confideration, that it is furprifing how fo many Princes have eafily taken fuch a Refolution.

I am perfuaded, that if Kings were to fee a true and faithful Picture of the Miferies that are brought

upon

Authority to a new Prince. The present Opportunity therefore should not be let pass; that *Italy*, after so long Expectation, may at length see her Deliverer appear.   Nor can it be expressed, with what Affection, with what Thirst of Revenge, with what Fidelity, with what religious Attachment, and with what Tears, such a Champion would be received in all the Provinces that have suffered by these Inundations of Foreigners.   What Gates
would

upon a People by a Declaration of War, it would not fail to move them.   Their Imagination is not lively enough, to give them a natural Representation of those Calamities which they never felt, and against which they are protected by the Eminence of their Rank. How can they feel those Taxes and Duties which overload and oppress the People? The Scarcity of Inhabitants, when the young Men are carried off to recruit their Forces? Those contagious Distempers which sweep off almost intire Armies ? The Horror of Battles, and the still greater Horror of bloody Sieges? The Misery of the Wounded; when the Sword of the Enemy has deprived them of those Limbs which were the only Instruments of their Industry and Subsistence ? The Grief of Orphans, who, by the Death of their Fathers, have been deprived of the only Support of their Weakness? Or the Loss of so many Men who were useful to the State, and whom Death has mowed down in their Youth?

Princes

would be shut against him? What People would deny him Obedience? What Malice would oppose him? What true *Italian* would refuse to follow him? Every one abhors and nauseates this Domination of *Barbarians*. Let your illustrious Family therefore undertake this Enterprize with all that Courage and Confidence wherewith just Enterprizes are attempted; that under your Banner this Country may be ennobled, and by the

Princes whose only Aim it is to make their People happy, ought well to consider, before they expose them to every thing that human Nature has most Occasion to dread.

Others who look upon their Subjects as their Slaves, endanger them without Pity, and see them perish without Regret; but those Princes who consider Men as their Equals, and look upon their People as a Body of which they themselves are the Soul, are as sparing of the Blood of their Subjects, as of their own.

To conclude this Work, I would beseech all Sovereigns not to take Offence at the Liberty with which I speak to them: My sole Design is to make them acquainted with Truth, to animate them to Virtue, and to flatter none. The good Opinion I have of the Princes who reign at present in *Europe*, makes me believe them worthy to hear the Truth: It is only to a *Nero*, to an *Alexander* VI a *Cæsar Borgia*, or a *Lewis* XI. that there would be Danger

in

the Favour of your auspicious Fortune it may be truly said with *Petrarch*:

Virtù contr' al furore
  Prendrà l' arme; & fia il combatter corto,
Che l' antico valore
  Ne gl' Italici cuor' non è ancor morto.

True Courage then shall furious Rage oppose,
  Nor shall it long for Victory contest;
Our Foes shall feel that antient Valour glows,
  With *Roman* Warmth, in each *Italian* Breast.

in telling it. Thank God, we can reckon no such Men among the Princes of *Europe* in our Days; and the greatest Encomium that can be given them, is to say, that in their Presence one may boldly condemn all those Vices which degrade Royalty, and are inconsistent with the Sentiments of Humanity and Justice.

F I N I S.

Devotions applicable to the Troubles of the Times. In Folio.

N. B. None of these Pieces were ever printed before, and the Original Manuscripts in his Lordship's Hand-writing may be seen at *T. Woodward's*.

III. The History of *Japan* · Giving an Account of the antient and present State and Government of that Empire; of its Temples, Palaces, Castles, and other Buildings, of its Metals, Minerals, Trees, Plants, Animals, Birds and Fishes; of the Chronology and Succession of the Emperors, Ecclesiastical and Secular; of the original Descent, Religions, Customs and Manufactures of the Natives; and of their Trade and Commerce with the Dutch and Chinese. Together with a Description of the Kingdom of Siam Written in High Dutch, by Engelbertus Kæmpfer, M. D. Physician to the Dutch Embassy to the Emperor's Court; and translated from his original Manuscript, by J. G. Scheuchzer, F. R. S. and a Member of the College of Physicians, London; with the Life of the Author, and an Introduction. To which is added, A Journal of a Voyage to *Japan*, made by the *English*, in the Year 1673. Illustrated with many Copper Plates. In two Volumes, Folio.

IV. Cato's Letters in four neat Pocket Volumes, with a Character of the late John Trenchard, Esq,

V. A Collection of Debates in the House of Commons in the Year 1680, relating to the Bill of Exclusion of the then DUKE OF YORK, containing the Speeches of the Lord Russel, Sir Henry Capel, Sir Francis Winnington, Ralph Montague, Esq; Henry Booth, Esq; Sir Gilb. Gerrard, Sir Lion.

Lion, Jenkins, Sir Thomas Player, Sir Richard Graham, Sir Will. Pultney, Daniel Finch, Efq; Hugh Bofcawen, Efq; John Trenchard, Efq; John Hampden, Efq; Sir Roger Hill, Sir Will. Jones, Sir Richard Mafon, Laur. Hide, Efq; Coll. Leg, Sir H. Capell, Edward Dering, Efq; Coll. Birch, with many more; and a Lift of the Members that compofed that Houfe. To which are added, The Debates of the Houfe of Commons affembled at Oxford, March 21. 1680. As alfo an Introduction, fhewing the Progrefs of Popery from the Reformation to this prefent Time.

VI. A Collection of feveral Pieces of Mr. *John Toland*, with fome Memoirs of his Life and Writeings. In Two Volumes. Vol. I. Containing, 1. A Specimen of the Celtick Religion and Learning; with an Account of the Druids, or the Priefts and Judges; of the Vaids, or the Diviners and Phyficians; and of the Bards, or the Poets and Heralds of the antient Gauls, Britons, Irifh and Scots. 2. An Account of Jordano Bruno's Book, of the infinite Univerfe, and innumerable Worlds. 3. A Catalogue of Books mentioned by the Fathers, and other antient Writers, as truly or falfly afcribed to Jefus Chrift, his Apoftles, and other eminent Perfons. 4. The Secret Hiftory of the South-Sea Scheme. 5. The Scheme of à National Bank; with other Pieces. Vol. II. A Letter concerning the Roman Education. 2. A Differtation, proving the received Hiftory of the Death of Atilius Regulus, the Roman Conful, to be a Fable. 3. Several Letters of Pliny, tranflated into Englifh. 4. A new Defcription of Epfom. 5. The Primitive Conftitution of the Chriftian Church. 6. Some
Me-

Lightning Source UK Ltd.
Milton Keynes UK
21 October 2010

161668UK00005B/45/P